Glove Puppetry

Margaret Arney

Copyright © 2017 Margaret Arney

All rights reserved. No part of this book may be used or reproduced by any means, graphic, electronic, or mechanical, including photocopying, recording, taping or by any information storage retrieval system without the written permission of the publisher except in the case of brief quotations embodied in critical articles and reviews.

This is a work of fiction. All of the characters, names, incidents, organizations and dialogue in this novel are either the products of the author's imagination or are used fictitiously.

Glove Puppetry books may be ordered through booksellers or by contacting:

Making Magic Happen Academy
www.makingmagicacademy.com
hello@karenmcdermott.com.au

Because of the dynamic nature of the Internet, any web addresses or links contained in this book may have changed since publication and may no longer be valid. The views expressed in this work are solely those of the author and do not necessarily reflect the views of the publisher and the publisher hereby disclaims any responsibility for them.

The intent of the author is only to offer information of a general nature. In the event you use any of the information in this book for yourself, which is your constitutional right, the author and the publisher assume no responsibility for your actions.

ISBN: 978-0-6481030-1-1 (sc)
ISBN: 978-0-6481030-2-8 (e)

Designed in Australia

Printed on sustainable paper

INTRODUCTION

This glove manual is the second in a puppetry series of which Introducing Puppetry is the first.

It is fun creating an object and then giving it a life and character of its own. You can make it do things that you are unable to do yourself.

It is wonderful to act it in a make believe world and create all sorts of magic.

All ages love doing or watching puppetry.
Many people fondly remember making a puppet sometime in their life and seeing puppet plays they've never forgotten. It is beneficial to everyone.

I hope this manual, with its simple and illustrated text, will help would-be puppeteers and audiences experience the joy it brings.

A recording of the puppet songs has been included to help you know where the words go in the tunes.

I would love to hear from you.

ACKNOWLEDGEMENTS

I wish to thank Cliff, my husband, for writing all the verses contained within the manual. They are always a delight.

Thanks to my sister Robin for her encouragement, ideas, art, corrections and so much invaluable assistance in the production of this book.

A big thank you to Sue Dupont at a local Primary School for trialling the manual with the grade 5 children in her art class, checking the manual and for her invaluable input.

Tom from Midland Photographers, with his mouse companion, for the fantastic cover photo.

The lovely colourful photos taken by Celine certainly show how delightful puppetry can be.

Once again I wish to thank Colleen Rintoul for her painting of scenery, props and puppets whilst giving me secrets on how to achieve simple effective outcomes.

Thank you again to Karen at "Making Magic Happen" for her skill in publishing this book and further improving my computing skills.

CONTENTS

This manual and using the scripts	1
Puppets used in this theatre	3

SECTION 1: THEATRE — 4

1. Puppet theatre design	6
2. Theatre extension, riser and transportation	7
3. Theatre layout	9
4. Purchase of aluminium or substitute	10
5. Tools required	12
6. Assembling the theatre	13
7. Strengthening and stabilising the theatre	14
8. Scenery rack	15
9. Blockout covering	16
10. Mounting the curtain track	17
11. Front curtains	18
12. Scenery curtains	19

SECTION 2: MAKING PUPPETS

1 Puppetry program	22
2 Puppet cones	23
3. Puppet heads ~ paper	25
~ polystyrene	26
4. Using cones, marking faces	27
5. Hair ~ paper	31
6. ~ other materials	33
7. Human face ~ making	35
8. ~ templates	36
9. Animal heads ~ paper	37
~ polystyrene	38
10. Glove ~ pattern and making	39
11. ~ Joining head and glove, puppet rack	43
12. Hands, paws, hoofs and templates	45
13. Set materials and effects	48
14. Scenery backdrops	50

SECTION 3: Doing puppetry

The Three Pigs ~ script	54
Making the ~ pigs	57
~ wolf	59
Puppet photos	61
Scenery and props	63
Photos of final results	66
Music	67
Three Billy Goats Gruff ~ script, verses and music	68
Making an animal snout	73
Making ~ a goat head	74
Templates ~ little, middle and big billy goat	75
Troll and polystyrene heads	79
Photos.	81
Scenery and props	83
Final results	84
Goldilocks and the Three Bears ~ script, verses and music	86
Making Goldilocks	89
Making a bear	91
Templates ~ baby, mother, father	93
Polystyrene heads	96
Puppet photos	97
Scenery and props	99
Final results	101
Gingerbread Man ~ script, verse	103
How to make a straw and lengthen a kebab	106
Making the ~ little old woman and little old man	107
~ boy and girl	109
~ cow, horse	111
~ cat, dog, fox	114
~ Gingerbread Man, polystyrene heads	117
Puppet photos	121
Scenery and props	124
Final results	128

Little Red Riding Hood ~ script, verses and music   131
    Making ~ Red Riding Hood,   135
        ~ mother   137
        ~ grandma   138
        ~ woodsman   138
        ~ making a bun   139
        ~ polystyrene heads   140
        ~ wolf and polystyrene wolf   141
    Puppet photos   143
    Scenery and props   145
    Final results   153
Acting, choreography, extras, performance, review   155
Summary   158
Appendix   Cost of theatre

Advantages of glove puppets

Actions ~ use of the hands and head eg. the puppet can carry objects.

Eye level ~ puppet and scenery is directly in front of the puppeteer.

Visibility ~ the puppet is visible but the puppeteer is hidden.

Team Work ~ is essential in the limited environment.

Consequences~ each facet of the whole production has to be completed in a set order.

Thoroughly prepared puppet performances provide positive motivation in many subject areas and personal issues.

A simple story with puppets creates developmental opportunities, in a fun environment, for personal growth and confidence in children with difficulties.

Puppetry with gifted children stretches their initiative, imagination, problem solving and physical skills.

Puppetry also strengthens teamwork and leadership.
Puppetry inspires ordinary people to do extraordinary things.

This manual and using the scripts

There are full instructions on how to make glove puppet heads and bodies (the glove) and scripts to provide a medium for learning how to use and act these puppets.

The first two plays have only one scene and require 4 puppeteers.
The third play has two scenes with props to use. It needs musical interludes.
The fourth introduces scene variations and more puppet interactions.
The fifth can have extra acts added into each scene.

The Three Pigs incorporates simple entries, puppet interactions and hasty exits. The play can be expanded with the wolf coming through, sniffing the trail and speaking his thoughts. The pigs may meet before hurrying into the house when they see the wolf coming. See how active your puppet can be whilst it is on stage. Use it, enjoy it, exaggerate fear, excitement, victory.

The Three Billy Goats Gruff teaches the need to have a discussion before taking action and confronting the troll. Dramatise actions which show fear, bravery and encouragement.
The troll has to become bolder and roar louder at each Billy goat. Celebrate the victory on and off the bridge.

Goldilocks and the Three Bears needs a musical interlude during the scene changes. Start with mother in the kitchen. The puppets have to use the chairs and act at the table.
Goldilocks is curious about everything and talks aloud as she explores the cottage.
The bears should show their mounting distress and reactions, then astonishment at finding it is just a little girl.

The Gingerbread Man has the opportunity to make the chase very interesting and varied in pace. The smallest puppet has to be a very boastful lively biscuit with a lot to say. He is the one who can make the play hilarious. GBM can be well ahead, stop and act at each meeting. In between, the others could cross the stage complaining, shouting, talking, etc. Puppets keep their order crossing the stage and all end up on the stage at the end. Large props have been added to this play to provide more interest and acting opportunities,

Little Red Riding Hood provides two scenes which can have a couple of simple acts or extra acts added in to both scenes to build up the intrigue and suspense. The wolf can run off. After LRRH has picked her flowers and gone on her way, the wolf can return talking about his plans and sniffing the trail. The big props create more varied exits and interactions for your puppets.

Ask these questions with each story.
How? Why? Where? are they going, walking, running, acting, dancing, standing, sitting, feeling, talking, shaking, doing, laughing, crying, shouting....
How do they enter and exit - walking, running, happy, sad....

Suggestion

Do these plays simply. Then add in humour, characterisation, clever acts, etc.
If possible have 2 groups do the same play but in totally different ways.
Then they can watch the other performance and have an audience experience.
If some do not want to act their puppet, find them other parts to do eg. scenery changing.
Usually, once they have seen the performance, they want to be a puppeteer.

Extra acts, for exaggerated drama and character building, can be added to all the plays.

Puppets that suit this theatre

Solid or transparent Shadow puppets   Sock puppets

Human glove puppets   Animal glove puppets

Human and animal marionettes if the extra theatre parts included in the marionette manual are added.

Theatre

I used to be called Pucinella
Back in sixteen fifty two
Now I'm better known as Punch
Because it's what I often do.
It comes from the Italian word for chicken
Because I have a squeaky voice.
I'm good at getting plots to thicken
Yes! I'm the puppet of your choice.
I used to be a marionette
Now I have no strings attached.
And every joke you get
Has a Punch line for you to catch!

Design
Material purchases
Tools required
Assembling the theatre
Scenery rack
Blockout covering
Curtains, scenery and props

Puppet theatre design

1. **Simple** ~ easy to put together, store and use.
2. **Large** ~ to allow for more children and lots of action.
3. **Light weight** ~ easy to handle and can hurt no one if it falls over.
4. **Collapsible** ~ it can be stored or transported very easily.

The theatre turned upside down so that the proscenium is suitable for shorter children.

The top and bottom must be flat to be able to do this.

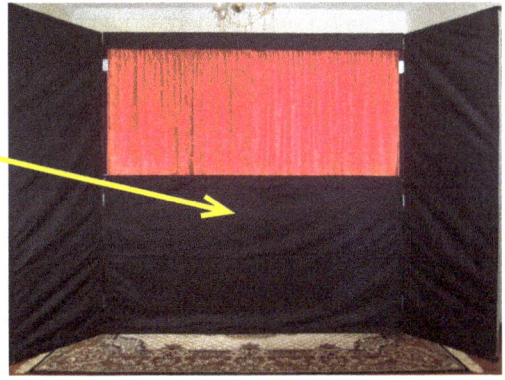

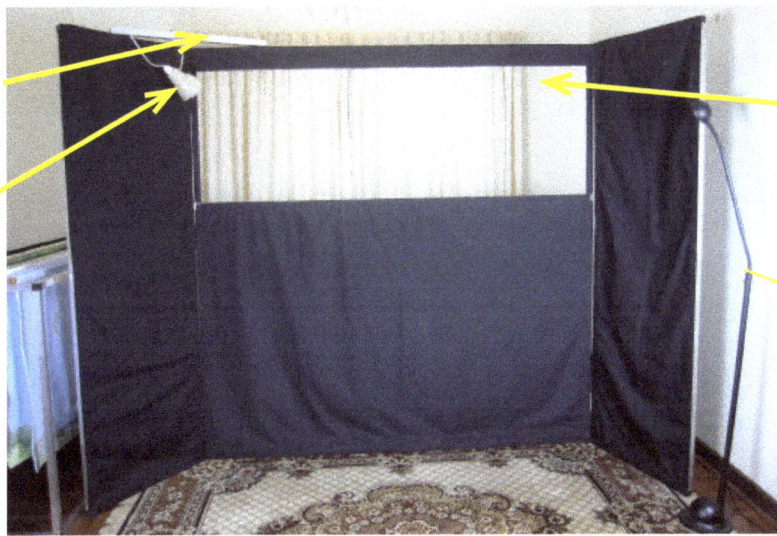

Curtain rod mounted behind

Flexible light, standard or hanging, on both sides.

Proscenium is high enough to have good scenery.

Standard light

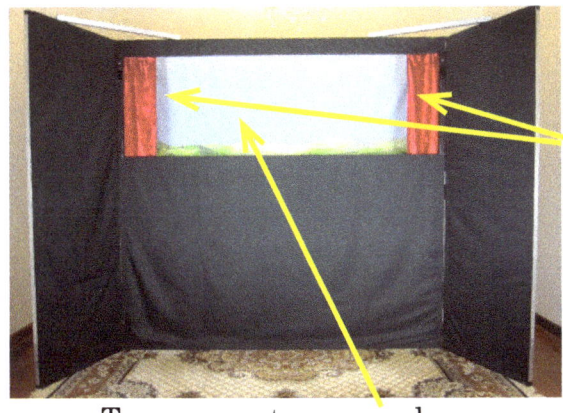

Two curtains that can be drawn apart.

Transparent scenery drop – puppeteers can see their puppets.

Block out – so no light comes through behind the puppeteers.

Any theatre with these components will work well.

This theatre is built with Qubelok (an aluminium modular framing system). There are similar systems in other countries and it can also be built in wood.

Theatre extension

The theatre can be extended to give more acting space or to suit adults.

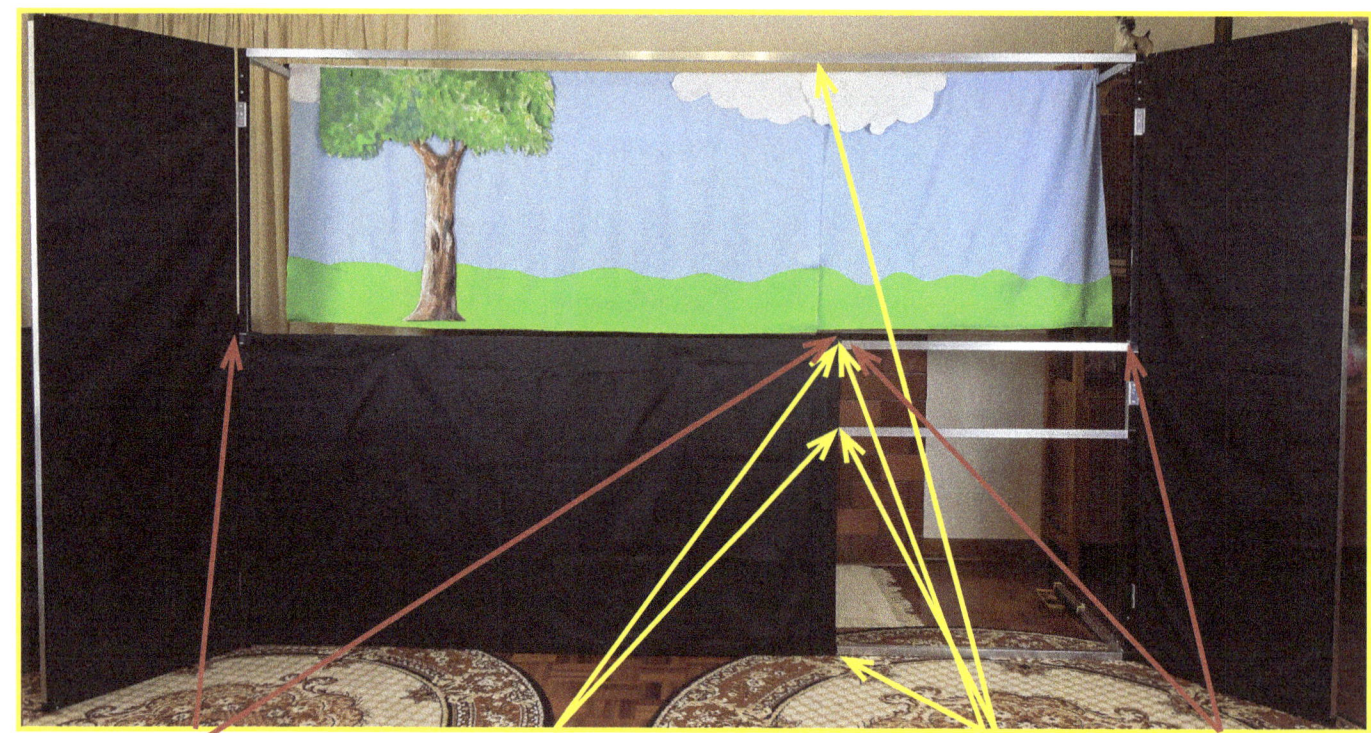

180cm original theatre   24cm or your measurement between these   The 4 x 'T' connectors   90cm extension

One 6.5m length of Qubelok and 4 x 'T' connectors will extend the theatre.
The simplest way to extend the scenery and blockout is to join on 90cm more of each so either theatre can be used. The bottom leg of the 'T' can be cut off or left on 'e' and 'h' facing back. This is the strongest position for the joiner.

The theatre can be placed on a riser to enable adults to use it.

Pop riveted strap on the sides of the top riser rail form a channel for the theatre to sit in. When the theatre is put on top of the riser the back ground supports must be moved down to the 3-way connectors on the riser.

2 x 90cm pieces joined into the riser for larger theatre.

The height of the riser can be changed by altering the length of the uprights.

The side wing sitting inside the channel.

Bolts can be put through this or straps put around it to hold the theatre in place.

One hinge joins side wing to the middle section of the riser.

Aluminium needed for extension ~ 4 x 90cm pieces and a 24cm piece (check your length) to go between 'f' and 'g' joining the two 'T's and strengthening the middle section. Need 4 x 'T's.

90cm	90cm	90cm	90cm	24cm	180cm	
					262cm left for risers cut at 180cm	

Aluminium needed for riser ~ 2 x 6.5m lengths of Qubelok and some 50cm wide strapping.

180cm	90cm	55cm	55cm	180cm	
				268cm left for risers cut at 180cm	
180cm	90cm	55cm	55cm	180cm	
				268cm left for risers cut at 180cm	

The leftover pieces will be a bit less than shown because of the fraction lost in all the cutting. Cut them at 180cm for storage and use them for sets of different length risers.

Connectors needed for the riser are;- 10 right angles, 2 x 'T's and 2 x 3-way.

The versatility of this theatre is more than doubled when using the extension and the riser.

Theatre transportation

As mentioned on page 9, if the theatre is too big to transport, separate it as shown below.

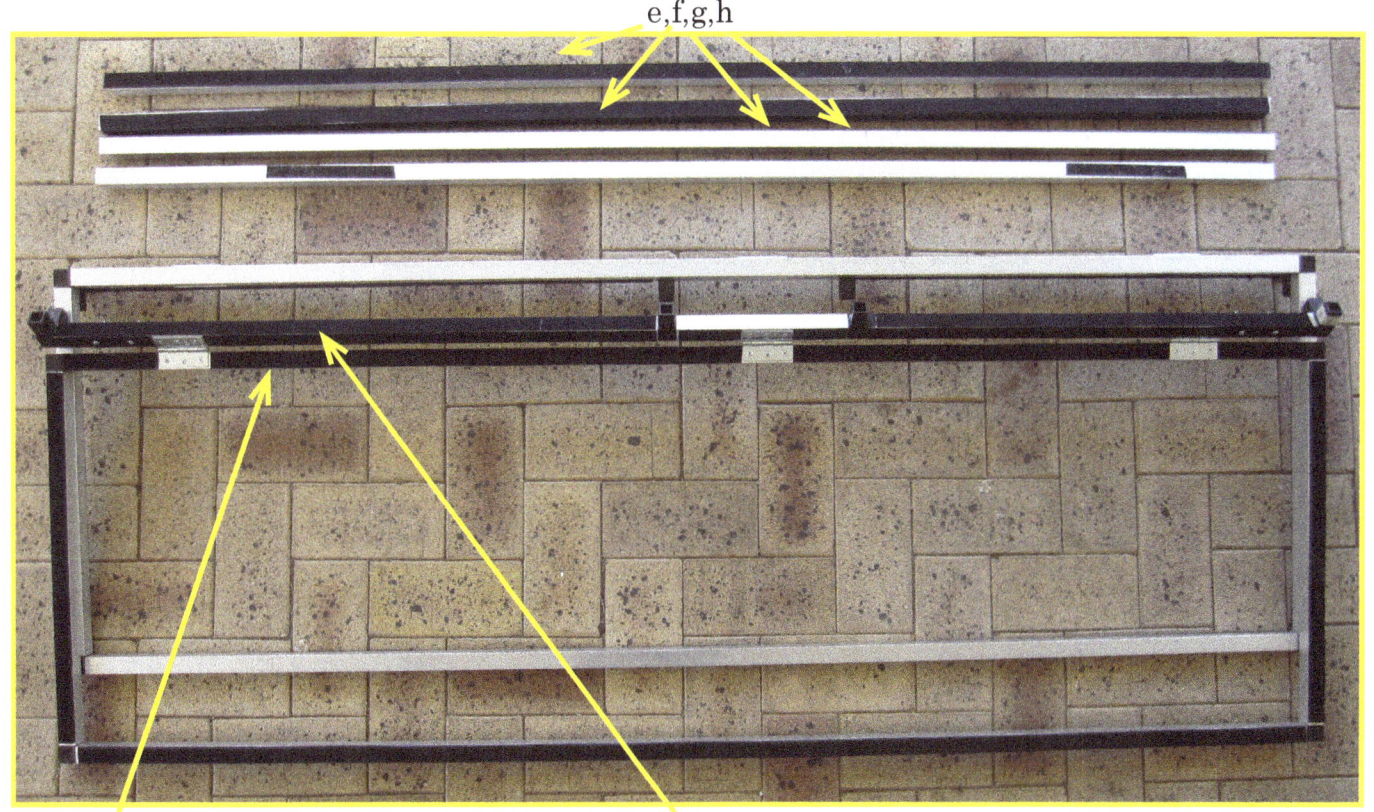

e,f,g,h

The side wings stay joined to their middle uprights.

REMEMBER to file the connector arms down a bit as shown on p 9 so they do not break when separating the joint.

WHEN REJOINED screw in the corner angle brackets to keep the theatre tightly together.

Glove theatre layout

If the centre section (180cm x 180cm) is too big for transport, remove 'e, f, g, h' and it is then two sections 65cm x 180cm in size.

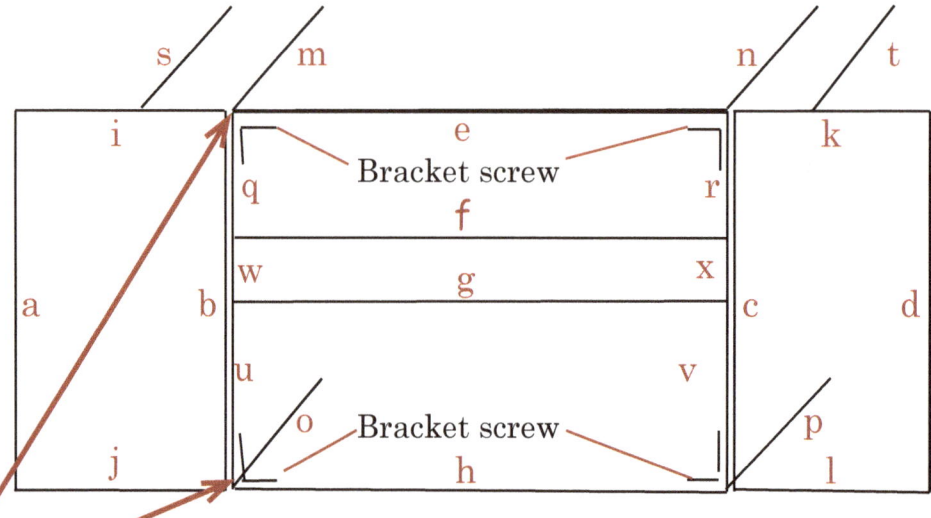

Pieces in alphabetical order

One small bracket in each of the four 3 W corners of the middle section will keep the theatre firmly together. Use small self tapping screws.

Remove the bracket screws in 'e' and 'h' if separating theatre for travel.

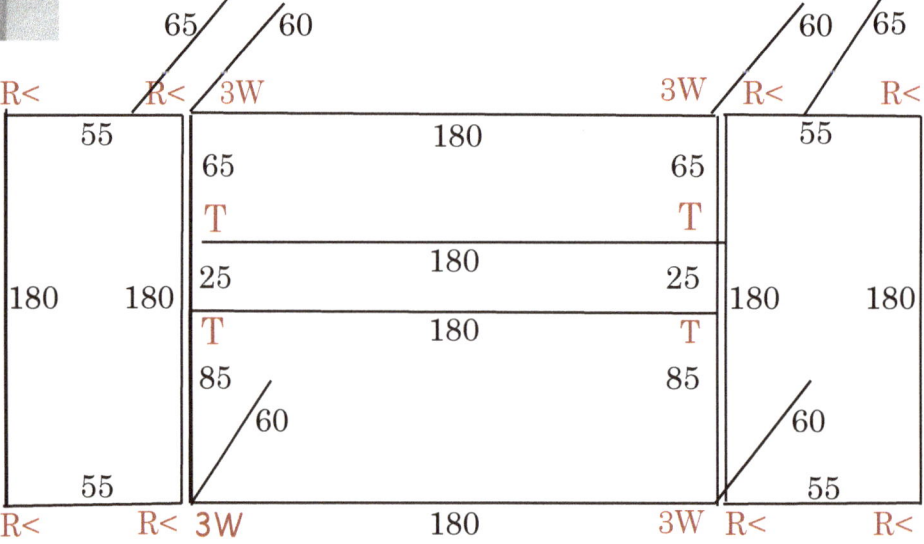

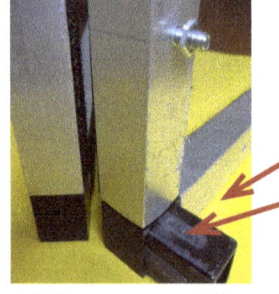

Lengths are in centimetres
Connectors : Right angle = R < ; Tee = T ; 3 way = 3W
File the ridges off the back leg of the 3W connectors at the 4 corners so the supports come off easily for transportation or to turn the theatre upside down. Leave 4 corner brackets on uprights as shown above.

* The top and bottom of the theatre is kept perfectly straight so it can be turned upside down, thus providing two different heights of proscenium. Step 23 on p 14 is put velcro on the top and bottom of the theatre, then the front stays can be used.
  The top front stays and back ground supports keep the theatre upright and safe p 14.

Aluminium puppet theatre
Ordering information

This theatre design is stable, uses 180cm measurements so as to keep cutting simple and it can be turned upside down to accommodate shorter children.

The aluminium pieces and plastic connectors are called QUBELOK.

The plastic connectors needed are:-

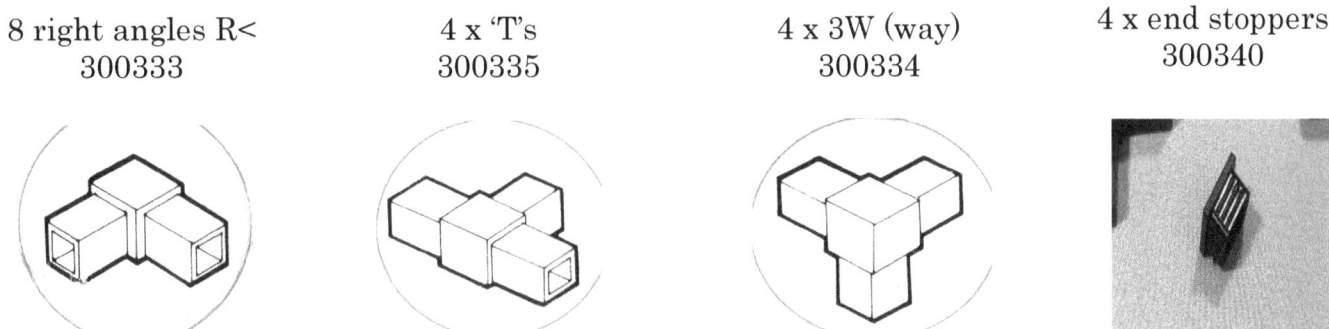

| 8 right angles R< | 4 x 'T's | 4 x 3W (way) | 4 x end stoppers |
| 300333 | 300335 | 300334 | 300340 |

The aluminium and plastic joiners can be ordered from Capral in any Australian capital city. They will cut and package it for you if you present this cutting diagram. (For schools this service might even be free)
They will deliver Australia wide.
I have dealt with Welshpool Capral, Perth, WA. (08) 9356 7811 or email - capral.com.au

MAKE SURE YOU ASK FOR ALL THE OFFCUTS as you will need them. Capral do not cut anything shorter than 50cm.

CAPRAL cutting instructions

The 4 lengths are designed to be cut simultaneously for each of the 180cm, 180cm, 55cm, 60cm and 65cm measurements, thus providing 4 of each that are exactly the same length.

Then cut only 2 together for q and r = two 85cm pieces.

a to d make the four side wing verticals.

e to h the four horizontals in the middle section.

There should be approximately 2 x 37cm and 2 x 118cm pieces left over, KEEP THEM.
When making the theatre, cut two 25cm lengths out of the two 37cm pieces and keep ALL the remaining pieces in case you do the marionette theatre conversion.

2 x 6.5m lengths of 16mm piping = 6 x 190cm curtain rods for scenery drops + 2 offcuts.

If making the large theatre add in the Qubelok from p8.

Also remember the Qubelok for the scenery rack on p 15.

CAPRAL cutting layout for glove puppet theatre

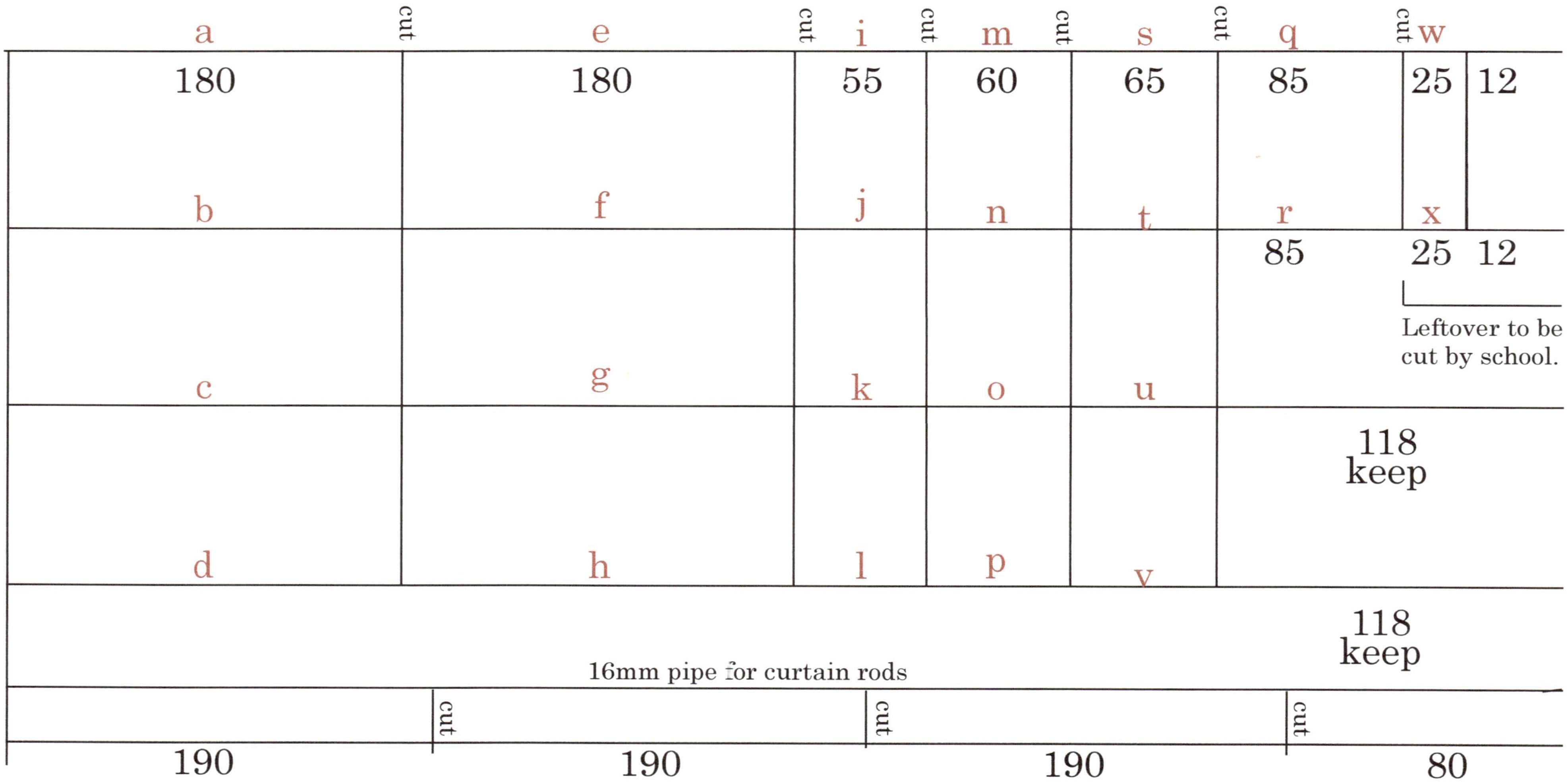
a
cut
e
cut
i
cut
m
cut
s
cut
q
cut
w
180
180
55
60
65
85
25
12
b
f
j
n
t
r
x
85
25
12
Leftover to be cut by school.
c
g
k
o
u
118 keep
d
h
l
p
v
118 keep
16mm pipe for curtain rods
cut
cut
cut
190
190
190
80

All parts are in alphabetical order to match the theatre layout.
Measurements are in centimetres. Keep all offcuts/leftover pieces.
If you are going to make the larger theatre add in the Qubelok from p 8.

Tools required

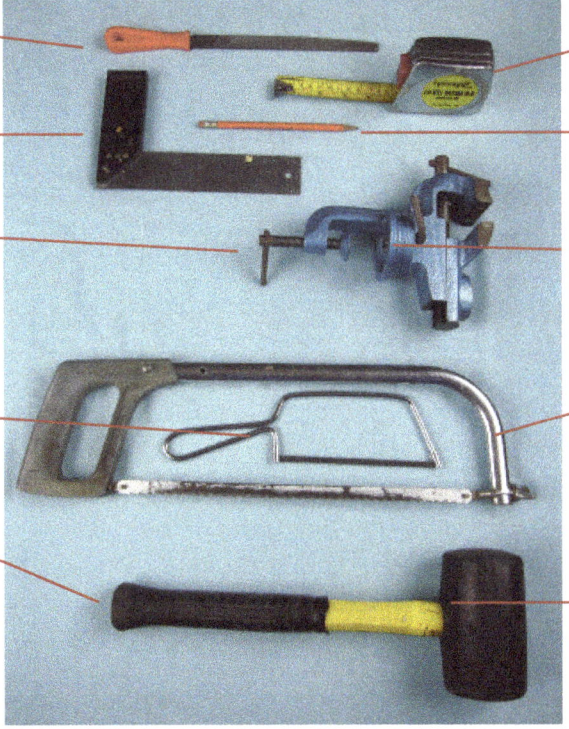

- Metal rasp to file the rough ends smooth.
- Set square to mark the 'w' and 'x' cuts square.
- This is a small vice that clamps onto a bench or table, the top swivels.
- A full-sized or small hacksaw.
- Be very careful when taking joints apart as the connectors can break and be stuck in the tube. First use a flat screwdriver in the corner to ease it off, then gently wiggle and knock it apart right in the corner.
- Tape measure
- Pencil or marker
- Vice to hold Qubelok when doing holes, brackets and hinges.
- Hacksaw to cut 'w' and 'x' pieces out of leftovers.
- Rubber mallet to knock the Qubelok together.

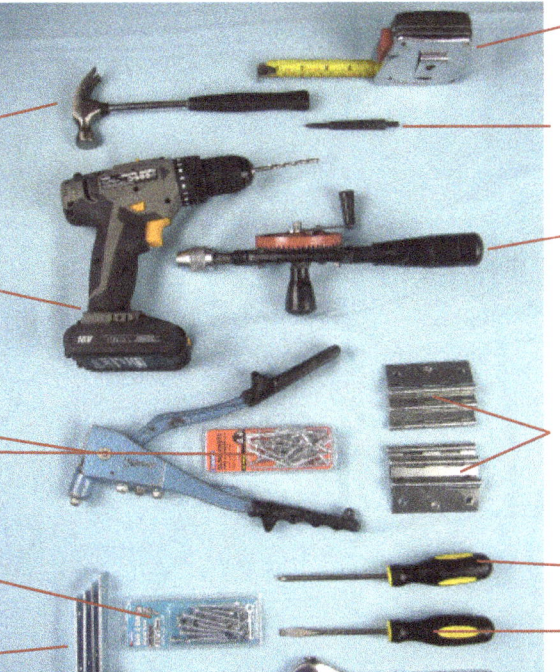

- Hammer to hit the centre punch.
- Electric drill and 3mm, 4mm, 5mm drill bits
- Pop rivet gun and 4 5mm x 6.5mm blind rivets
- 18 x 5mm x 38mm nuts and bolts
- 4 x 10cm x 10cm brackets or larger 12.5cm x 12.5cm
- Tape measure
- Centre punch to make a centre point for the drill bit.
- Hand drill if you do not have an electric one.
- Six 85mm hinges
- Philips screwdriver
- Flat screwdriver
- Shifting spanner

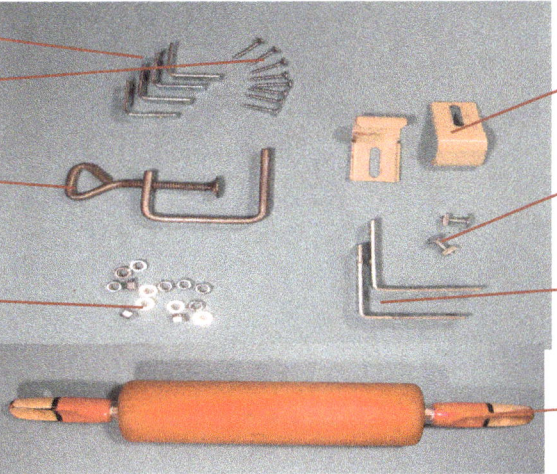

- 4 x 25mm x 25cm angle brackets and self tapping screws
- A small clamp to hold the bracket while you drill and bolt it in place.
- 5mm lock nuts for the bolts holding the brackets on the uprights.
- The 2 curtain rod attachments are bolted to the brackets with 2 x 5mm nuts and bolts.
- Two 5cm x 5cm brackets to hold the curtain track.
- Rolling pin to roll the adhesive velcro hook.

12

Assembling the pieces

rough edges

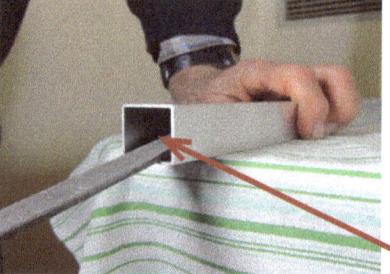

1. File all the rough edges inside and outside.

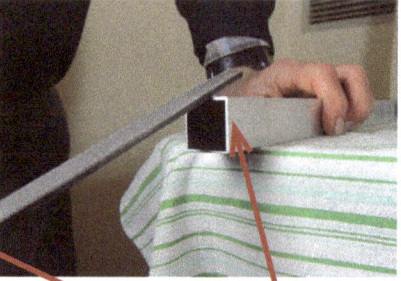

smooth edges

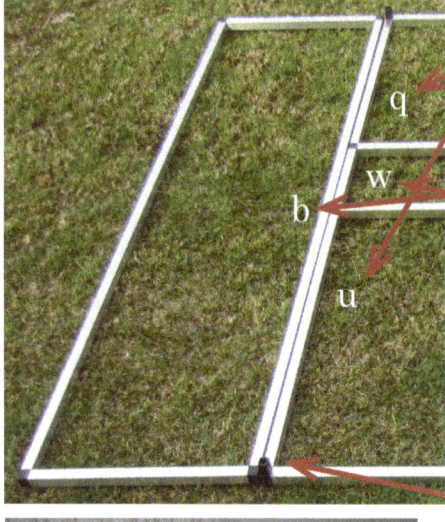

2. Knock 'T''s into q, u, r, v with a rubber mallet.
3. Place next to b and c in their positions.
4. Check length of w and x in case it is not exactly 25cm. Cut them out to your measurement from the two 37cm leftover pieces.
5. Screw in corner brackets.

Keep the leftovers.

Knocking together with a mallet.

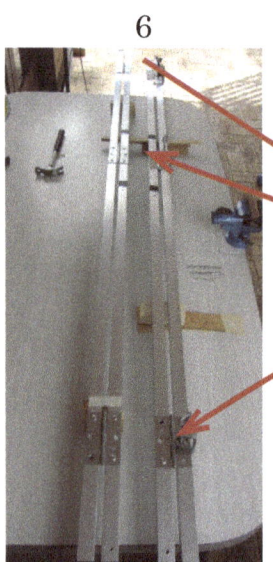

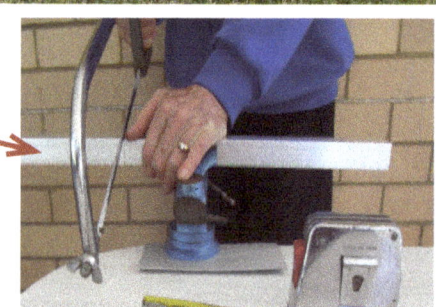

6 7 8 9

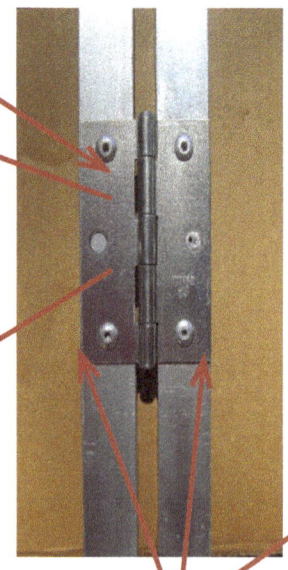

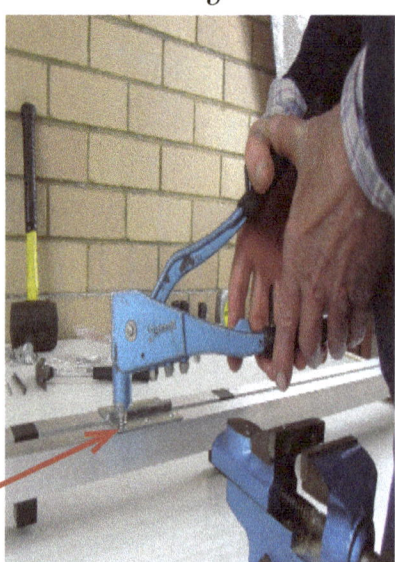

6. Join centre to side wing with 85mm hinges near top, bottom and on 'w' and 'x'.
7. Line hinges up with the outer edges leaving a gap in between uprights for material.
8. Drill holes for rivets.
9. Use 5mm x 6.5mm blind rivets.

Strengthening & stabilising the theatre

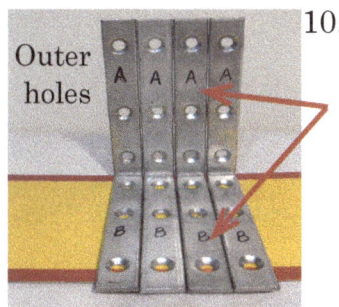
Outer holes

10. The holes on the bracket arm are usually spaced slightly differently, so line them up together with the same arm up and mark those arms with an 'A' and the arm lying down 'B'.

Always bolt this arm 'A' to the theatre front and the other arm will automatically be on the addition so the bolt holes will always line up.

These brackets are essential to strengthen the connectors.

Upright

11. Hold the 'A' arm of a 10 x 10 x 2mm or larger bracket level with the top end of 'q+w+u' upright. Centre punch the two outer holes.
12. Drill a 5mm hole right through the tube.
13. Use 5mm x 38mm bolt to hold it in place.
14. Put another bracket 'A' arm on the bottom end of 'q+w+u' using the same steps.
15. Repeat top and bottom upright 'r+x+v'.

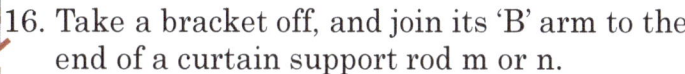

16. Take a bracket off, and join its 'B' arm to the end of a curtain support rod m or n.
17. Repeat this for the other curtain support rod.
18. Repeat for bottom theatre supports 'o' and 'p'.

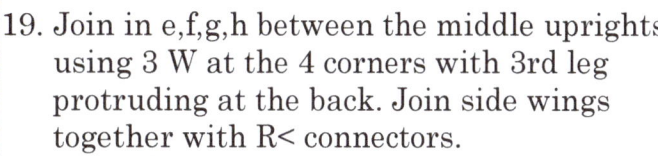
Support rod

19. Join in e,f,g,h between the middle uprights using 3 W at the 4 corners with 3rd leg protruding at the back. Join side wings together with R< connectors.
20. Put adhesive velcro hook on all the front surfaces and go over it with a roller.
21. Put adhesive velcro hook on the top of the curtain support rods m and n.

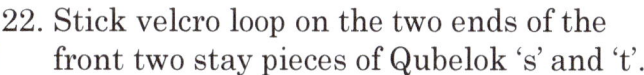

22. Stick velcro loop on the two ends of the front two stay pieces of Qubelok 's' and 't'.
23. Stick velcro hook on top of 'e' and bottom of 'h', also side wing tops 'i', 'k' and bottoms 'j', 'l' where the stays will sit.
The stay stops the theatre falling forwards.
24. Join curtain and bottom supports back to the uprights and bolt with lock nuts.

Make sure you have filed the ridges off the 3W connectors as shown on p 9 so these stays and supports come off easily and the connectors do not get broken.

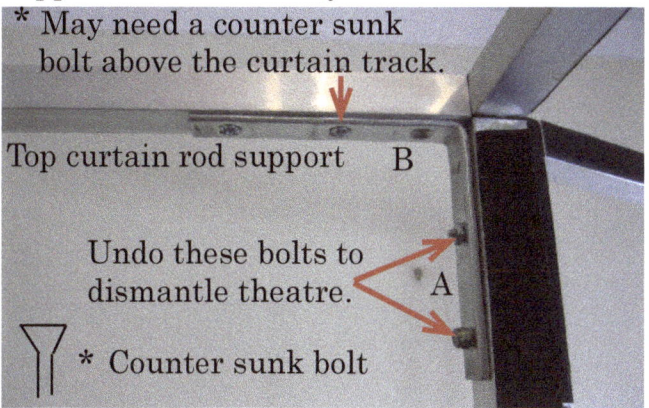
* May need a counter sunk bolt above the curtain track.
Top curtain rod support   B
Undo these bolts to dismantle theatre.   A
* Counter sunk bolt

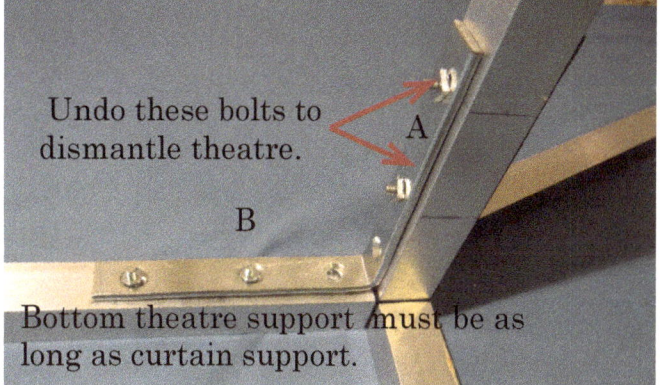
Undo these bolts to dismantle theatre.   A
B
Bottom theatre support must be as long as curtain support.

Scenery rack for small theatre

Here is a cheap simple scenery rack built from two 6.5m lengths of Qubelok Aluminium plus eight 3W connectors.

Cutting instructions. Capral will cut these.

1. With the two lengths together cut them in half.

| 325cm | 325cm |

2. Then place all 4 pieces together and cut at 180cm, then 90cm and 55cm will remain.

| 180cm | 90cm | 55cm |

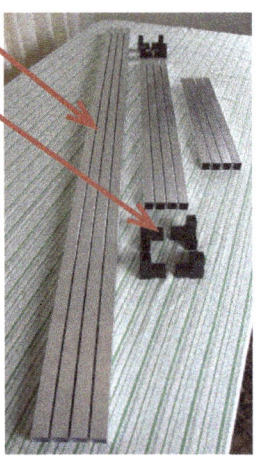

Qubelok and connectors

3

4

3. File the rough bits off inside and outside of the ends.

4. Knock together, as shown, with a mallet.

5

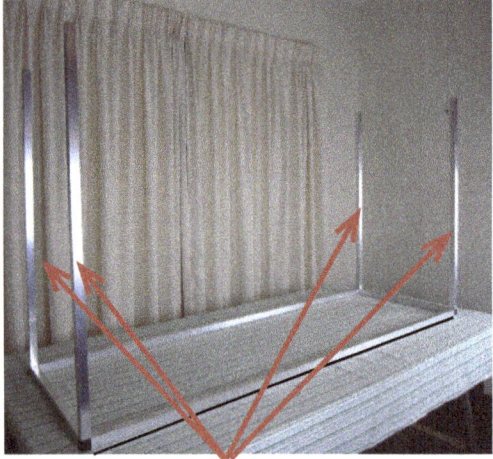

6

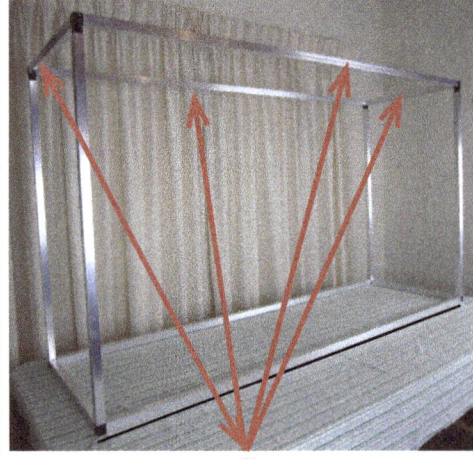

7

5. Knock top and bottom frames together.
6. Knock uprights onto bottom corners.
7. Knock top frame into place on top of these uprights.
8. Stick velcro loop along top two ends of the frame.

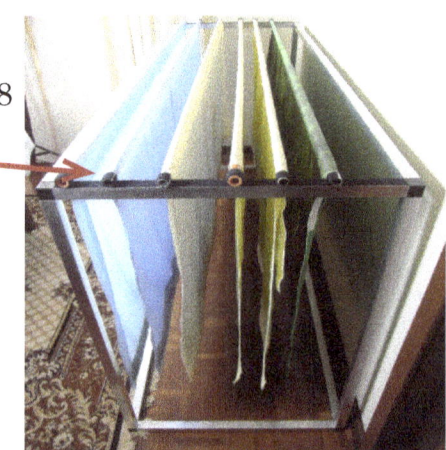

8

Scenery in finished rack.

Large flat hanging props can also hang in this rack on the scene or extra rods.

Blockout covering

Materials needed:

* One 25m roll of self-adhesive velcro hook.

* One 25m roll of sew-on velcro loop.
  (Velcro available at www.tapesonline.com.au)

* 6m of 150cm wide black blockout material.

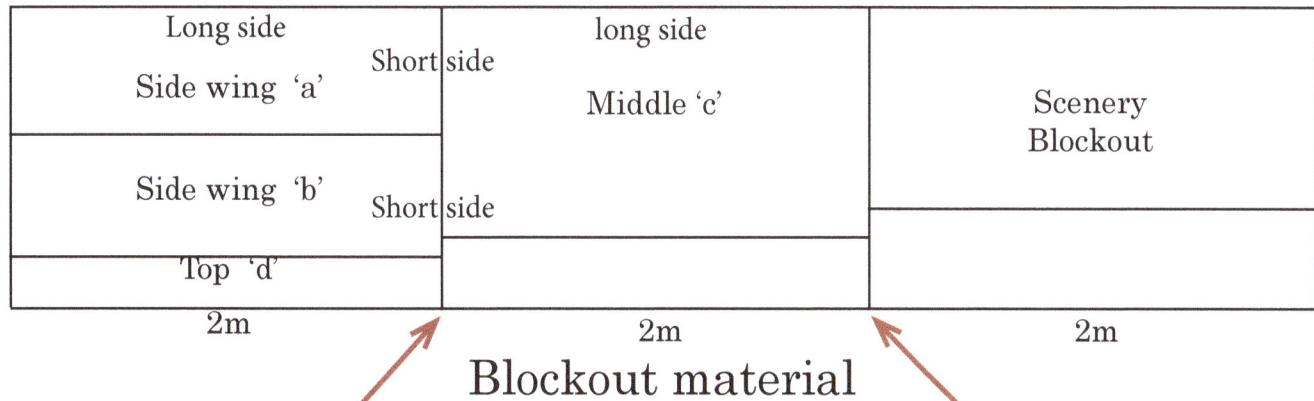

Blockout material
Divide the length of fabric into thirds and cut.

Check your theatre measurements. Add at least 3cm each side (may differ slightly to manual).

1st third ~ side wing frame plus 3cm all round for a single hem so it will = 193cm x 67cm.

1. Draw the measurements on the back of the material and cut it out.
2. On opposite sides 1 and 2 of the side wing 'a' and 'b', turn a single 2.5cm wide hem (the same width as the velcro) and machine the loop onto it. Do the same on sides 3 and 4.
3. Take the leftover 'd'. Turn a double hem on the two short sides and then one long side.
4. On the last long side turn a single hem and stitch loop on to it.
   This piece goes on the top rail to hide the curtain rod.

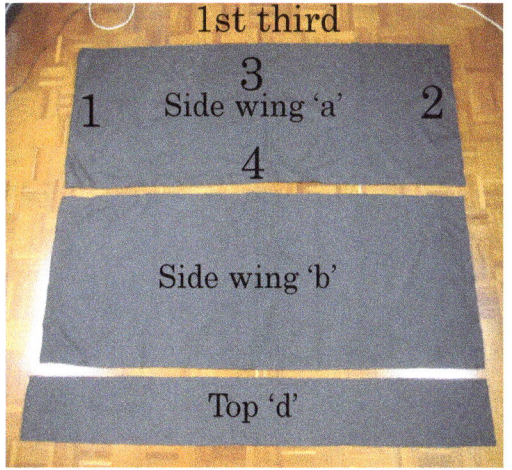 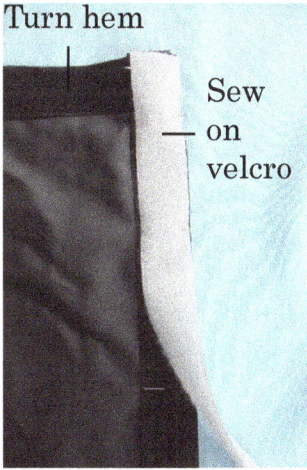 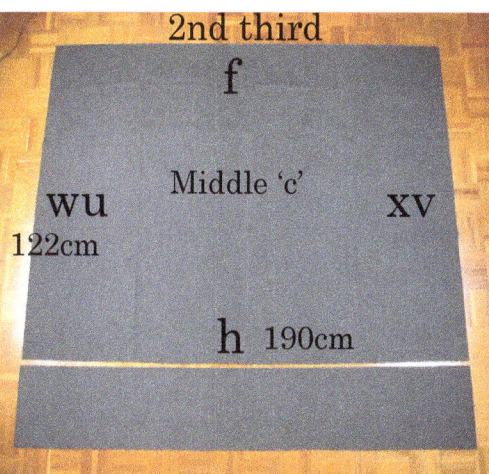

2nd third ~ middle section measure 'f' down to 'h' by 'wu' across to 'xv' (including frame) add on 2cm to both totals for a single hem allowance. It is about 122 x 190cm. Cut it out.

1. Turn a single 2cm wide hem, the same width as the velcro, along one side and machine the loop onto it. Do this on every side. Refer to theatre layout p 9.

3rd third ~ keep for the back blockout scenery curtain.

Velcro frames, if not done yet, as instructed on p 14, step 20. Lie the theatre flat on it's back on the ground, support frame, apply velcro to front surfaces and roller to seal it on.

Blockout curtain

1. Cut the third piece of blockout material 200cm x 120cm.
2. Sew a double 5cm hem on both short sides 'd' and 'b', then long sides 'a' and 'c'.

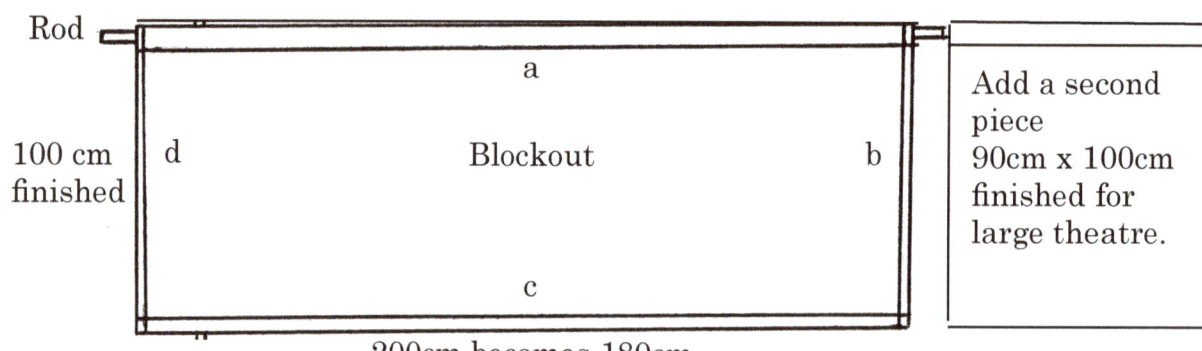

Rod

100 cm finished

a

d   Blockout   b

c

200cm becomes 180cm

Add a second piece 90cm x 100cm finished for large theatre.

Mounting the curtain track

Purchase an adjustable 2.4m track for the small theatre, so the curtains can be opened right back to the sides, or a 3.5m track that will do for both the small and the large theatre.

1. Mount two 5cm x 5cm brackets on the frame above the proscenium, hanging down 10cm in from each side using a 5mm x 38mm nut and bolt.

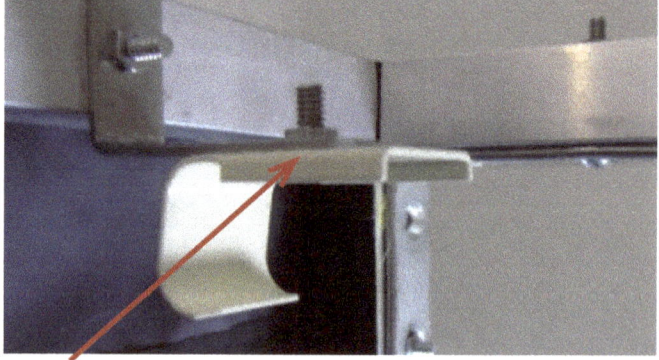

2. Bolt the curtain mounting bracket to the end bracket hole and space it out from the frame to allow curtain to gather.

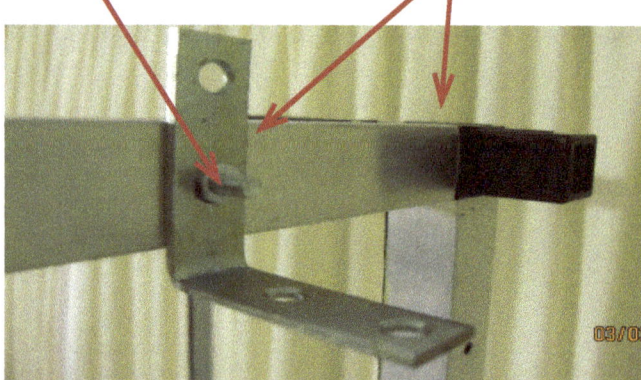

3. Clip track into bracket.

   Use this system because trackgliders/runners will catch on any screws put in the back of the track.

4. Take the leftover blockout piece 'd' and turn a double hem on the two short sides and on one long side.

5. On the last side turn a single hem and stitch loop on to it.

   This strip goes on the top rail to hide the curtain rod.

Front curtains

Make bracket holes 10cm in from each side as in no.1 on the previous page, in the bottom theatre frame. The curtain can be hung there when the theatre is used upside down.

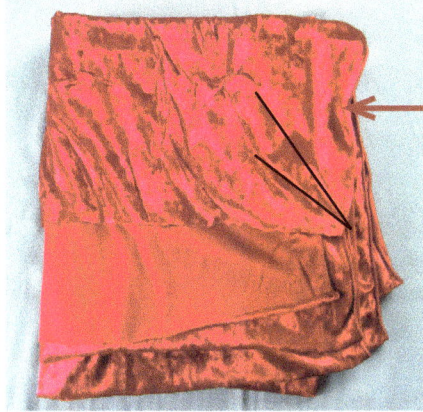

Purchase

200cm x 150cm of fabric for two 100cm x 150cm curtains or a 300cm x150cm to do the large or small theatre.

300cm gathering tape for small
450cm gathering tape for large
50 or 80 steel curtain hooks.

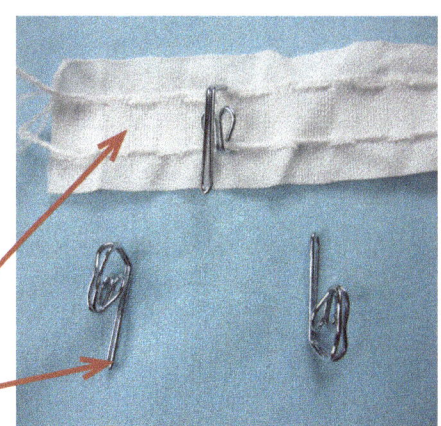

1. Cut material into two (100cm x 150cm) pieces. or add 100cm x 150cm to each of the above drops for large theatre.

2. Double hem (turn material twice) sides 'b' and 'd' of curtains.

3. Turn a single 2.5cm hem, (width of the gathering tape), along top 'a', 150cm side.

4. Pin the gathering tape to the hem on the wrong side.

5. Machine along both sides of the tape.

6. Space hooks evenly along the tape.

7. Attach them into the track runners.

8. Tighten the gather of the tape on each curtain to fit across a little over half the stage.
9. Curtain length needs to be 90cm, so measure it and turn up the bottom side 'c' then hem. It can then be used in all three theatres, that is the plate, gloves and the marionette one.

Sometimes it is better to have no curtains, to allow more room for the puppetry.

Scenery curtains

1. Choose a see-through piece of coloured material suitable for an inside or outside scene.
2. Cut it down to 200cm wide and 110cm deep, then it will suit both prosceniums.

3. Sew a double 5cm hem on both short sides 'd' and 'b'.
4. Sew a 6cm hem along the bottom side 'c'.

5. Fold side 'a' at 75cm from side 'c'. Machine along 5cm in from the fold with a gather stitch (which can be easily pulled undone and restitched to suit the deeper proscenium 90cm drop) leaving the excess to hang down behind. (Curtain is now 180 x 75cm finished)

6. Sketch scenery ideas and hold a puppet in front of it to check that the scenery is the right scale/size for the puppet.

7. Don't overload your scenery back drop with objects. Puppeteers need to see their puppets.

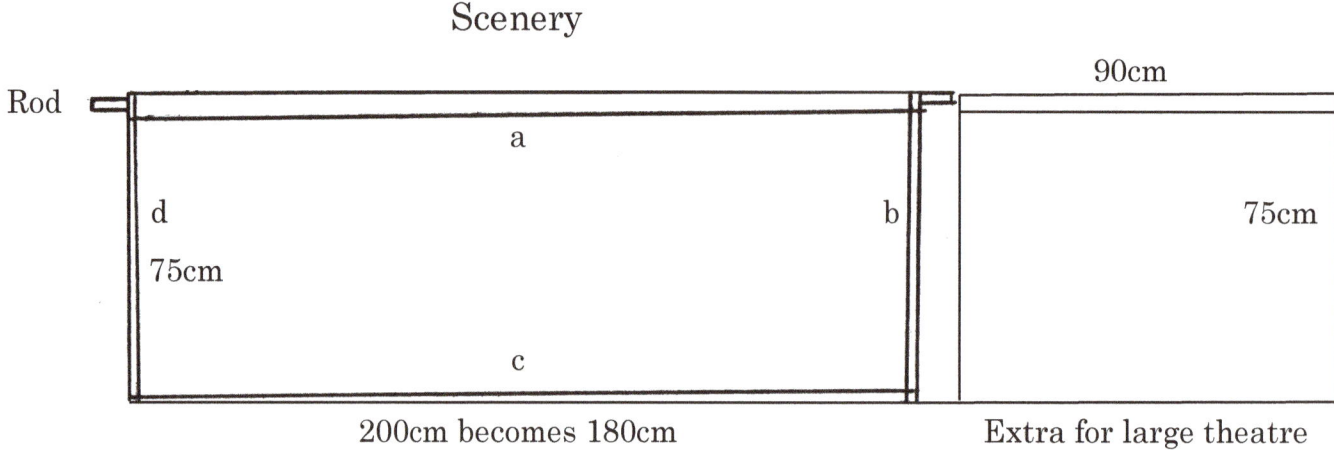

Scenery

200cm becomes 180cm   Extra for large theatre

8. Stick self-adhesive hook on the top side of curtain support.
9. Put velcro loop around the ends of the 190cm rods.
10. Push a rod through the top hem of each curtain.
11. Locate blockout on the back end of the curtain support.
12. Put scenery curtain approximately 23cm from the front end of the curtain support.

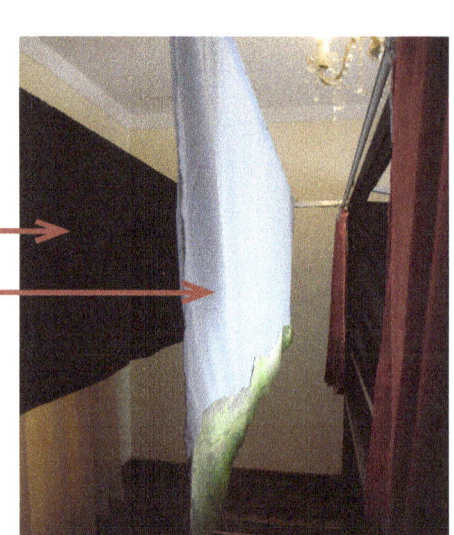

The puppeteers stand between the black curtain and the scenery curtain so they can watch their puppet through it.

The black curtain blocks any back light so the puppeteers are hidden.

Standard lights, or reading lights clamped to the front stays,

NEED TO BE FOCUSSED ON THE SCENE

so the puppeteers can see their puppets.

Making Puppets

Later on I wed Dame Joan
Her name was later changed to Judy.
Boy! Does she ever make me moan.
Stirs me up but to treat her crudely
I hit out with my famed slapstick.
Now it's quite well known like me.
More amusing than a donkey's kick,
You've all heard of slapstick comedy.

Choice of play

How to make your puppet

~ human or animal.

Production details

~ acting, choreographing and music.

Performance

Puppetry program

Every group will progress at their own rate according to many factors. Stages are listed (below) and each can be ticked off when completed.

The theatre is best made beforehand and used to illustrate puppetry. Otherwise it needs to be made quickly to maintain the momentum.

Play

1. Gather versions of suitable stories for glove puppets from your school, home, libraries and the web.
2. Select simple plays to try for puppetry that younger children will enjoy.
3. Show pictures from these resources to illustrate scenery and characters.
4. Using your collection, create the script. This can be an English exercise.
5. Invent your characters, set the scene, add fun as you go along.

    Puppet plays benefit from short, action-packed interaction, not l-o-n-g speeches.

6. Introduce puppets by showing one you bought or made.
7. Demonstrate puppetry fun and your invisibility with a performance of a short play.
8. Sort out the characters and match them with your puppeteers.
   You can have two or more different puppets for a character to be used in different scenes, (e.g. Cinderella dressed in rags and Cinderella at the ball).
9. Put the puppeteers into groups according to acts or scenes.

Puppet making

Gather the materials needed for the puppets.

Paper head ~

Balls 60 - 80mm, up to 100mm for a troll.

Newspaper and starch or water-based glue.

Cardboard and water based glue
Paint and brushes

Face ~

Pens, fine brushes, cardboard.

Polystyrene head ~

Balls - 60 - 80mm plus 100mm for Troll.

Cardboard and water-based glue.

Paint and brushes.

Face ~

Pens, fine brushes, cardboard.

Glove ~
A selection of materials and trims such as buttons, braids, lace, ribbons, etc.

Now it is time to make the puppet.

45 - 70cm puppet cone

A simple cone to make out of any cardboard.
Rest the puppet head on it at any angle when wanting it to be held steady to work on.
Use it to store heads on a shelf.
Put puppet's/puppeteer's name on it.

Head can sit in the 45cm diameter end.

1. Cut out the template.
2. Draw round it on cardboard and cut it out.
3. Curl it round twice, mark where the ends sit.
4. Glue the ends in place.
5. Clamp until dry.
6. Write your name on it.

Rest the head on the 45cm or 70cm end to work on the face or hair.

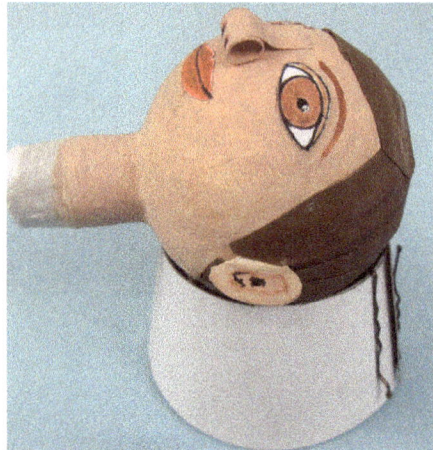

60 - 80cm puppet cone

1. Cut out the template.
2. Draw round it on cardboard and cut it out.
3. Curl it round twice. Mark where the ends sit.
4. Glue the ends in place.
5. Clamp until dry.
6. Write your name on it.

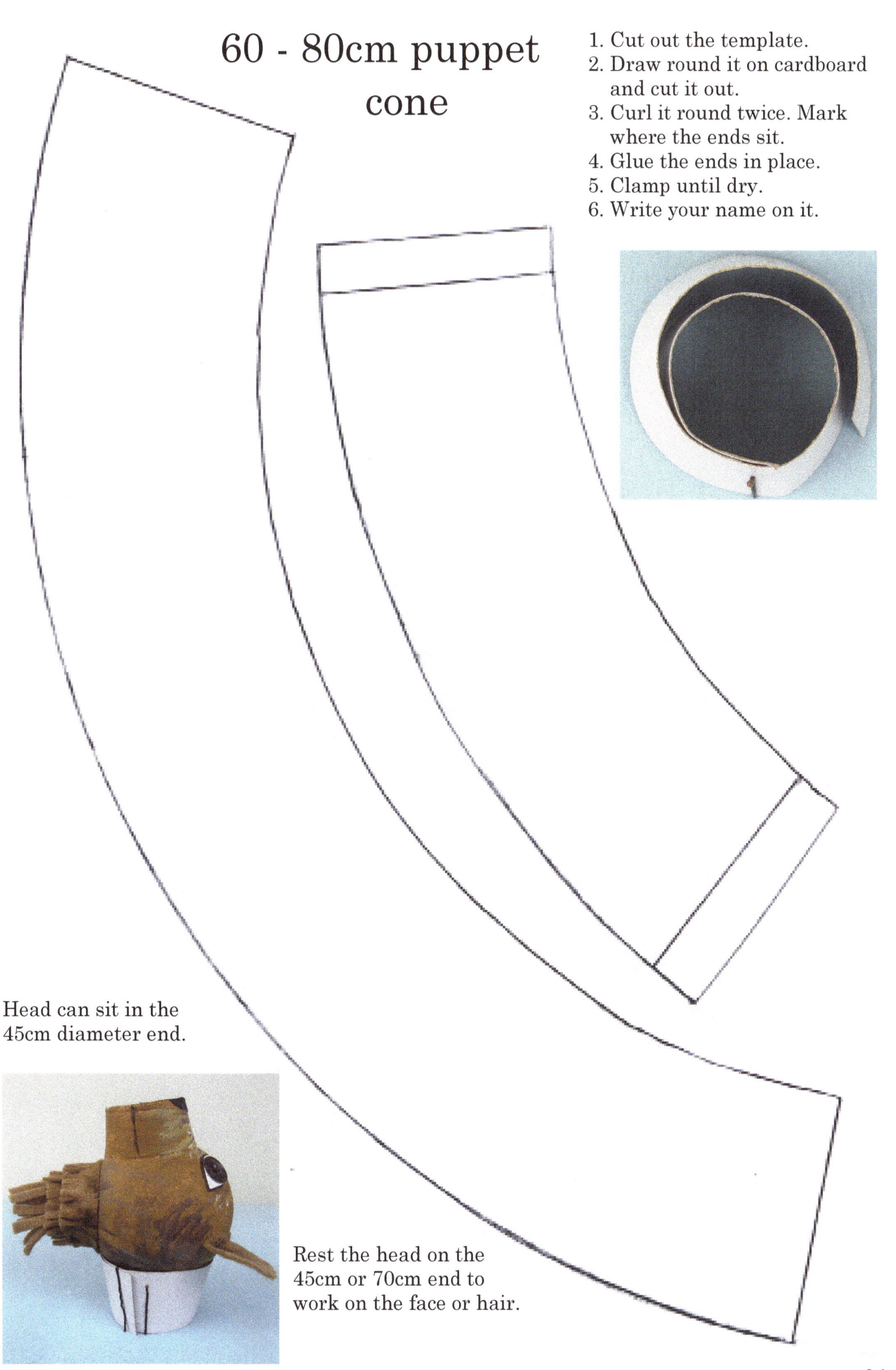

Head can sit in the 45cm diameter end.

Rest the head on the 45cm or 70cm end to work on the face or hair.

Making paper heads

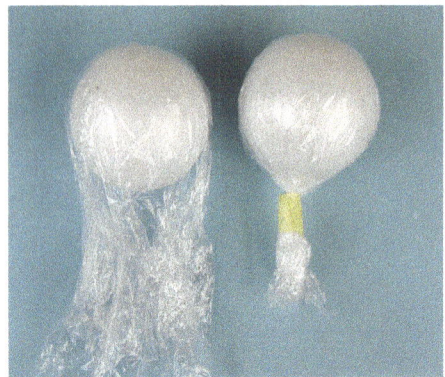
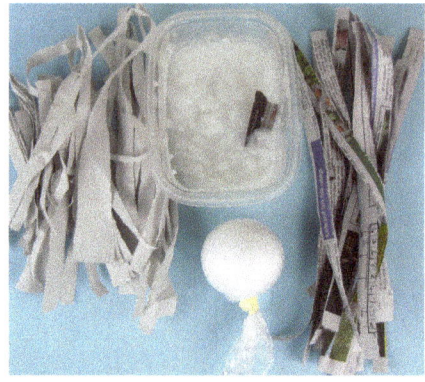

1. Draw a hole, a bit bigger than your pointer finger, on the outside of the ball.
2. Cover ball with glad wrap.

3. Tear 10-15cm strips of butchers paper and newspaper.
4. Make starch or get glue.

5. Glue strips or pieces over ball but not the hole. Do 5 layers alternating plain and newspaper.

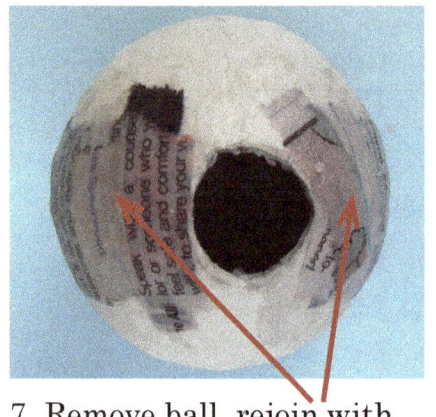
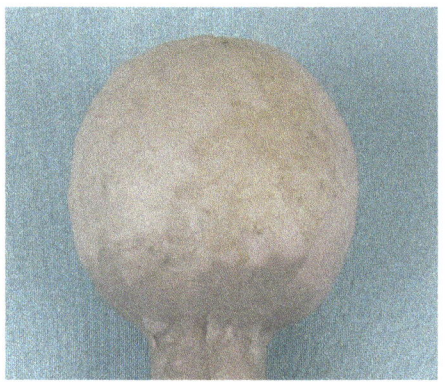

6. Cut the dry ball in half passing through the hole.

7. Remove ball, rejoin with 5 layers of paper pieces.
8. Finish with plain paper.

9. Make a neck and join it in (5 layers of paper pieces).
10. Finish with plain paper.

Neck

11. Cut a cardboard rectangle 14cm by the diameter of the ball + 4cm.

12. Roll it up to fit over your pointer. Put it in the hole and right across the middle to the top of the ball. It should stick out about 4cm at the bottom.

13. Join it into the ball with 5 layers of paper from ball to neck and finish with plain paper.

14. Undercoat it with white paint so the colours go on better.

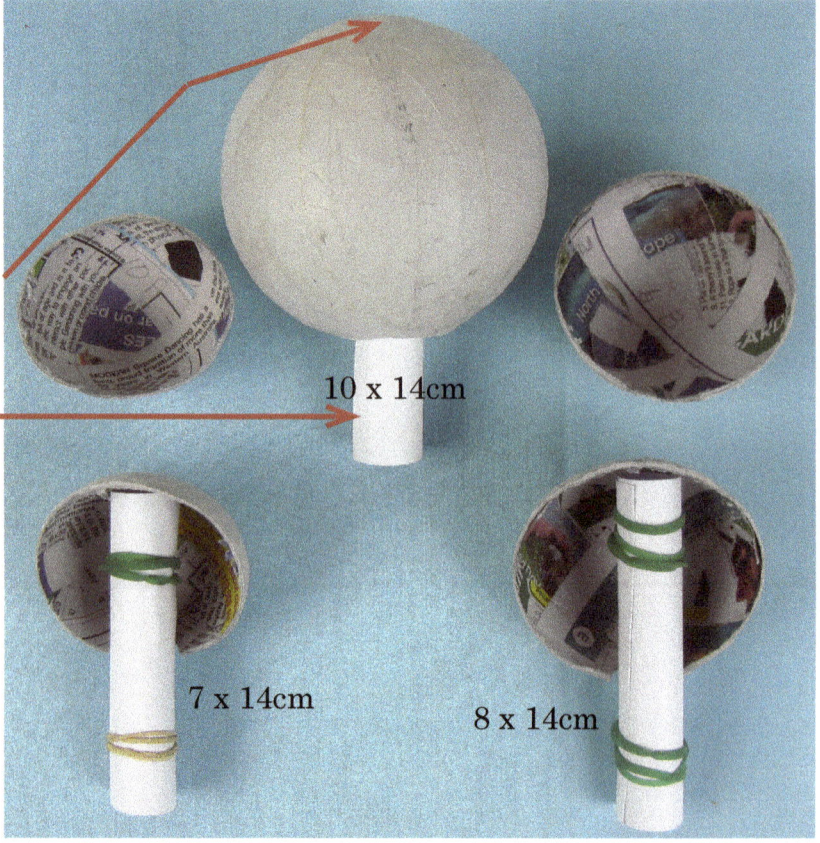

Making polystyrene heads

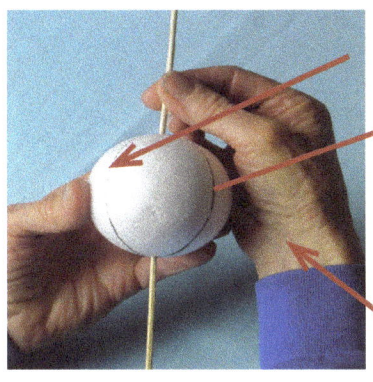
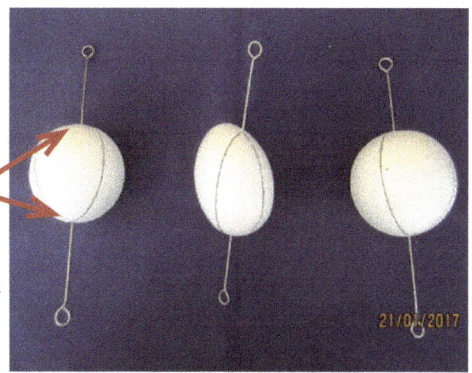

1. Draw a line down the seam of the ball from top to bottom and another at 90 degrees. (a 1/4 slice)

2. Insert a skewer top and bottom.

3. Push the top skewer towards you lining up with the lines and the bottom skewer until it reaches the middle of the ball.

4. Remove this skewer.

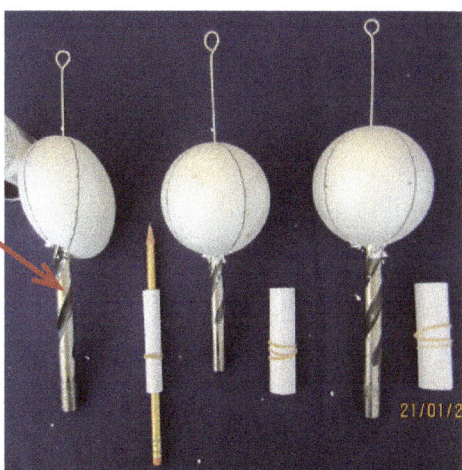

5. Turn the ball on a small drill bit, while lining it up with the marks and remaining skewer, to increase the size of the hole.

6. Increase bit size each time from 3mm to 5mm, 13mm and 19mm.

7. Enlarge the hole until it is loose on your pointer/first finger.

8. Cut a rectangle of thin cardboard 7cm x 15cm on a guillotine or individually.

    Pattern is opposite for an A4 page.

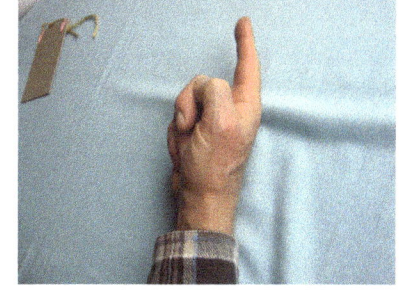

9. Roll the rectangle of cardboard up on a pencil. Slide it off.

10. Insert it into the hole and let it uncurl.

11. Check it fits over your pointer finger.

12. Enlarge the hole if necessary.

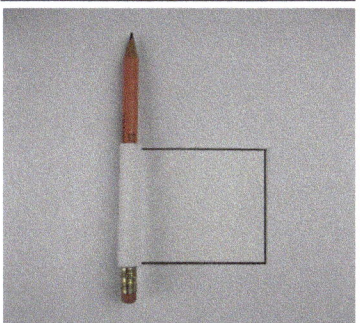
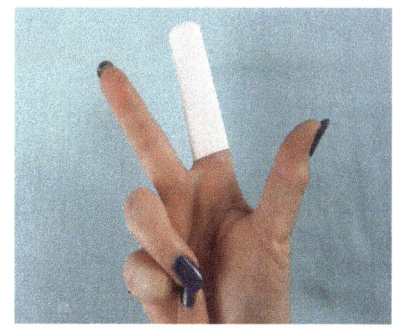

13. Put some water based glue in the hole.

14. Curl the tube tight again.

15. Push it into the hole then let it uncurl.

16. Once again make sure it fits over your finger.

17. Leave it to dry.

18. Paint it white, when dry do main colour.

19. Leave it to dry.

20. Puppet head rack ~ dowels in a piece of wood.

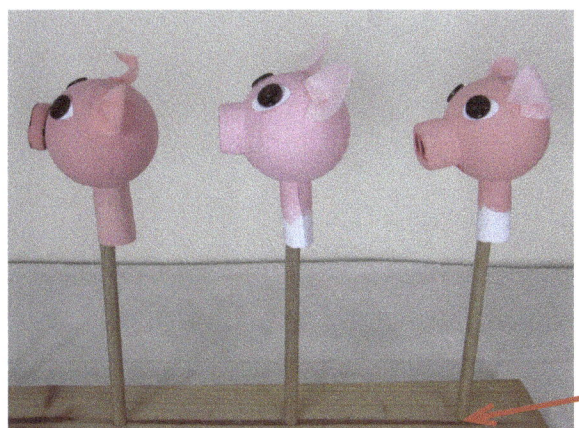

Using the cones

45cm - 70cm diameter cone for small and medium puppet heads.

The small cone makes it possible to work on small heads much more easily.

Puppets stand very well in this small one if the neck is short enough.

Medium puppets rest more securely on the wide base. Small ones on narrow top.

60cm - 80cm diameter cone suits the medium to larger puppet heads.

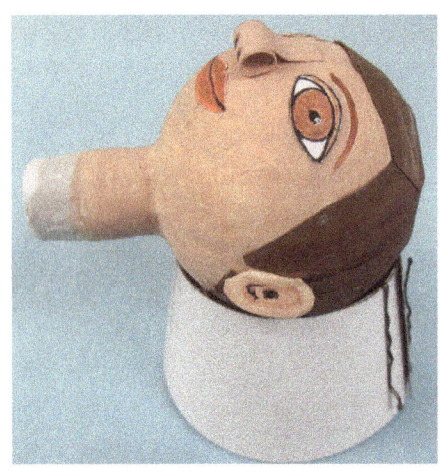

Smaller heads fit well in the smaller end.
It is very stable up this way.

Larger heads can stand in the smaller end.
Write owner's name on cone.

The large heads sit in firmly up this way. They can go on their side too.

Nose cone p 36. Cone can be made wide or narrow and any part used. Pinch it into shape. Cut the section you want longer than required. Then shape the bottom end.

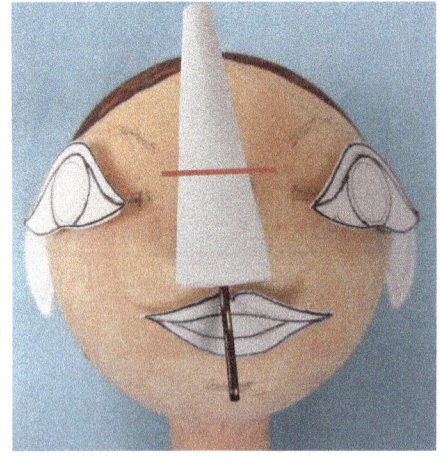
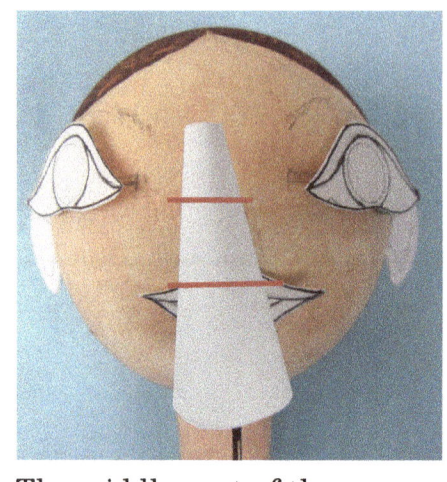

The bottom part of the cone.

The middle part of the cone.

The top part of the cone.

How to use the templates on the next pages

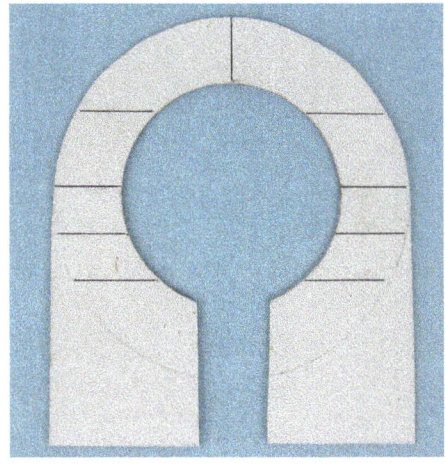
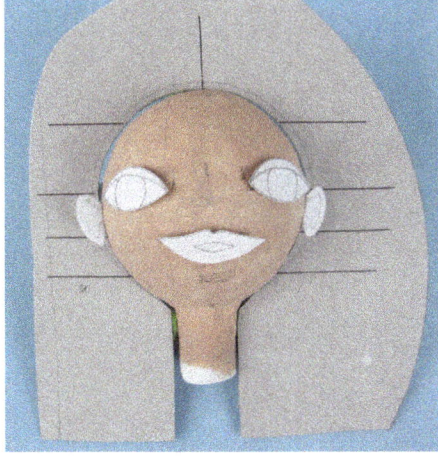
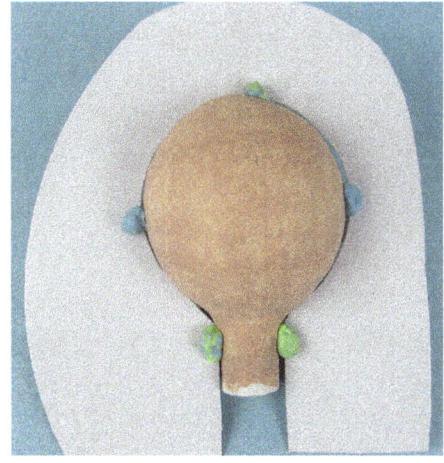

Draw on medium cardboard. Cut it out, adjust if needed. 2 sizes on next pages.

It fits over the head like this.

It can rest on small bits of Blu-Tack if necessary.

Middle of face

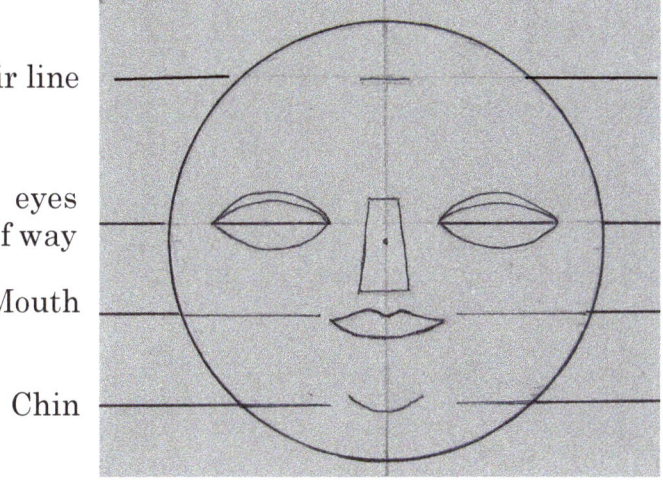

Hair line

eyes half way

Mouth

Chin

Middle of face

Rest the puppet head on the cone.

Place the card over the head.

Hold the 1/2 card vertical on the top and bottom lines and mark the centre down the face.

Then hold the card vertically on the lines going across the face and carefully mark where the hair line, eyes, mouth, chin go. The ears sit between the eye and mouth lines in front of the large flat card.

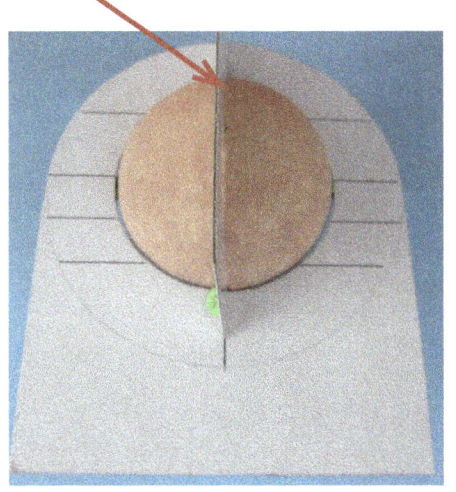
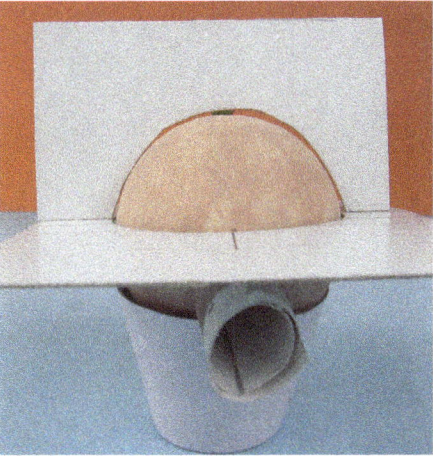
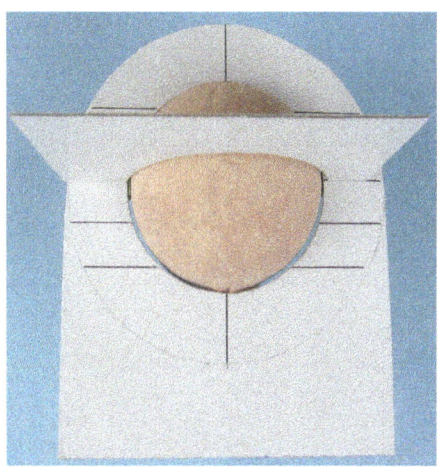

Large flat card with the small card sitting vertical.

Head on the cone. Large card on head. Small card over it.

The small card sitting vertical on the lines.

Templates for marking the face.

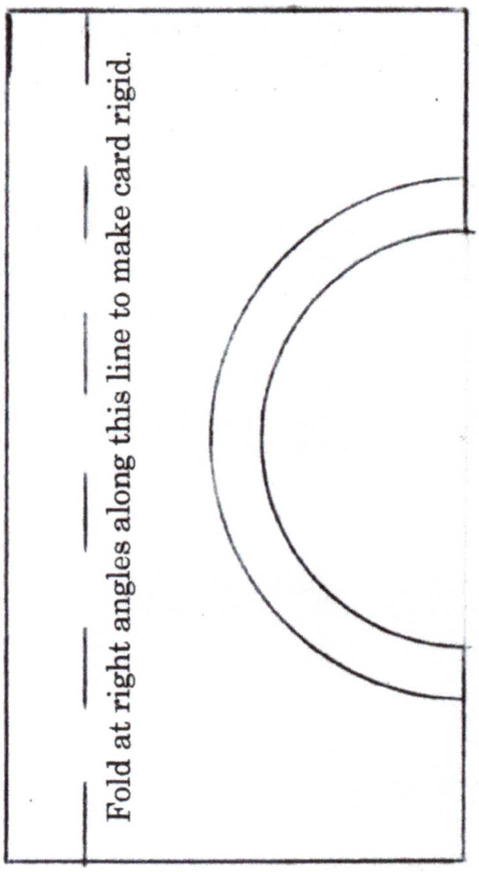

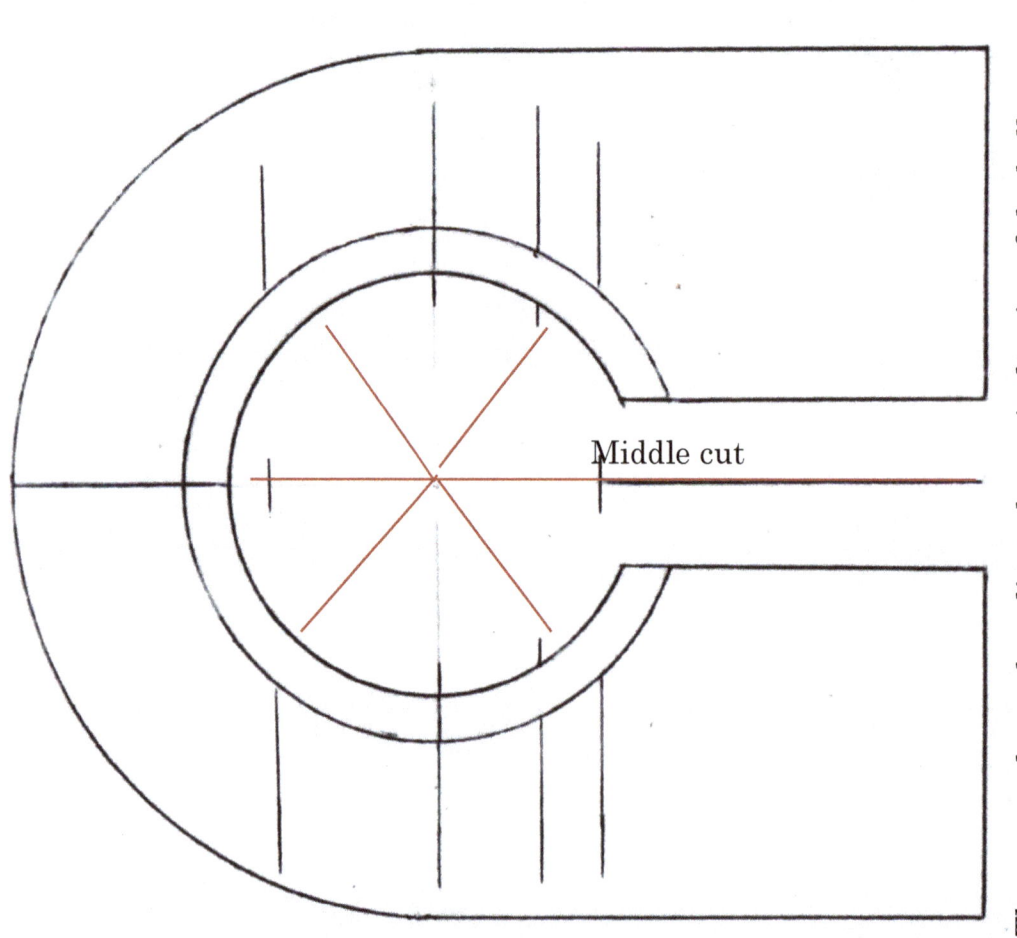

Fold at right angles along this line to make card rigid.

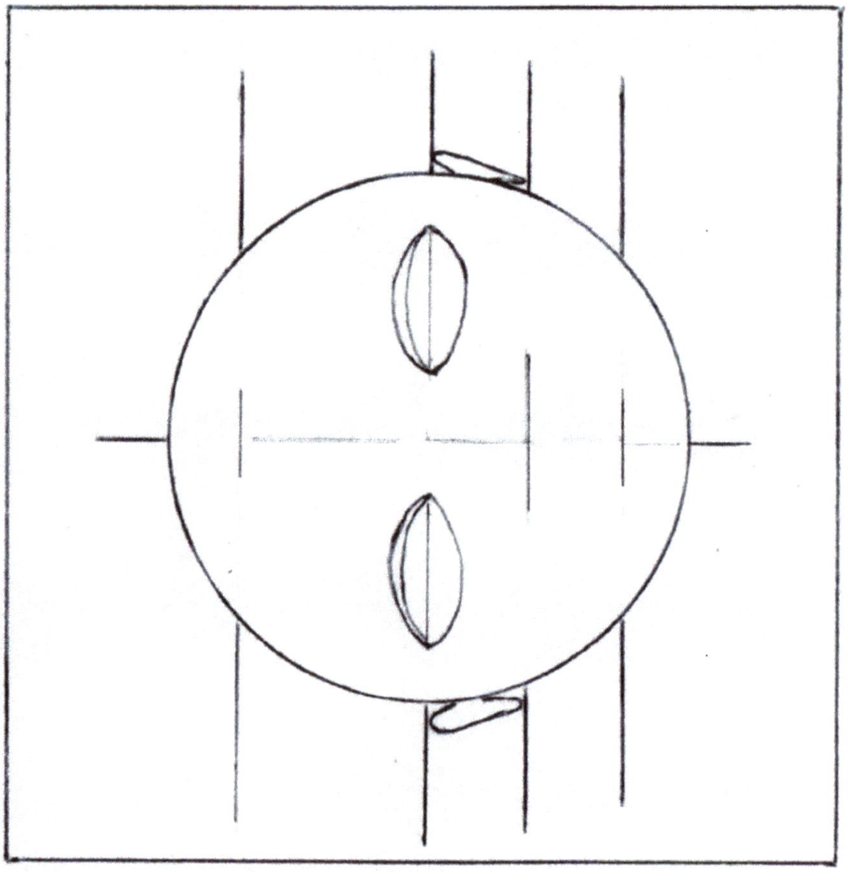

These can always be adjusted to suit the size of the ball.
The double lines at the centre circle give a choice, if in doubt cut out the small one. Then cut it back to the larger one if needed.

If the card is thick, cut up the middle of the neck and straight across to near the top of the circle.
Then cut out from the centre of the circle to near the edge 4 times (red lines). This will make it easier to then cut around the circle from the neck as the card will bend out of the way.

Middle cut

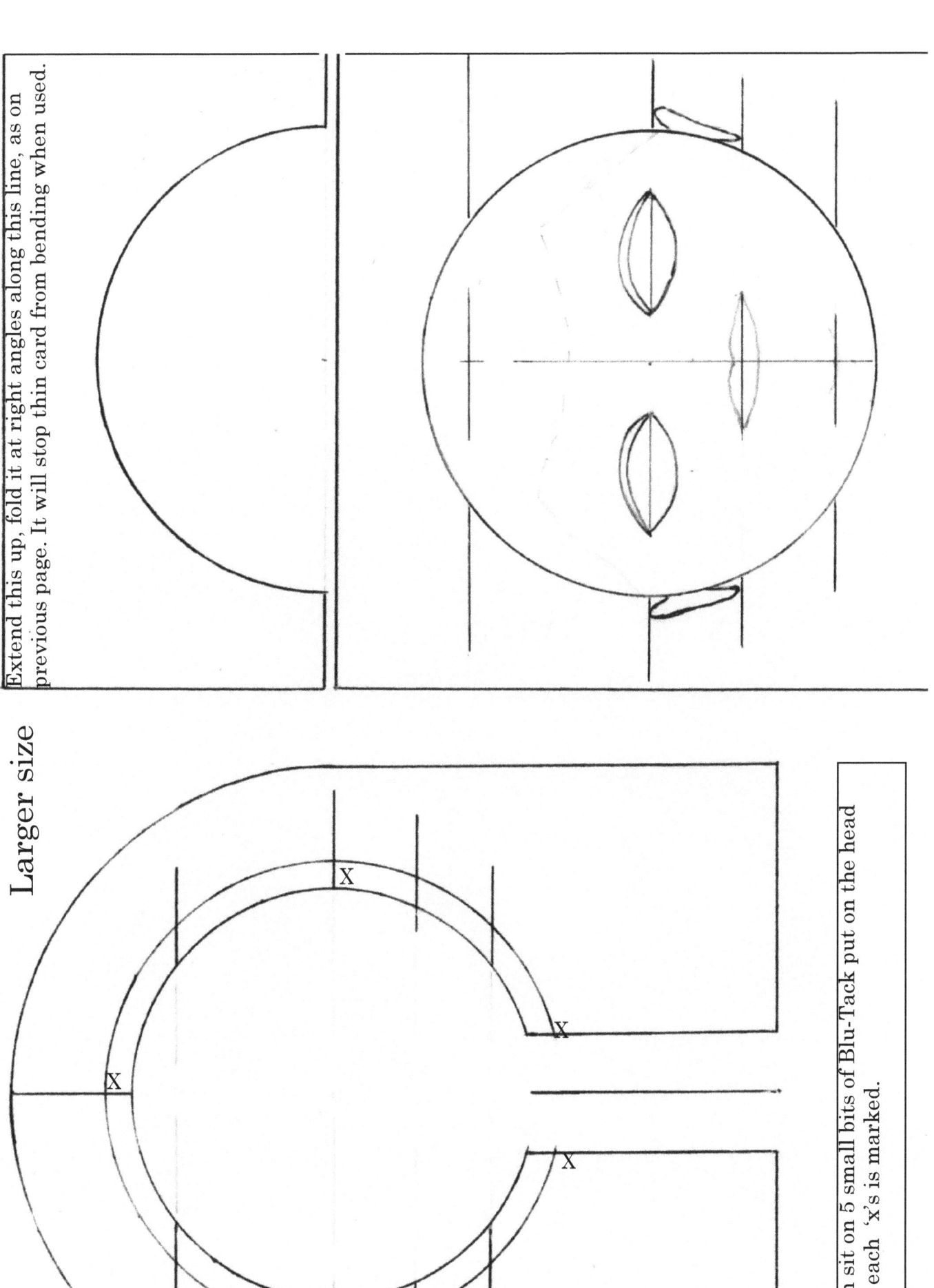

Extend this up, fold it at right angles along this line, as on previous page. It will stop thin card from bending when used.

Larger size

This card can sit on 5 small bits of Blu-Tack put on the head under where each 'x' is marked.

Goldilocks with strips of card curled tightly.   Girl with straight

Goldilocks with strips curled and stretched out.   Boy with a straight

Red Riding Hood with a crepe paper pony tail.

R R H's Mother with a cardboard looped pony tail.

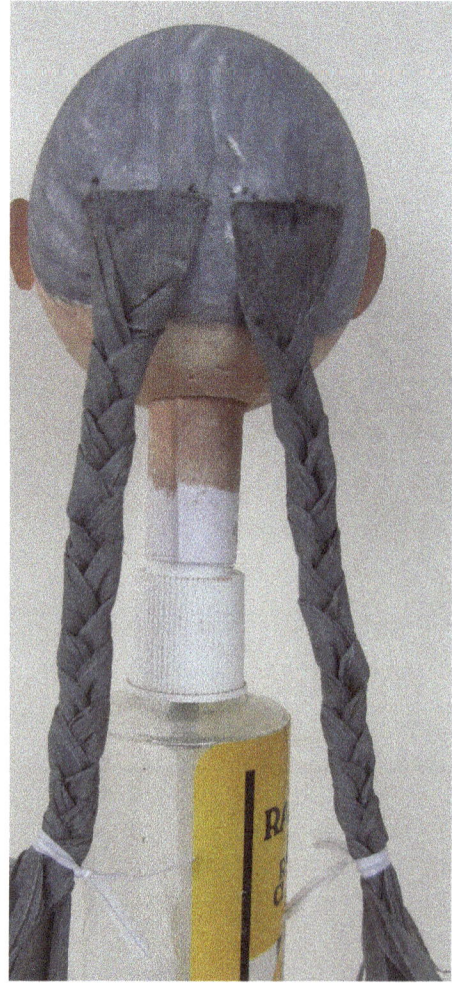

Old woman's crepe paper plaits

cardboard hair and a fringe.

Cardboard curls over the head.

cardboard short hair cut. The woodsman - hair made to fit the head, not cut in strips.

Painted grey hair with a small crepe paper bun.

The old man with white crepe paper hair, eyebrows and beard.

Painted crepe paper hair and pony tail.

Grandmother with white painted hair and a larger crepe paper bun.

Hair with other materials

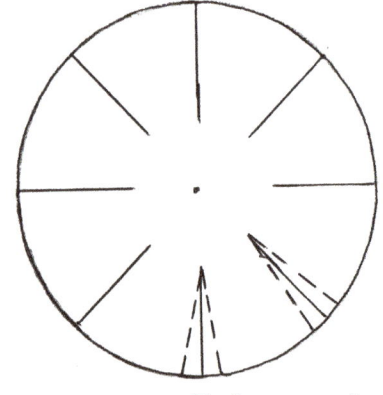

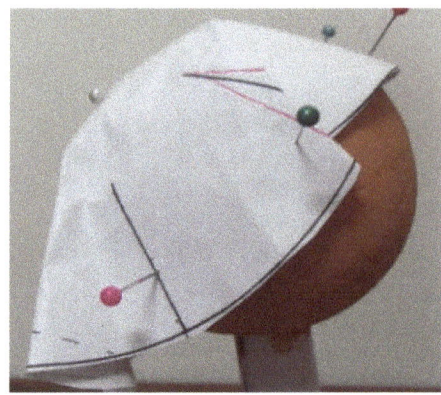

Paper pattern. Enlarge to ball size.   Pinned onto the head.

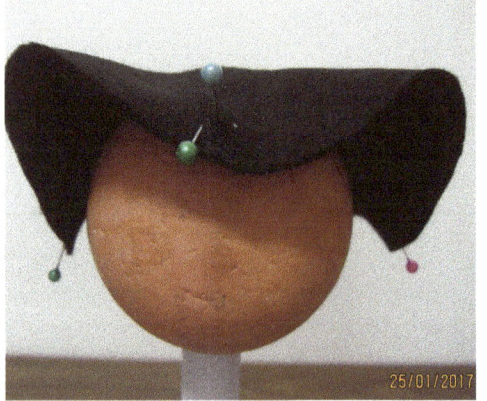
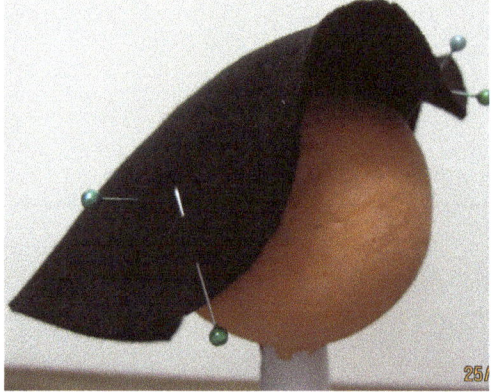
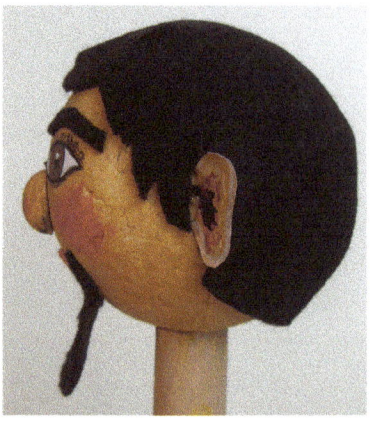

Frontview   Made in felt.   Side view   Finished product.

Attach piece of wool along the top with paper clips. Wind wool over the card.   Glue along top edge, knot the top piece, glue it to the wool.   Lengths cut.   Hair parting

Wool hair

Strands of unravelled wool.

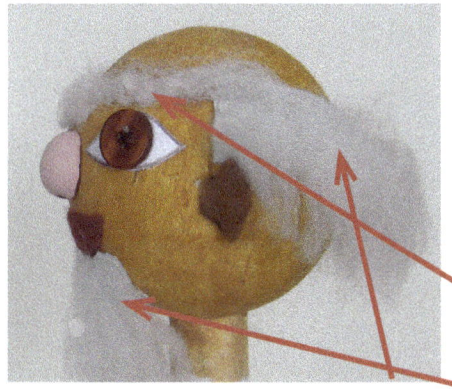 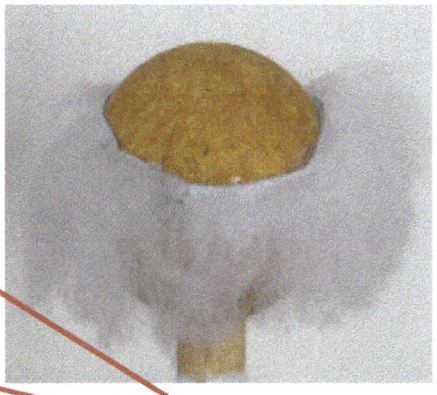 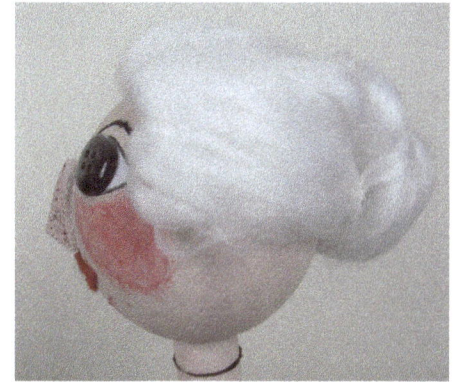

Sheeps wool for hair, beard and eyebrows.

Part of a Father Christmas beard for her hair.

 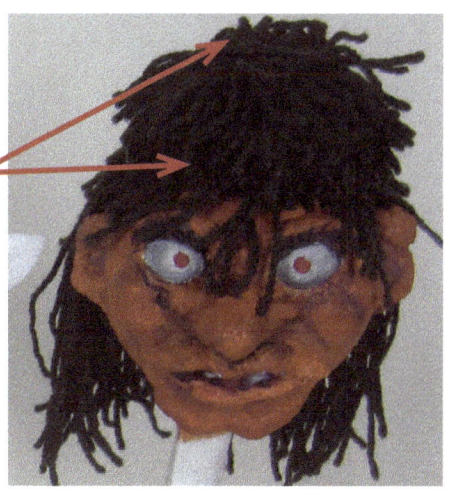

Long pieces of wool stuck on.

Two pom poms were made for the Troll's wild hair - it is illustrated on p 77, 78.

Unravelled wool wound around a card.

Top piece of wool tied off, cut and stuck on the head.

Looped back up at the nape of neck using a rubber band.

The daughter has a pony tail.

Then a ribbon tied around it.

Wool (fine not thick), on a long card was needed for these plaits.

It also required a short layer underneath to add density at the sides and back.

Making the human face

* Teach the basics. Then variations can be made..
* Have pictures of the characters in your plays.
* The shapes on the next page can be photocopied.
* Use the hands and ears as templates to make them in stronger materials.
1. Select and colour in the eyes and mouth from the template on the next page.
2. Cut out the rectangle they are in and then cut out the shape. Work from point to point.

3. Mark the front hair line and the chin. Her fringe reaches her eyes.

4. Pin the eyes about half way between hair line (not fringe) and chin.

   Leave room for the bridge of the nose between the eyes.

   Big eyes are happy eyes.

   Eyes and mouth when slightly lower down look younger.

5. Cut out the mouth.

6. Pin it half way between the eyes and the marked chin.

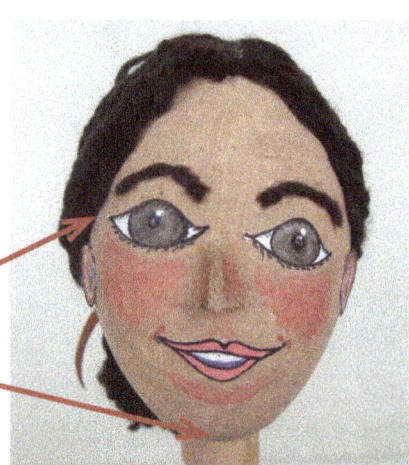

7. Make ears.

8. Put them on the sides of the head between the two lines drawn out from the eyes and the mouth.

9. Pin on the nose and make or draw the eyebrows.

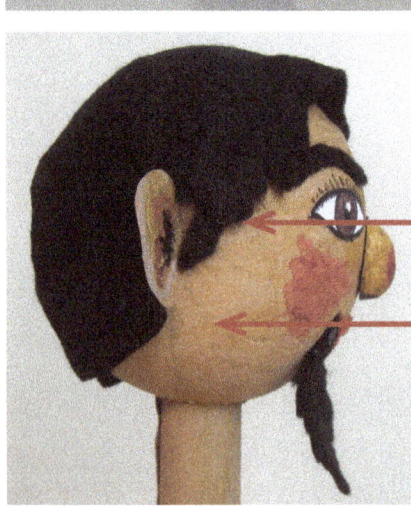

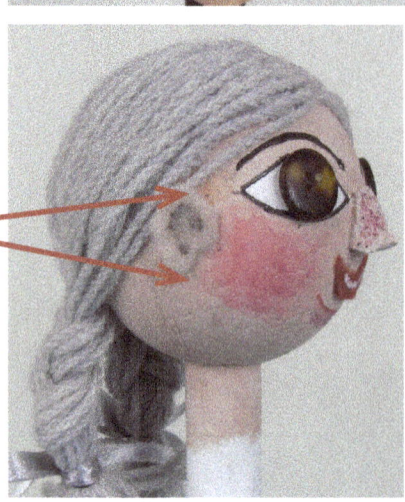

Check and discuss the finished product and make alterations if necessary.
Stick all the features on.

Some things to use for the features.
Eyes ~ drawn on paper, buttons or painted on.
Nose ~ pinched foam, cardboard, half bead, shaped polystyrene or paper mache.
Eyebrows ~ pipe cleaners, wool, pen and paint.
Hair or beard ~ wool, felt, sheep skin, cotton wool and fur.

Paper templates for human face

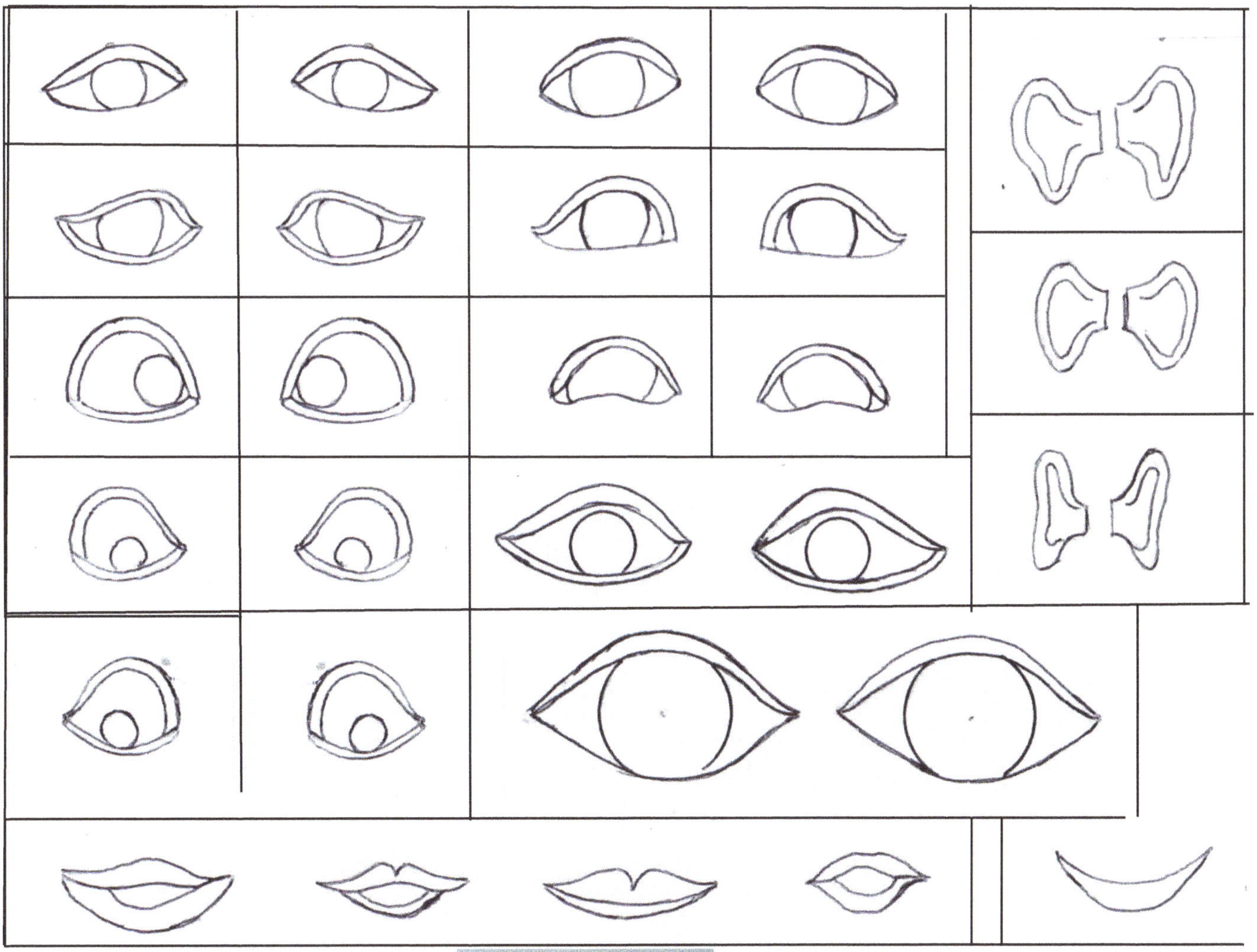

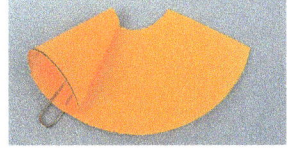

Use all or part of this to make a cone in paper or cardboard.

These are just some shapes that can be made bigger or smaller to suit the size of the head you are making.

Make a narrow or wide cone. Use any section. Shape and cut the front end to be a pointy witch hat or a big rounded clown nose, etc.

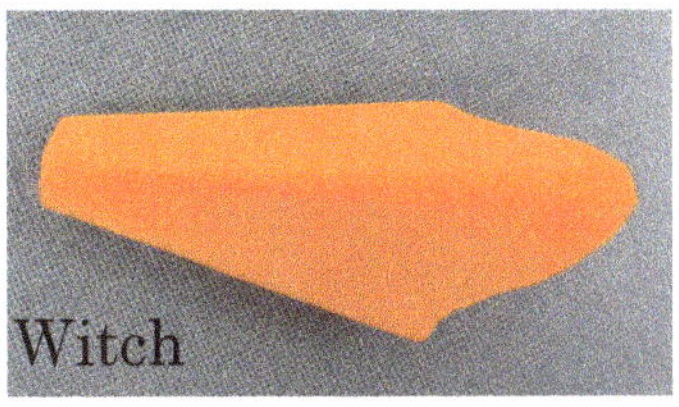

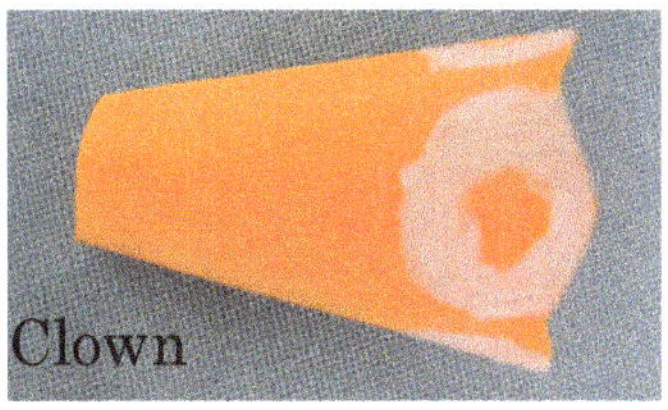

Adjust this size to fit your ball.

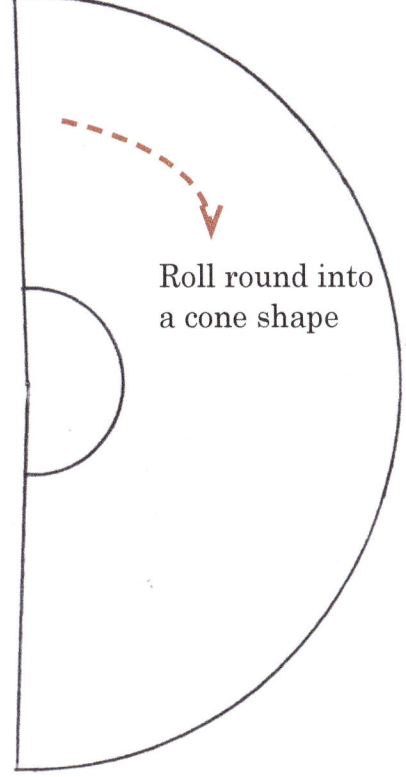

Roll round into a cone shape

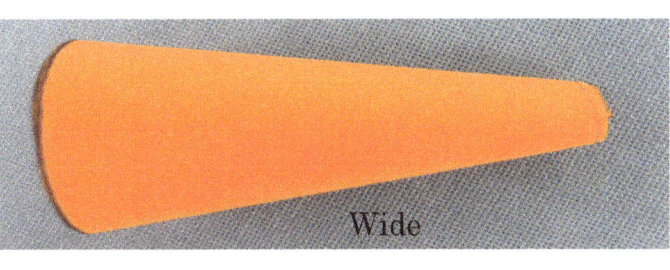

Wide

Narrow

Witch

Clown

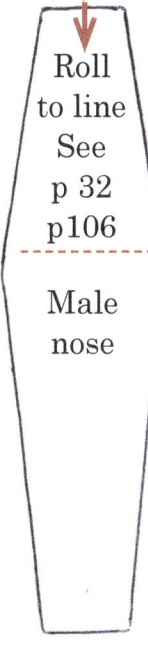

Roll to line See p 32 p106

Male nose

36

Paper animal heads

Pig snout

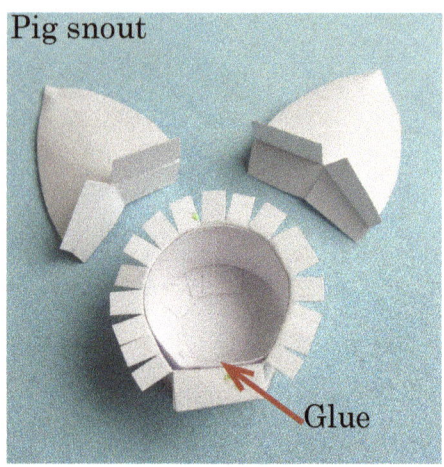
Glue

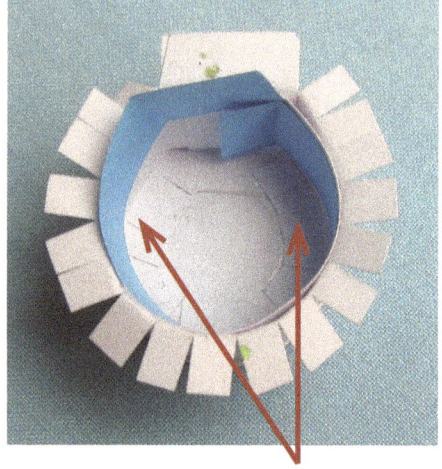

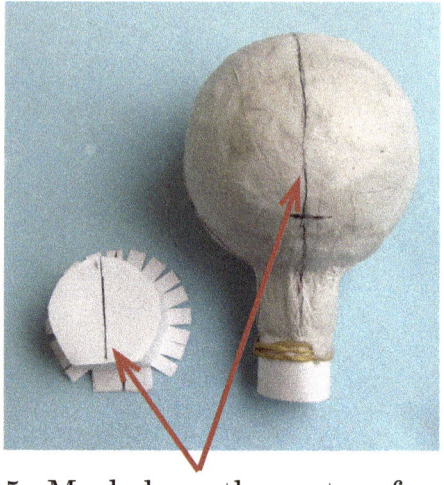

1. Glue 4 ears into 2 pairs, shape and flange bottoms.
2. Cut out snout, snip and bend flanges, then wrap round gluing the overlap.

3. Glue nose on, press down flanges for good contact.
4. Glue reinforcement strip (blue) inside snout.

5. Mark down the centre of the snout and around the ball.

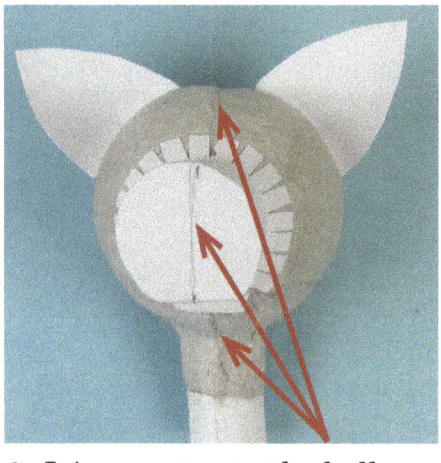

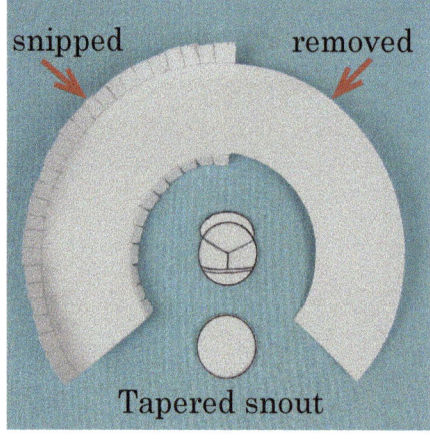
snipped   removed

Tapered snout

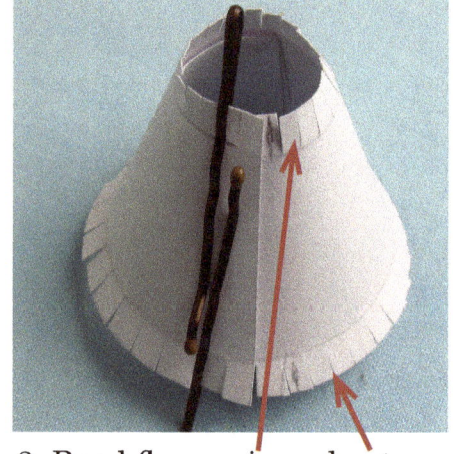

6. Join snout onto the ball. Match up the centre lines.

1. Cut out the template,
2. Remove the flanges on half, snip the other half.

3. Bend flanges in and out.
4. Wrap around twice, glue and clamp till dry.
5. Cut out and glue on nose.

Bear or goat

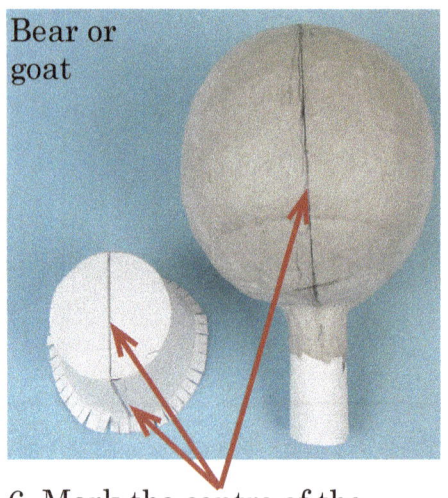

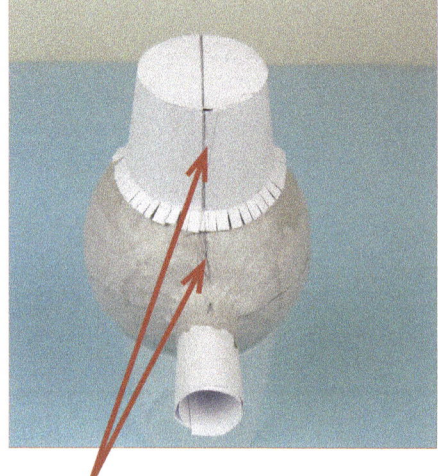

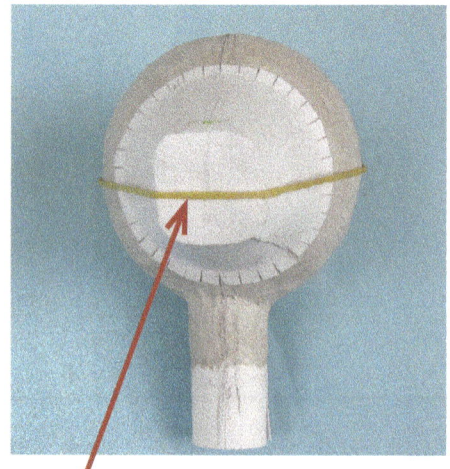

6. Mark the centre of the snout and around the ball.

7. Join the snout onto the ball, matching up the lines.

8. Hold in place until dry with an elastic band.

Paint with white undercoat. Individual templates are on each animal's instruction page.

Polystyrene animal heads

Round ball with neck undercoated white.

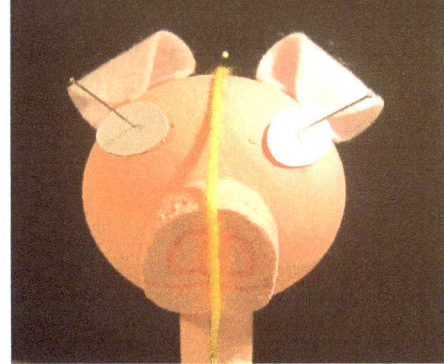
Felt ears, a cork for a nose, cardboard and button for eyes.

Painted mouth and cork nose.

A section of a poly drink cup stuck on the front.

Felt ears, button eyes, paper nose and cut felt around neck.

Painted fur over the head, felt ears and neck.

Polystyrene egg with cardboard neck.

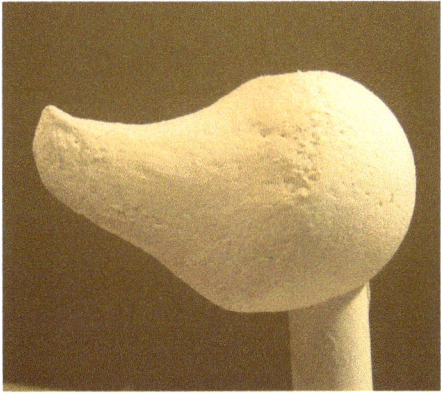
Egg shaped using a saw, rasp, sandpaper, then undercoated.

Both have painted head, eyes, nose, ears and neck.

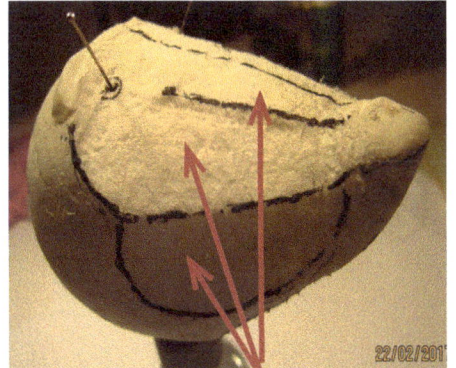
Sections cut off with a small saw then sandpapered.

A folded piece of felt stuck on and cut to be like hair around head.

Pattern for

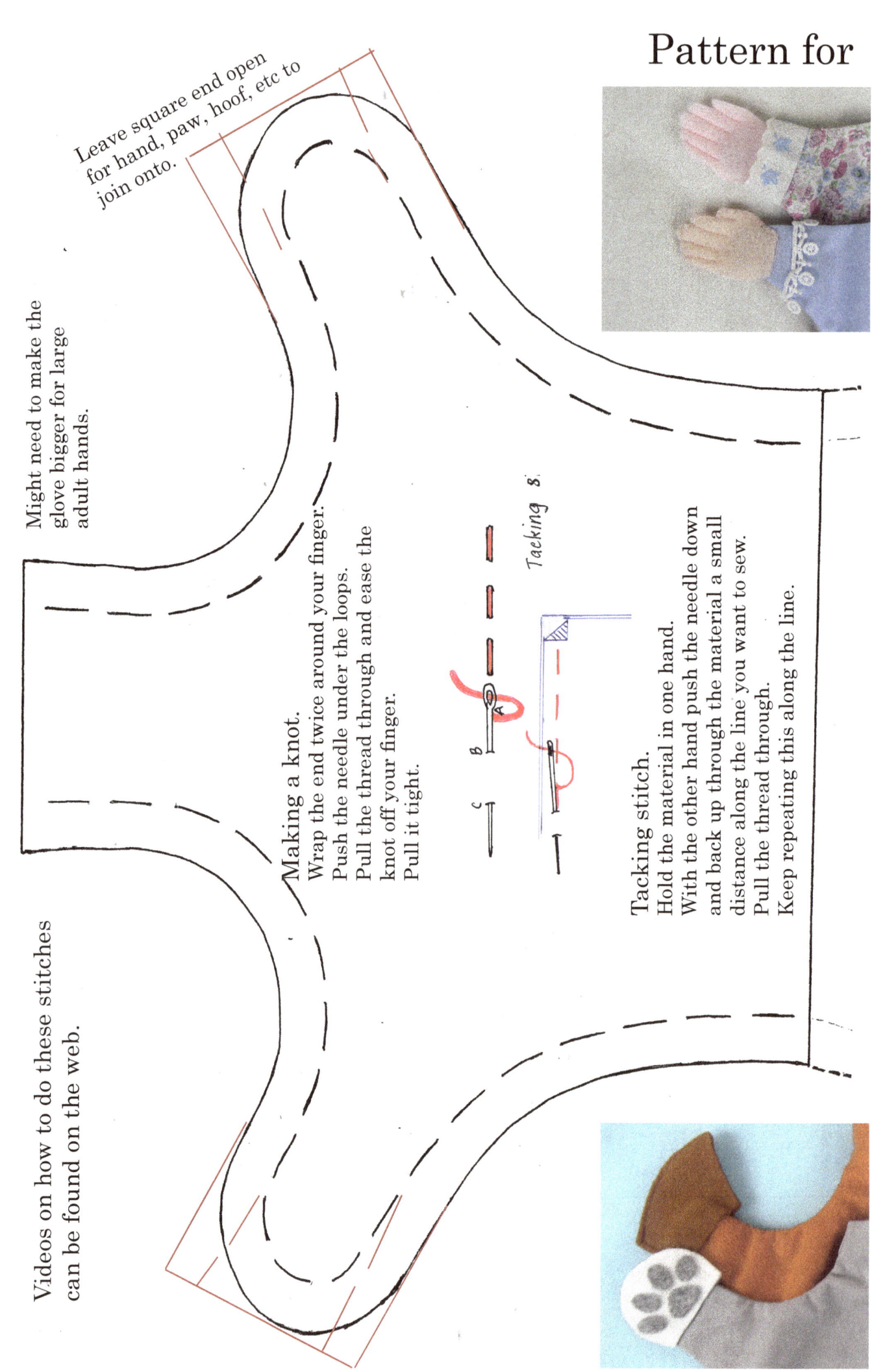

Leave square end open for hand, paw, hoof, etc to join onto.

Might need to make the glove bigger for large adult hands.

Videos on how to do these stitches can be found on the web.

Making a knot.
Wrap the end twice around your finger.
Push the needle under the loops.
Pull the thread through and ease the knot off your finger.
Pull it tight.

Tacking stitch.
Hold the material in one hand.
With the other hand push the needle down and back up through the material a small distance along the line you want to sew.
Pull the thread through.
Keep repeating this along the line.

making the glove

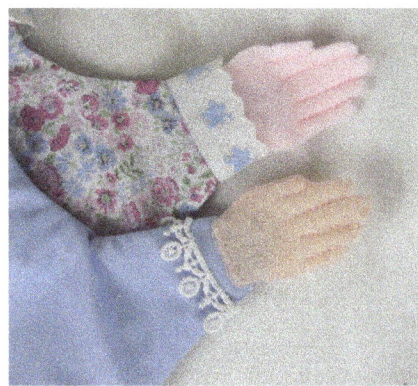

Videos on how to do these stitches can be found on the web.

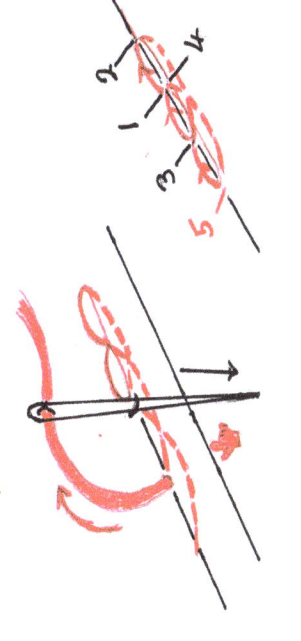

Back stitch.
Hold the material in one hand.
With the other hand, push the needle up through it at 1 and down at 2.

Come up again at 3 in front of 1

Go back down at 1 (your 4th stitch), and out at 5.
So you come out ahead and go back down where you came up for the last stitch.
Keep repeating this with small stitches along your line of sewing.

Sew a turned hem around the neck hole if you want to put elastic through it.

Otherwise cut off excess length or turn it in. Glue the glove to the neck.

Hem the bottom of the glove unless it is in felt material.

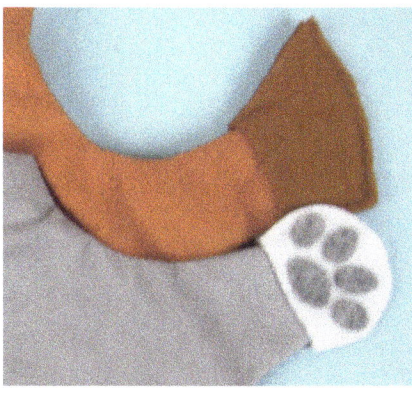

Hand extension

The pointer and thumb that go in the arms of the puppet can be extended with a cylinder of paper that fits them snugly. Allow for this when cutting out and sewing the glove. It enables the hand, etc to reach the head better and be more expressive with sweeping arm movements.
Keep the end of the arm square for this.

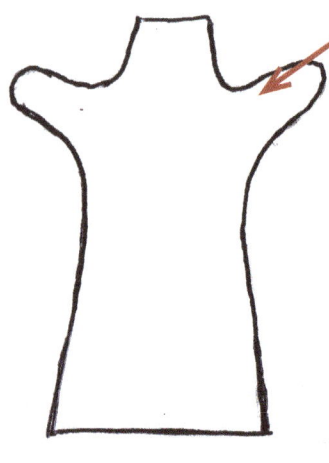
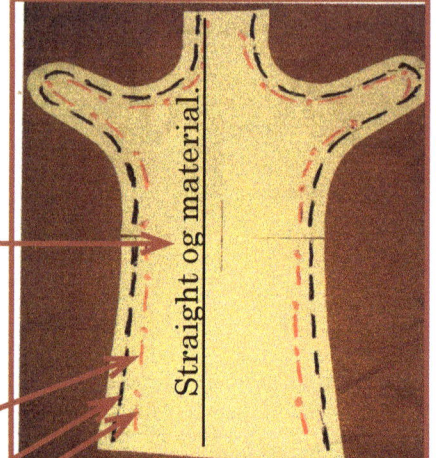

1. Make a paper pattern.
2. Choose material for each glove.
3. Fold enough material for the pattern with right sides together. Place on a table.
4. Put pattern on the straight weave of the material.
5. Pin it along each side.
6. Cut around the pattern.
7. Remove the pattern but keep the two pieces pinned together.
8. Tack them together.
9. Back stitch or machine them together along this line.
10. Make small cuts towards the seam on the shoulder and under the arm curves.
11. Trim the seam to 6mm around the end of the arm.
12. Turn right side out.

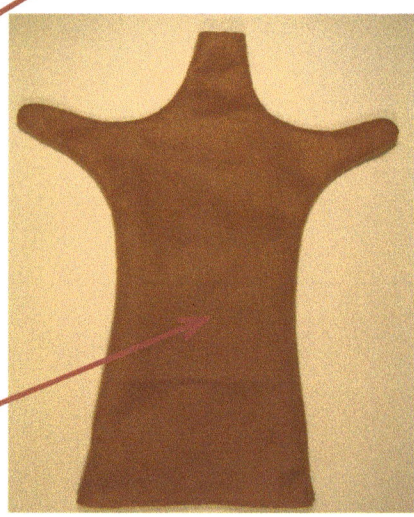

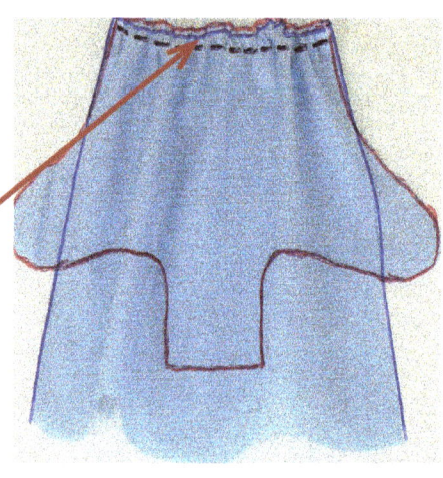

1. For a skirt/trousers or a blouse/shirt, cut pattern at waist. Add on 15mm to both for the joining seams.
2. With right sides together pin each top to a bottom at the waist and sew together.
3. Unfold them, put fronts right sides together and pin the sides.
4. Tack, then back stitch or machine down the sides.
5. Turn up bottom hem and sew it.
6. Turn right side out.
7. Turn in or trim neck.
8. Glue on hands (NB Put plastic inside the arm to stop glove sticking together.

Glove Ideas

Lace

Ribbon

Hood is one piece gathered through the middle.

Dress trimmed with lace and ribbon.

Light pink under glove so dress can be short for a little girl.

A waist apron.

Full length apron

Apron tied behind back.

White panel down front

Net train attached at the neck.

Always use thin soft material so you can get good movement.

Trims

Buttons, belts, red triangle scarf, a straight scarf or crevat, waist coat, a hat, cap or helmet, etc.

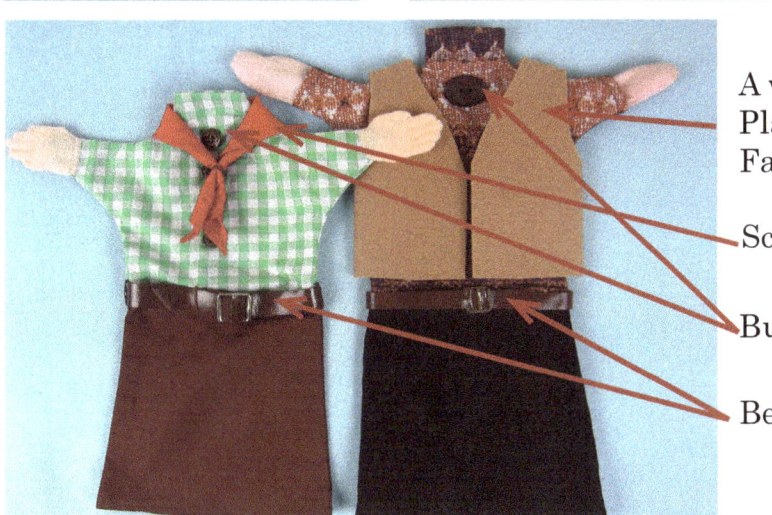

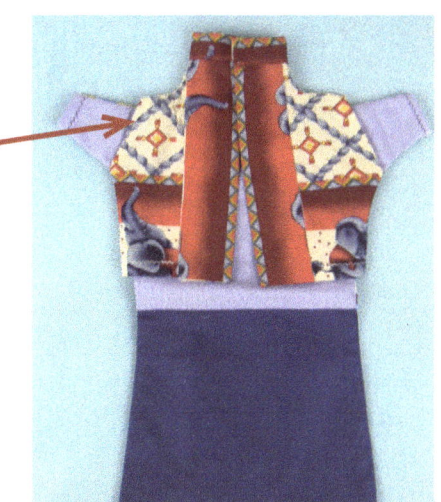

A waist coat
Plain
Fancy

Scarf

Buttons

Belt

Joining the glove to the head

The size of the neck will vary from small (child) to large (adult). Adjust it by sewing the seam in closer at the neck, gather or pleat the material, put ribbon/elastic through a hem and tie it.

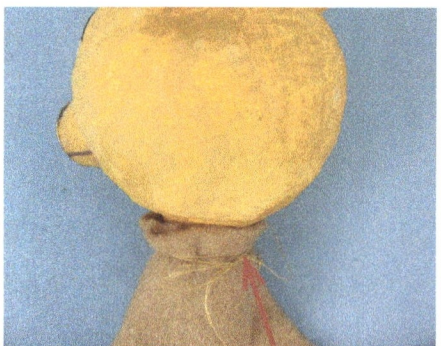
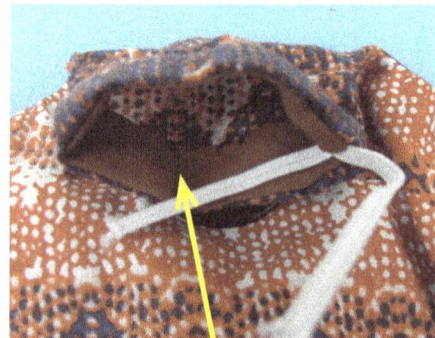

Use a double knotted thread. Use tacking stitch, starting at the center back. Leave some thread sticking out and go right around.

Gather it along the thread until it fits the neck. Tie half a knot, take both ends round the neck again and tie it off at the center back.

Fold material over and sew a hem right around neck. Thread elastic, thin ribbon, cord, etc through it. Gather the neck in and tie it.

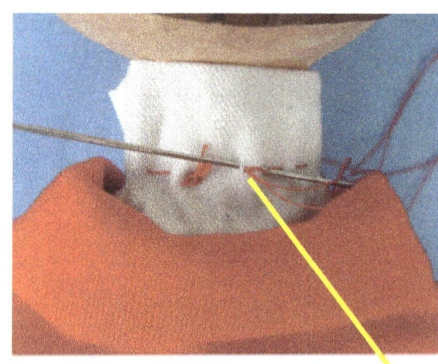

Sometimes it is easier to work on the neck if the glove is turned inside out. Halve velcro if it is too wide.

Tie the gather tight above a piece of adhesive velcro loop around the neck, not hook. Wind cotton round middle 3 times and knot to make sure it stays stuck.

Tack, gather, oversewn. Then oversewn onto scarf to keep the scarf in place.

If a lot of puppets are wanted on stage at the same time, a strong 3cm wide S card with a cross one can be used. Each puppeteer can hold their puppet and a card one in the other hand. Arms can be bent into a set position and used at different times or when needed.

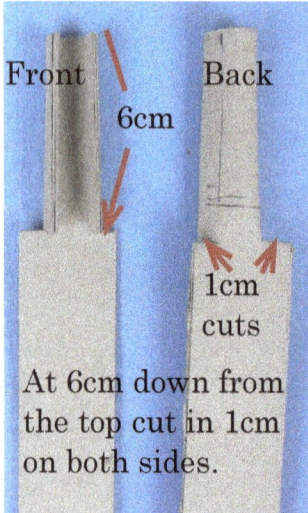
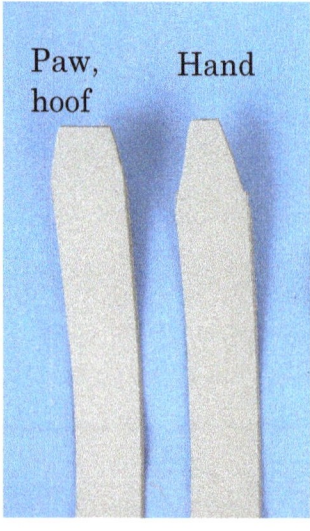

Front, Back, 6cm, 1cm cuts. At 6cm down from the top cut in 1cm on both sides.

Brush that top part with water and curve it to fit into the neck.

Paw, hoof — Hand. The arm strip goes right across and is tapered at the ends to fit hands, etc.

Put into 1st hand and bend/curve it into 2nd and then unbend, it will stay there.

Puppet 3.5cm x 50cm card body goes in behind the arm strip.

Assembling the puppet rack

Qubelok and connectors required to build this puppet rack.

1. Join the 4 feet into 2 pairs using the two 3 way connectors.

2. Join the two feet to the ends of the bottom bar.

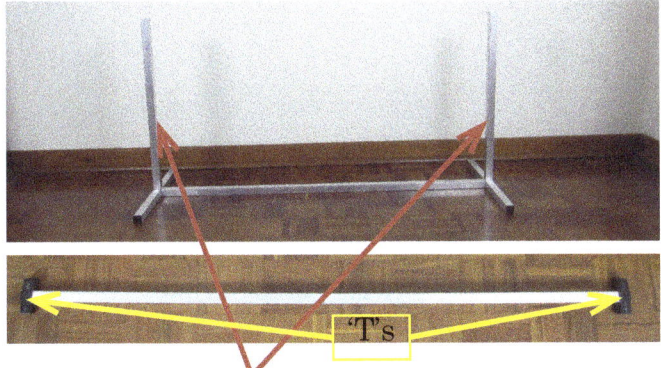

3. Knock two 60cm pieces onto the 3 ways and "T"s into the ends of the middle rail.

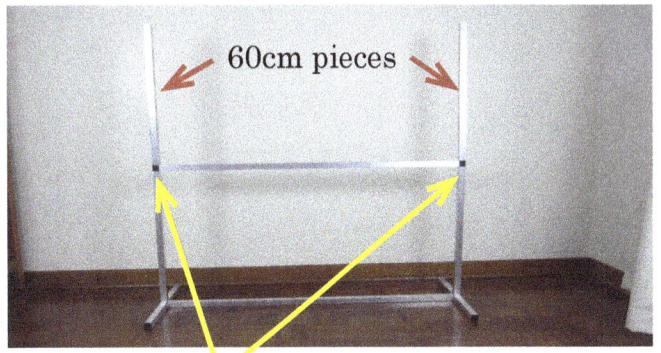

4. Knock the 'T's into the uprights and join the two 60cm pieces onto them.

5. Knock a rt < into each end of the top rail and then knock them into the uprights.

6. Put velcro hook on the front and back of the top and middle rails.
   Attach puppets on both sides of the rails.

7. Sew a 6cm piece of velcro loop in the center of the bottom and on the inside of the glove.

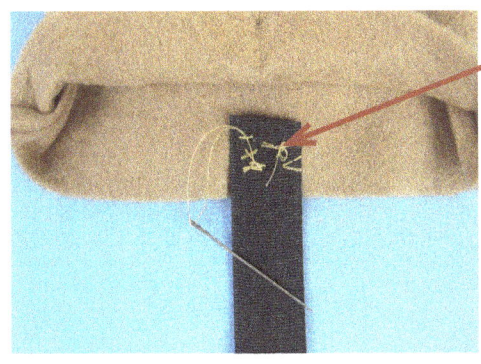

Stitch with a double thread and oversew it.

Put the loop to the outside.

Hang it down for 5cm so it sticks up above the rail, then it's easy to hold and put on or take off the rail.

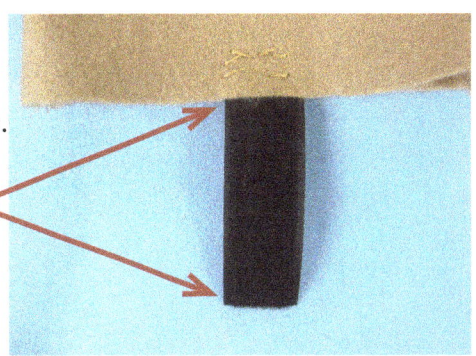

Hands, paws, hoofs and templates

Felt can be glued, painted, is easy to work with and won't fray, but it is not strong enough to be cut into pointy fringes.

Hand, paw and hoof templates are on the following pages and can be enlarged or shrunk. They need to be wide enough for the pointer and thumb to go into so they can be used.

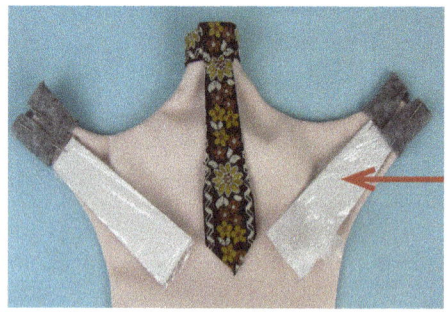

Put plastic covered cardboard in this position inside the glove arm so that it is not stuck together when gluing on the hands, paws or hoofs.

Glue together and clamp.

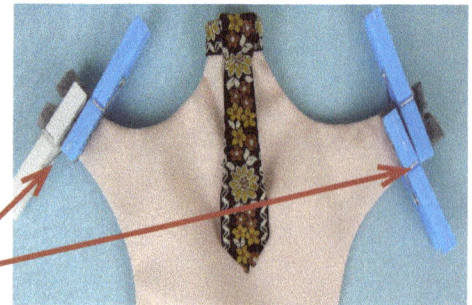

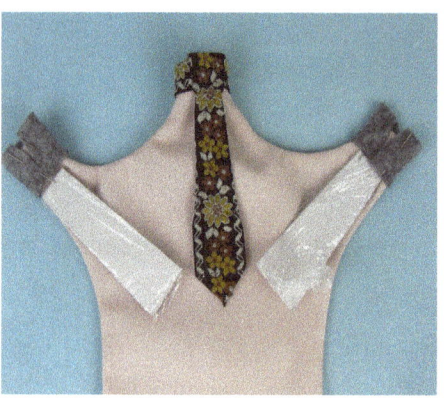

Hoofs ~ can be two pieces glued around the glove and meeting at the 'V'. See bottom p 45.

Or looking side on. See 2nd bottom p45.

They can be glued together at their ends but not essential.

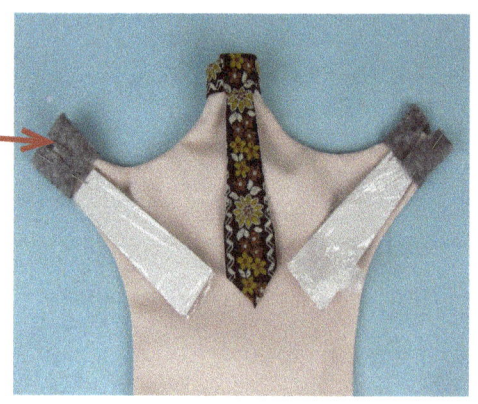

The wolf is treated separately on his instruction pages.

Hands ~ are 2 identical pieces glued together, so cut 4.
The adult puppeteer pattern needs to be larger for their fingers. Adjust if needed.

Woman   Man

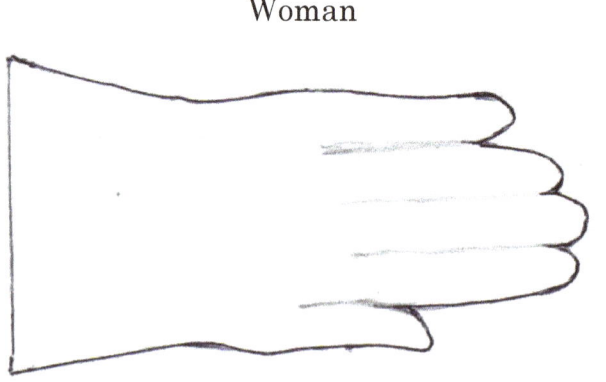 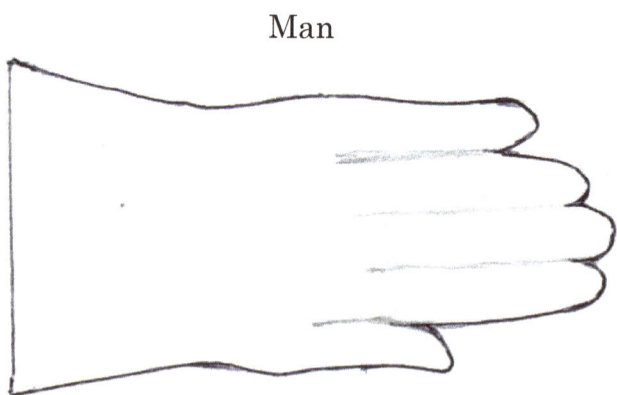

Girl   Pattern for a child puppeteers hand.   Boy

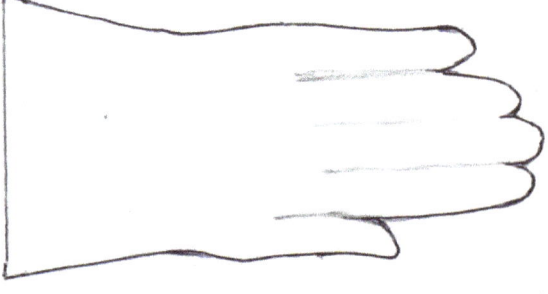 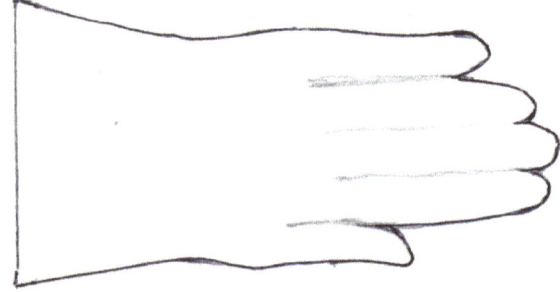

Paw templates

An underneath paw pattern glued onto the front of the glove and a patterned or plain top glued onto the back of the glove.

Then they are glued together around the edge.

Patterns can be painted on the felt or cut-out the felt and glued on.

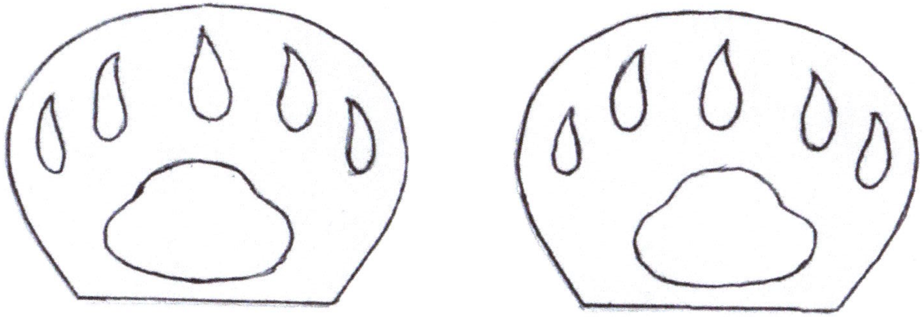

Dog paw

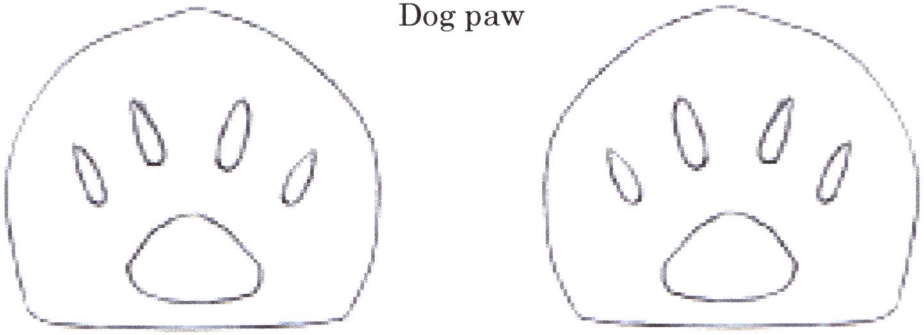

Cat paw

Fox paw

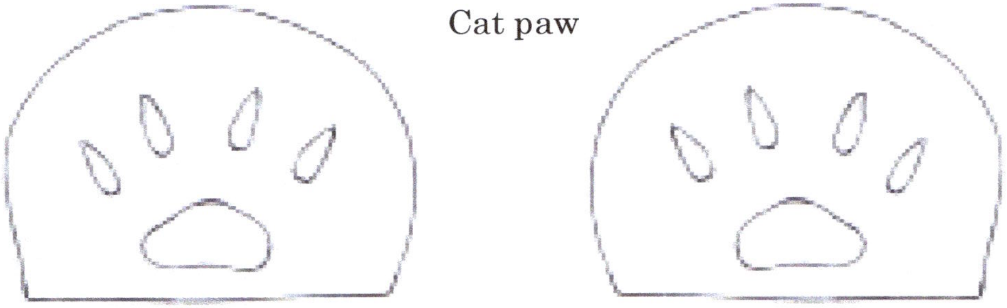

Fox paw

Cat paw

Baby bear paw

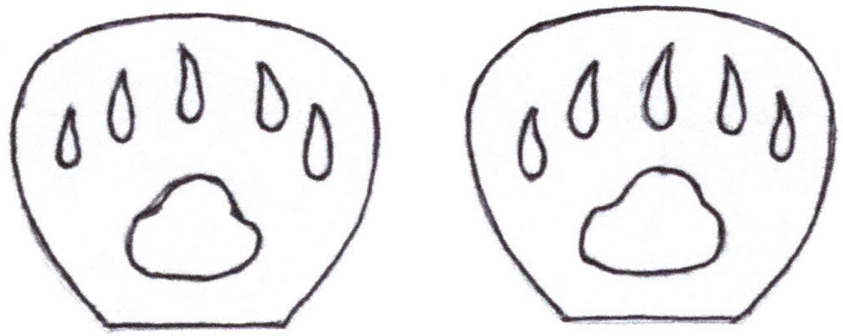

Mother bear paw

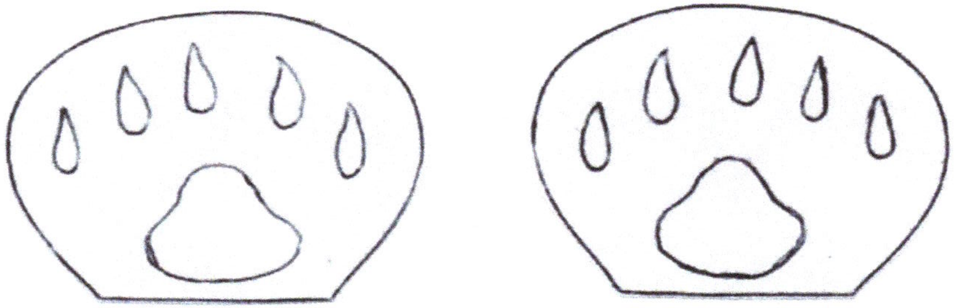

Father bear paw

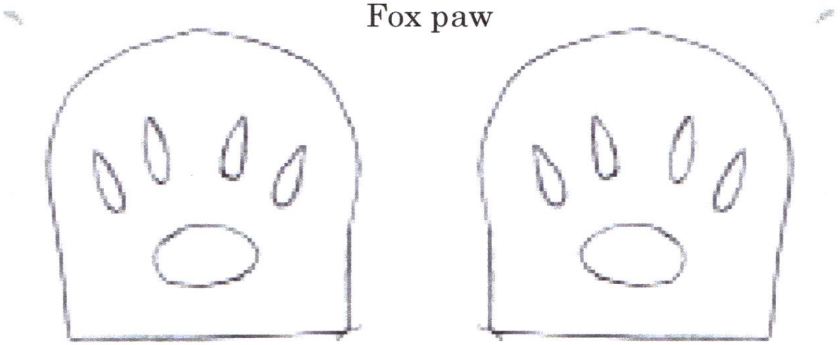

All of the side view hoofs allow for stitched sides but can be cut to a smaller size if wanted.

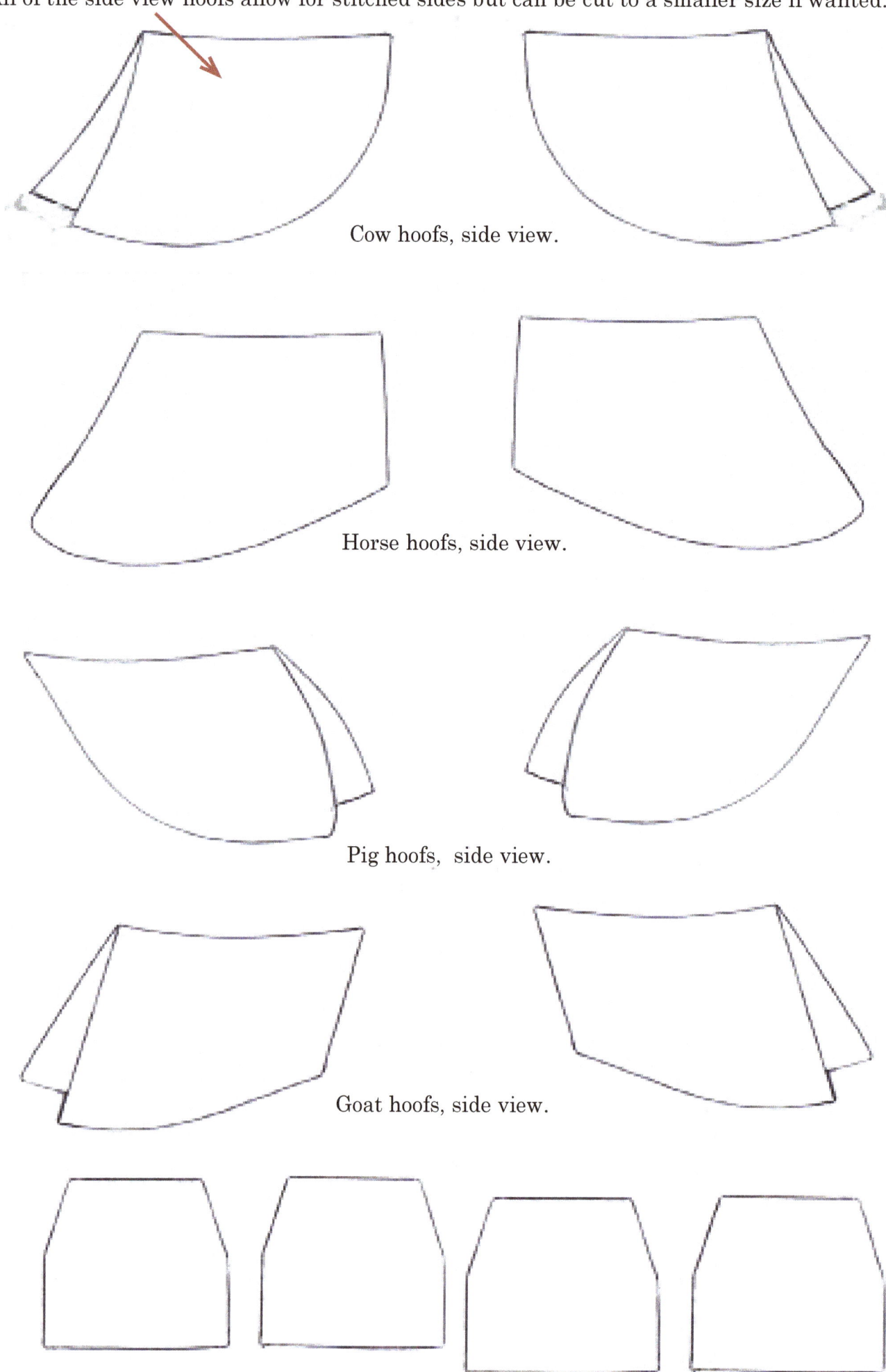

Cow hoofs, side view.

Horse hoofs, side view.

Pig hoofs, side view.

Goat hoofs, side view.

Pig and goat hoofs, front view. Fit around the glove arm meeting in the centre. See p43.

Set material

Paints

1. Acrylic water-based paints. School issue poster paints are available for most large background work and undercoats.

2. Student or artist quality tubes are better for effects, details and brighter areas or objects as they contain more pigment.

3. Acrylic house paint can be used. White to undercoat (gives good coverage, less colour is needed on top and the final colour is brighter) and for mixing to lighten colours.

Note:- For a pale colour, start with white and add small amounts of colour until it is right.

Colours needed

Red ~ bright (eg. flag red) ~ cadmium red
Blue ~ (eg. sky) ~ cobalt
Yellow ~ (eg. canary) ~ cadmium yellow
Black ~ can be house paint (small pot) or tube, or school poster paint which is much cheaper.
White ~ acrylic house paint is best. Decant some into smaller containers with lids.

Note:- Every colour can be mixed using different amounts of these, eg. green = yellow + blue.

Useful extras ~ Green (light and deep)   Purple
                  Brown (burnt sienna)   Orange
                  Deep yellow (raw umber or yellow ochre)   Turquoise
                  Indigo (very dark blue)

Note:- Meat trays and plastic plates are useful as mixing palettes.
When mixing, start with the main colour, then add small amounts of others to brighten and change it eg. white to lighten, indigo to darken, black to grey it down.
Mixing too many colours together will result in dirty brownish grey! Use black sparingly.

Crayons, water-based markers, textas and coloured pencils can also be used for smaller areas and outlines but will not show up as well as paint.

Brushes

* Small to medium house painting brushes can be used for large areas.
* Different sized cheap bristle oil painting brushes from hardware stores or art supply shops.
* Some fine and medium point, soft acrylic watercolour brushes. Cheap ones will do.
   Wash brushes between using different colours or use different brushes for each colour.

Other materials

Containers for clean and dirty water.
Spray bottle of water----to keep paint moist, spray mixed paint often and also when finished for the day. Then cover it with plastic wrap.

Rags for wiping brushes, hands, spills and mistakes.
Sponges for effects or soaking up excess.

Ruler or straight-edge. A large set-square or the corner of something big and flat eg. a sheet of cardboard/mat board.

Soft (4-6b) pencils for sketching before painting. Charcoal - but dust off before painting.

Set effects

Trees on light-weight cardboard.
Paint or wet both sides and dry flat under weights, then draw and paint the tree, etc.
This stops cardboard from curling. Can always rewet and dry again under weights.
Edges of trees, etc can be wriggly and random! No straight edges.
Yellow to deep blue/green for grass/foliage and bits of brown or grey, purple or deep indigo for shaded areas.

Scenery
Simplify, alter, improve or change illustrated scenery from books to suit your play.
If Jack and Jill's well is too high up for the puppeteers, drop the hill down but keep the well the same - it must be in the right proportion to the puppets.

Perspective
Paint front objects in strong colours and distant ones paler or slightly greyish, or pale purple/blue to give scenery depth.

Some techniques
Make 3D round objects (tree trunks, buckets, etc.) appear real by shading edge with different tones.

For rough surfaces stipple with darker/lighter paint using the end of a stiff brush, crumpled rag, or paper dipped in paint. Useful for trees, bushes, rocks, stonework, etc. Practise!

For wood ~ Apply main colour, then use a stiff brush with darker or lighter tones to mark wood grain. Don't over do it!

Note:-
In reality and nature because of varying light nothing is one flat colour all over.
3D objects on stage will create their own light and shade because of their shape.
Drawn and painted 2D objects need shaded and lighter areas to appear natural and 'real'.
It depends on what effect you need.
A row of perfectly flat looking daisies could be very effective in some situations, but to look natural they would have to be shaded and look flexible.
No straight edges in nature so perfection in everything makes it appear stiff and unnatural..

Use children's books with good illustrations for ideas.

Theatre scenery
Theatre scenery is amazing with its exaggerated perspective. Whether simple or very detailed it will have the incredible effect of depth and spaciousness.

Each type of puppet- cardboard, rod, glove and marionette- has required Colleen's thought and experience in live theatre to work out the right sizing. All the templates have the sizing written on them to give you an idea of size for your creations.

Looking ~ really looking at your scenery size and perspective is worth the effort to get it right. Study the perspective of the things in your visual world and try it in your theatre.

Scenery

Ground, trunks and canopy painted onto white undercoated blockout. The empty spaces were cut out. The trees were attached to the dark green see-through background.
This scene is more work to make but it is very effective when you want depth in a forest.

Low hills with an empty part in the middle where the bridge will sit. However it is worth doing the middle so the scene can be used as another back drop.

Low gentle hills (puppeteers can see their puppet over the top of them) for the three pigs back drop and the Gingerbread Man.

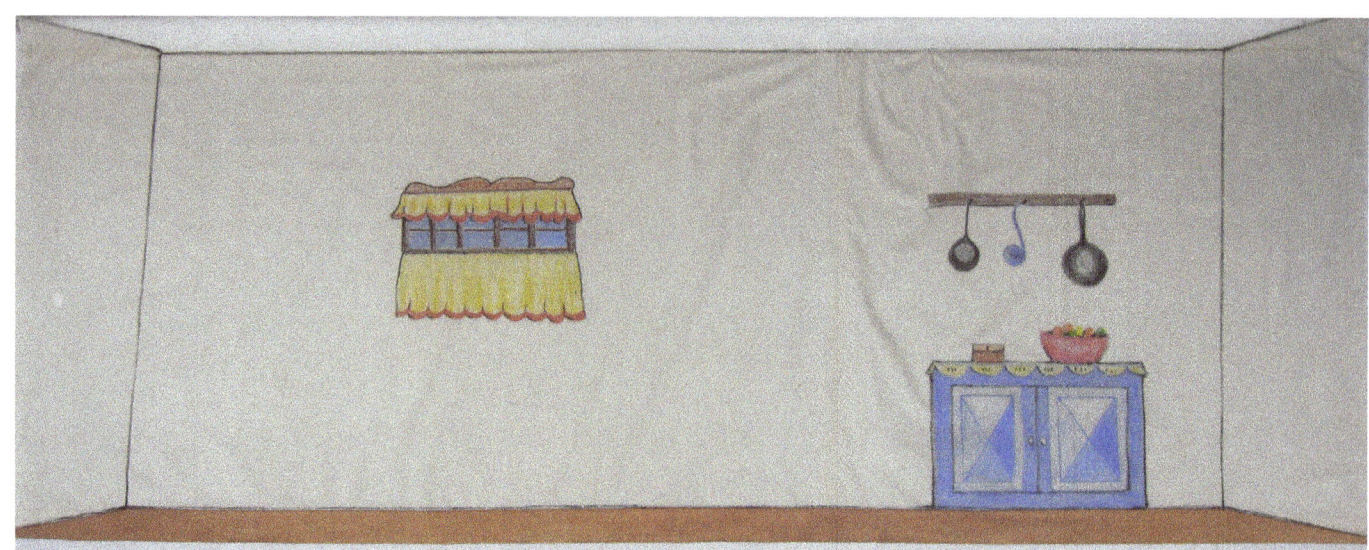

Painted white undercoated blockout for the floor and the ceiling. Wall, corners, window, cupboard and rack drawn on with fabric crayons. They need bold outlines to be effective.

A painted floor but no ceiling visible. This still gives a 3D effect. Once again the structure of the window and cupboard needs to be boldly outlined in order to stand out from the wall.

An old fashioned wash stand with a water jug sitting in a basin and towels on the shelf underneath. No walls, floor or ceiling for the 3D effect. The picture and stand definitely need to be bold or they would not be noticed.

Doing puppetry

We had a baby not long after
And I was ordered to baby sit.
I raised quite a lot of laughter
Thinking I had to sit on it.

Scripts

Three Pigs

Three Billy Goats Gruff

Goldilocks and the Three Bears

The Gingerbread Man

Little Red Riding Hood

The Three Pigs

Narr   This is a story about three little pigs who built their houses of straw, sticks and bricks to keep out the big bad wolf.

(Curtain opens on the first pig outside his house of straw.)

1st PIG   I love my little house of straw

It's warm and cosy behind the door

Keeps out the cold wind and the rain

It's the prettiest house, that's very plain. (repeat 1st 2 lines.)

(He goes into his house and looks out the window then settles in.)

(The big bad wolf enters.)

WOLF   It's time for breakfast and I'm hungry. I hope someone is home.

(He goes across to the house of straw and bangs on the door.)

1st PIG   Who is it?

WOLF   Let me come in, let me come in.

By the hair of your chinny chin chin.

Or I'll huff and puff and blow your house in

And chase your bacon all over town.

(1st pig is at the window.)

1st PIG   Not by the hair on my chinny chin chin!

WOLF   Well I want some breakfast! You asked for it. *(He takes a big breath and goes huff, puff and blows the house in.)*

(Squealing, the little pig runs off the stage and the wolf chases after him.)

WOLF   Run away will you. I'll catch you.

Curtain closes.

(The curtain opens on the 2nd pig outside his house of sticks.)

2nd PIG   I love my little house of sticks

It's firm and strong and easy to fix

Doesn't look too good but then again

(The 1st little pig comes running in and squeals.)

1st PIG   Quick get inside the big bad wolf is behind me. Shut the door! *(They run inside and shut the door - slam.)*

(The wolf comes running in, stops and talks to the audience.)

WOLF   Seeing I missed out on breakfast I can have two for lunch. After all I'm twice as hungry.

WOLF   It's the big bad wolf! Let me in, or I'll blow your house in!

2nd PIG   Not by the hair of my chinny chin chin! I'll not let you in.

WOLF   Hum. He won't let me in either. We'll see about that. This calls for double the action.

(The wolf steps back, takes a big breath then, he goes huff, puff, then huff, puff, again and he blows the house in!)

(They run off the stage as the house blows away.)

1st+2nd PIG   Help, we're out of here. Runnnnn!

WOLF   Bother I have two to catch, and I want my dinner. *(Wolf chases them off the stage.)*

Curtain closes.

(Curtain opens on the 3rd little pig outside his house of bricks.)

3rd PIG   I love my little house of brick

Hard work to build, but just the tick

Worth the effort, worth the cost

When a storm comes it won't get lost. (Repeat 1st 2 lines.)

(In run the two pigs.)

1st PIG   Quick into the house, the big bad wolf is coming. *(They run into the house.)*

2nd PIG   Shut the door! *(Slam.)*

(The mean old wolf comes running in, stands and looks at the house of bricks.)

WOLF   Hmm, a brick house..... this will be harder, but then the reward will be greater.

THREE pigs for my dinner, that will make up for no breakfast or lunch.

(He steps up to the door and bangs loudly.)

3rd PIG   Who is it?

WOLF	Let me come in, let me come in!
	By the hair of your chinny chin chin
	Or I'll huff and puff and blow your house in
	And chase your bacon all over town.
3rd PIG	Never will we let you in
	Not by the hair of our chinny chin chin
	You can huff and puff all through the night
	You'll not put this lot of bacon to flight!
WOLF	You asked for it. *(He takes a big breath.)* - Huff, puff, blow! Huff, puff, blow! *(The wolf walks towards the front.)* I see that I'll have to puff harder. *(Practices taking a big breath, then-)* Huff, puff, blow! This is no good. *(He sits down, looks at the house and scratches his head.)*
	Ha! I can't bring the house down so I'll go down into it, catch them and have a bacon breakfast in a nice brick house. *(He moves around the back of the house and we see him appear up on the roof.)* What a big chimney.... *(He looks down it)*...HERE I COME!
3rd PIG	Quick! Throw more wood on the fire. He is going to come down the chimney.
	(They pretend to throw wood on the fire and blow on it to make it flame up. The wolf's tail appears down the chimney.)
WOLF	Yowee! *(The tail disappears. The wolf comes out the top of the chimney.)* Ouch my tails on fire! *(He disappears down the back of the house then runs across the stage howling.)*
	(The pigs come out of the house and dance around singing.)
3 PIGS	He couldn't puff our brick house in
	All out of breath he could not win
	He tried the chimney, but let out a wail
	When he took off with a blazing tail.
NARR	And the wolf has not been heard of since!
	Curtain closes.

THE END

The tune for the house verses is at the end of this section on p 65.

Pig - paper head

Ball flanges

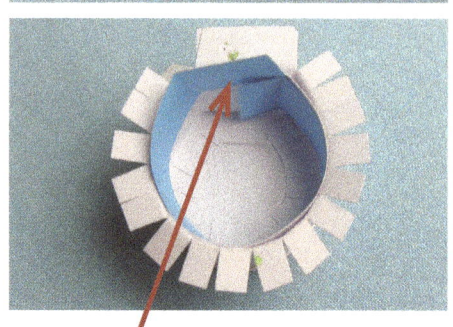
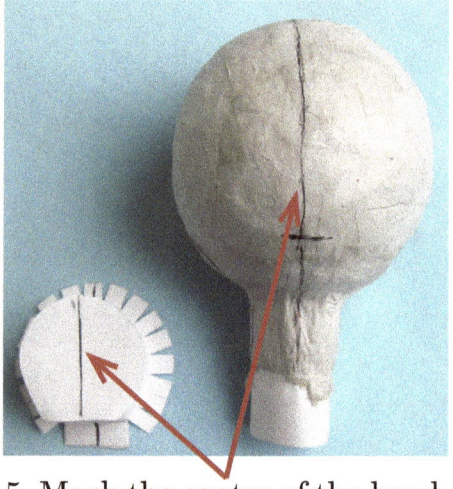

1. Cut out snout, nick edges, bend them opposite ways. Bend round, glue overlap.
2. Cut out 2 snout fronts.
3. Circle reinforcing and glue the overlap together.
4. Glue on one snout front to the inward bending card.
5. Mark the centre of the head and snout.
6. Glue the snout on, lining up on the centre.

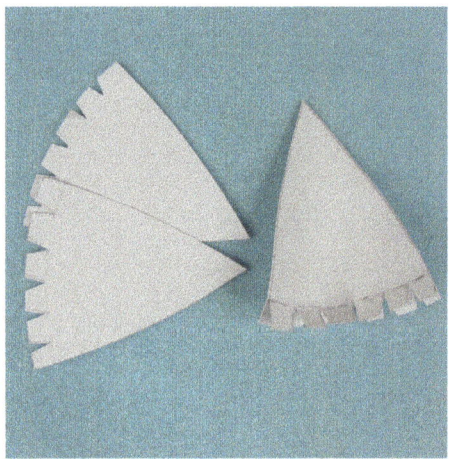

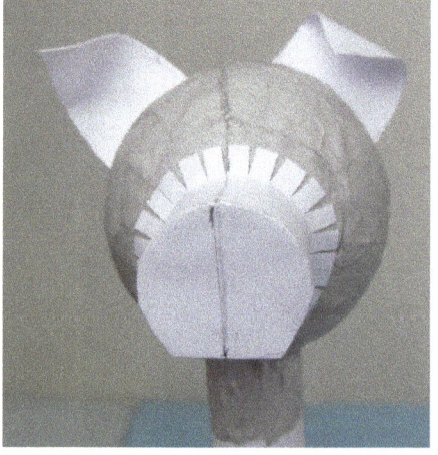

7. Cut out 4 ears, join the 2 pairs. Shape ears, bend bottoms to front and back.
8. Mark where the ears go, check them in place then glue them on.
9. Paint the head and neck white, then with colour. Finally paint inner ear.

10. Draw and colour in 2nd snout front. Glue in place.
11. Draw or paint a mouth.
12. Colour in or cut out coloured paper irises. Cut out the eyes.
13. Try them in place then glue them on.

Pig templates

The instructions are on the previous page.

Snout template

!st snout front

Snout reinforcing

Nose

Ears

Eyes

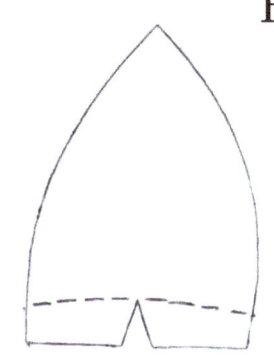
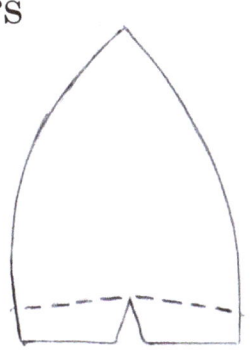

Polystyrene head

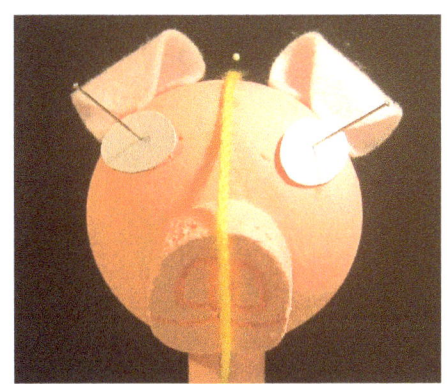

Round ball with neck undercoated white.

Glue on the snout and ears. Paint it all the skin colour. Do cardboard eyes.

Button/coloured paper irises. Paint cork nose, mouth and inside ears.

Wolf

Basic head instructions are on p 37, 38.
Also there are very full instructions on p 71 and 72 for a snout and the goat head which is very similar to the wolf.

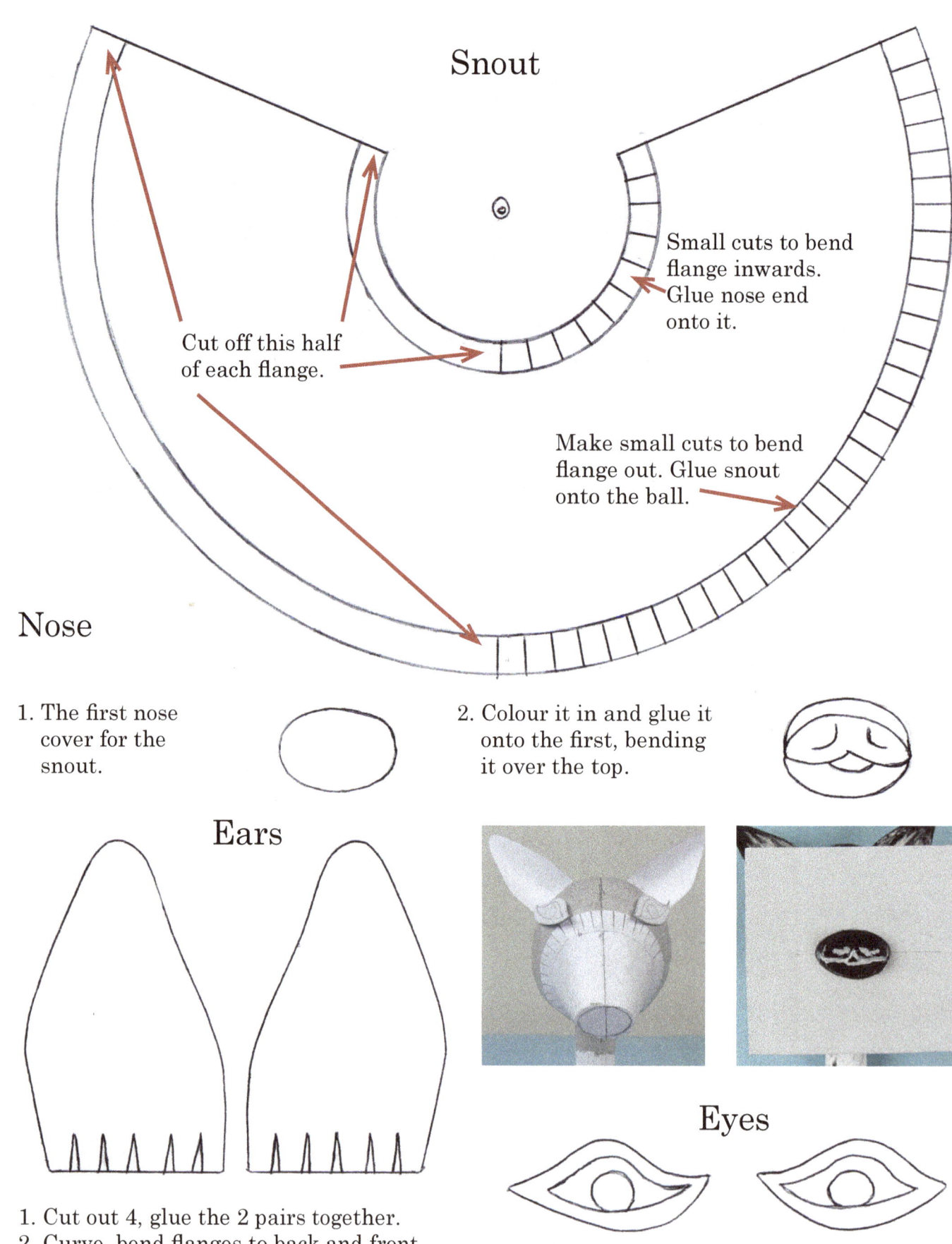

Snout

Cut off this half of each flange.

Small cuts to bend flange inwards. Glue nose end onto it.

Make small cuts to bend flange out. Glue snout onto the ball.

Nose

1. The first nose cover for the snout.
2. Colour it in and glue it onto the first, bending it over the top.

Ears

1. Cut out 4, glue the 2 pairs together.
2. Curve, bend flanges to back and front.
3. Glue the ear onto the head.

Eyes

Colour in or cut out coloured paper irises.

59

Polystyrene head

1. A cardboard neck glued into a polystyrene egg.

2. Centre and shapes drawn on the egg then cut off.

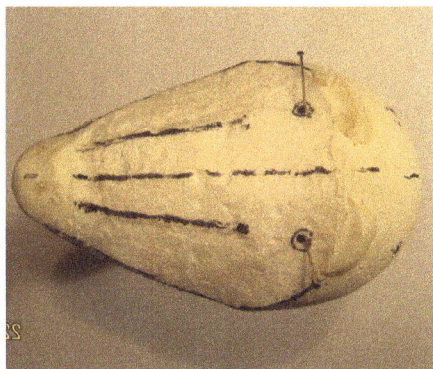

3. Sandpapered to gentle curves.

A folded piece of felt stuck on the head, cut and painted like hair around the head.

This makes him different to the one at the bottom of the following page with no trims.

A 14 x 5cm piece of felt cut and glued around the neck.

Cut 30 x 5mm strips. Glue it onto the head 5mm out from the neck. Glove fits in under it.

Continue all the way along

Trims for the paws and chest can be sewn or glued on before or after making the glove.

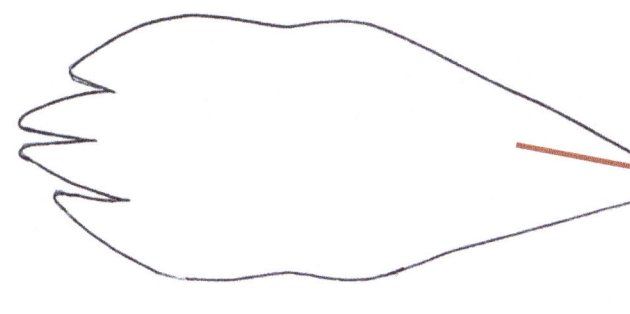

The white top for the front paw.

The bottom of the paw.

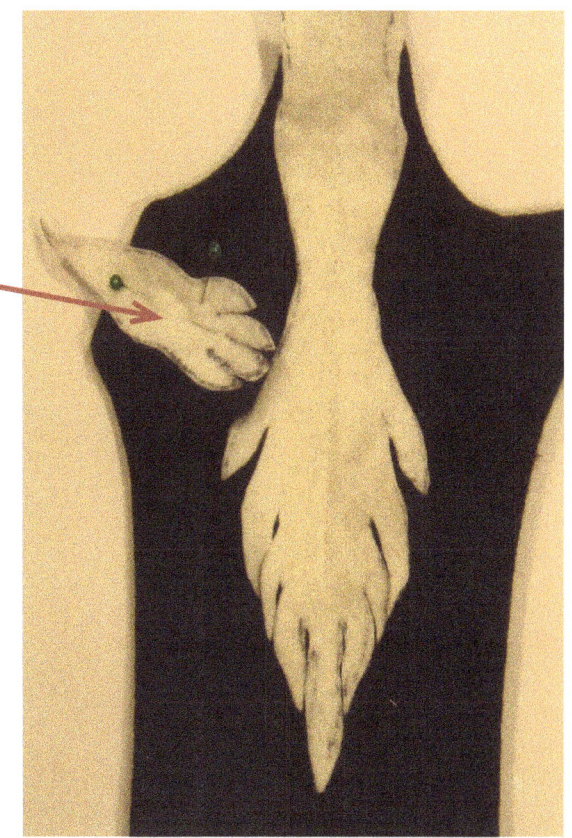

1st Pig

2nd Pig

Paper heads

3rd Pig

Wolf

1st Pig

2nd Pig

Polystyrene heads

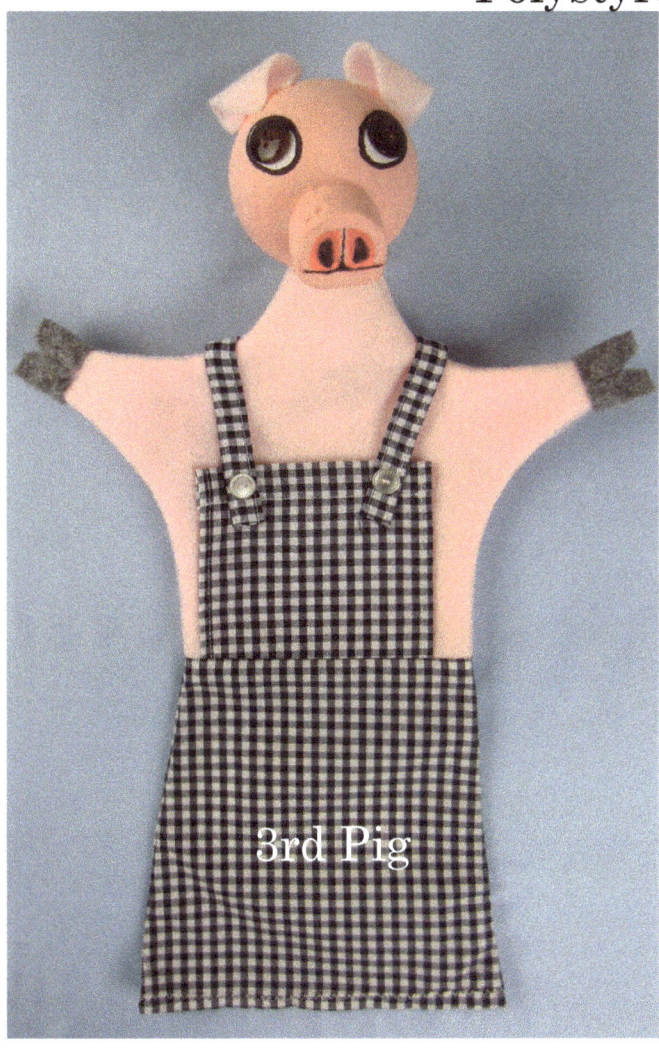

3rd Pig

Wolf

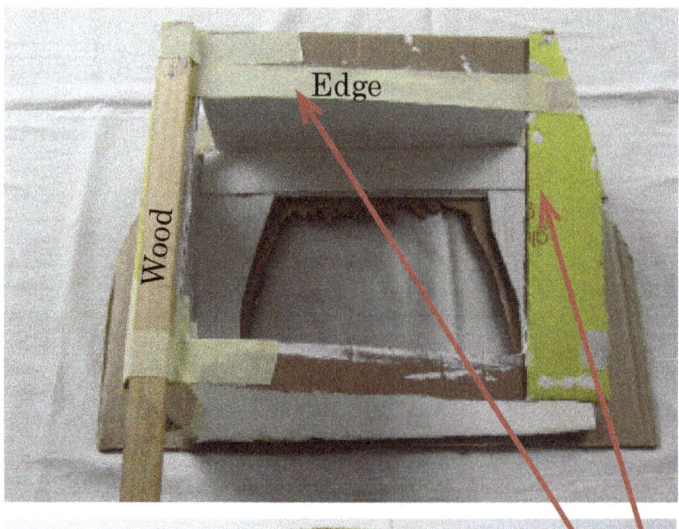

Straw house

1. On strong cardboard draw the curved outline of a house and window with jagged edges.

2. Paint it a straw colour.

3. Draw or paint curved uneven lines getting closer together at sides to show roundness.

4. Darken window frame on three sides to show thickness.

5. Cut out house shape and small window.

6. Glue onto prepared small box frame.

7. Attach see-through material for the back wall of the house to inside of this frame.

8. Tape or glue wood to the back side strip to use for holding up the house.

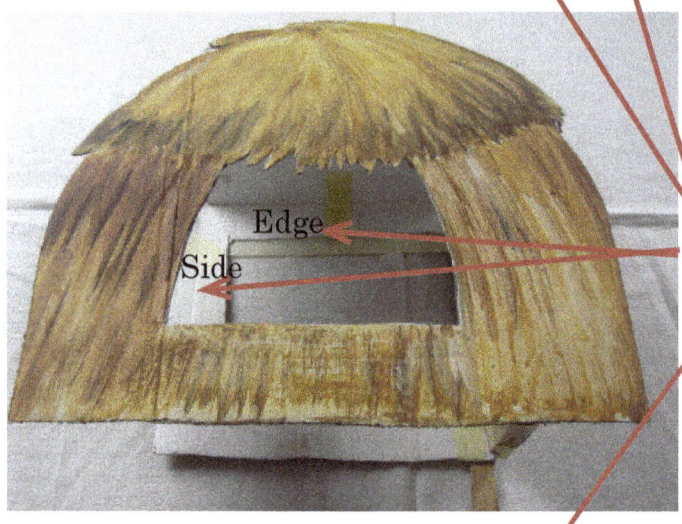

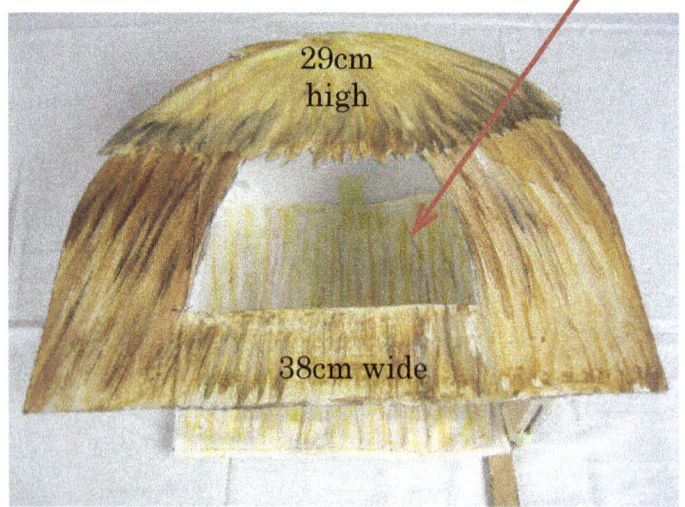

Box frames

View box from the back.

1. Remove right end, bottom and back (leaving top and side 2.5cm strips for strength).

2. Cut a window in the front side of the box to match your drawn cardboard front.

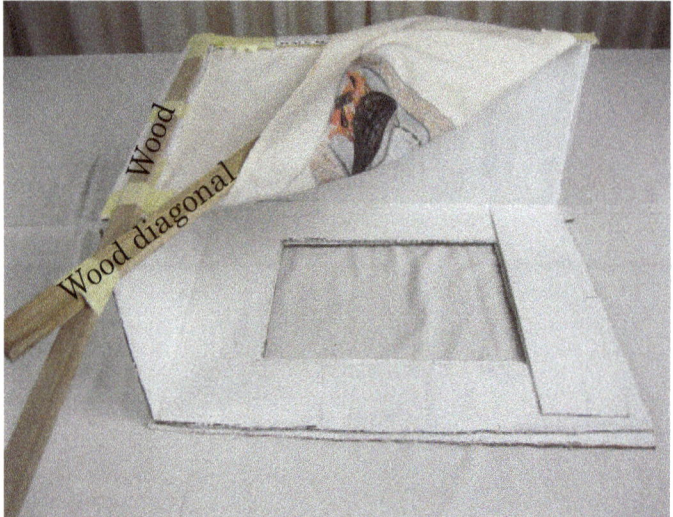

Brick house

1. Draw a brick house with a tile roof on a larger piece of cardboard, and a brick chimney on a smaller one to add on to it.

2. Cut a large framed window in the middle.

3. Paint walls and roof the basic colour.

4. Draw in imperfect bricks, making chimney ones smaller.

Stick house

1. On strong cardboard draw the outline with rough stick edges and an angled roof.

2. Paint with lightish brown.

3. Draw on sticks of different lengths and widths, darken some gaps between sticks.

4. Darken three sides of window frame to show thickness.

5. Cut out house shape and medium size window with bumpy edges.

6. Glue onto prepared medium box frame.

7. Attach see-through material for the back wall of the house to inside of this frame.

8. Tape or glue wood to the back side strip to use for holding up the house.

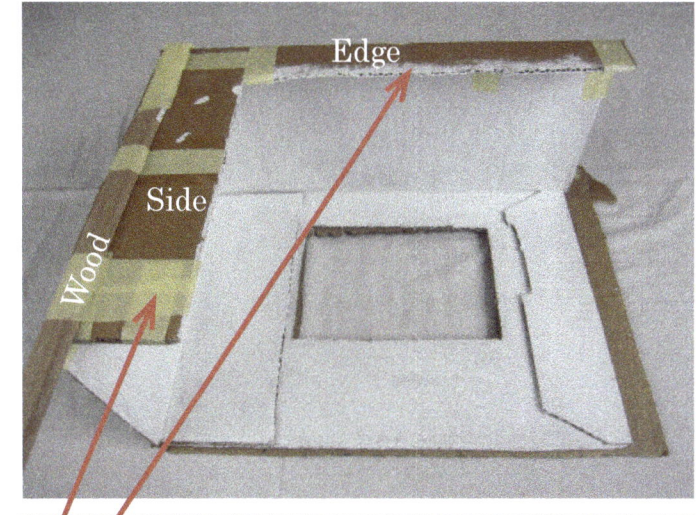

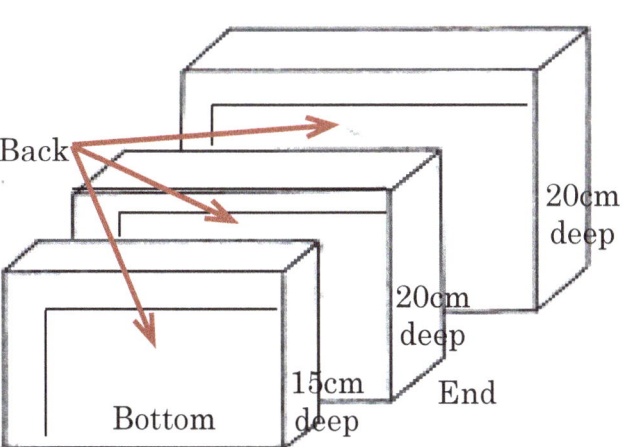

5. Roof tiles are shaded on one side.

6. Colour window frame.

7. Cut out and glue onto biggest box frame.

8. Fix a piece of wood across diagonally on the back to give strength.

9. Draw a fireplace on house backdrop.

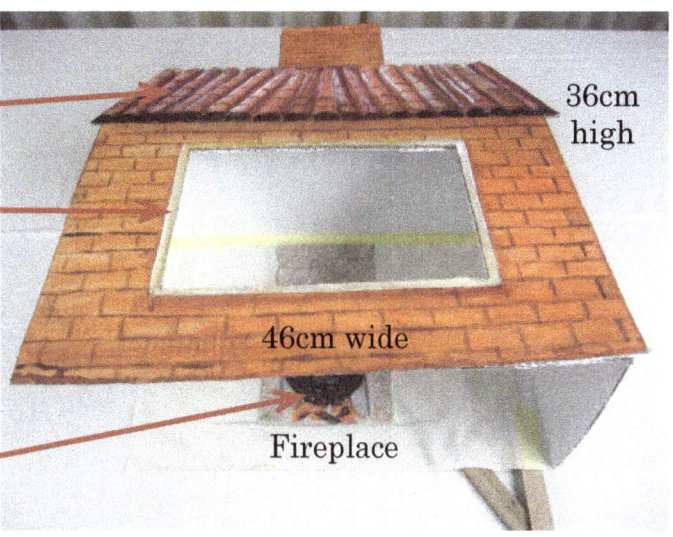

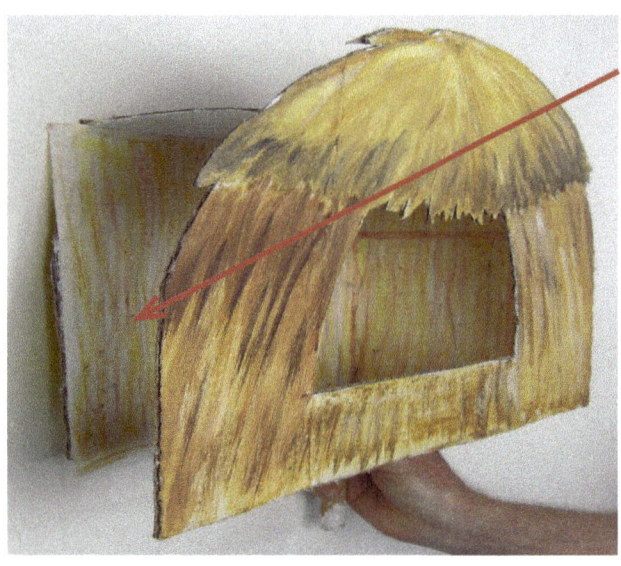 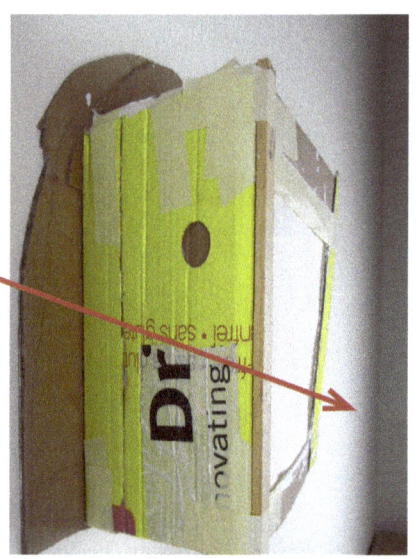

Puppets come in this side.

It is held from behind like in the picture on the right.

The house is blown out with the puppets in it.

The person holding the house stands at the side of the proscenium so the puppeteers can have all the space behind the house for their bodies.

Most people are right handed so they go across the stage from their right to their left. The pigs come out to dance and sing their final verse. Extras can be added to all these plays.

 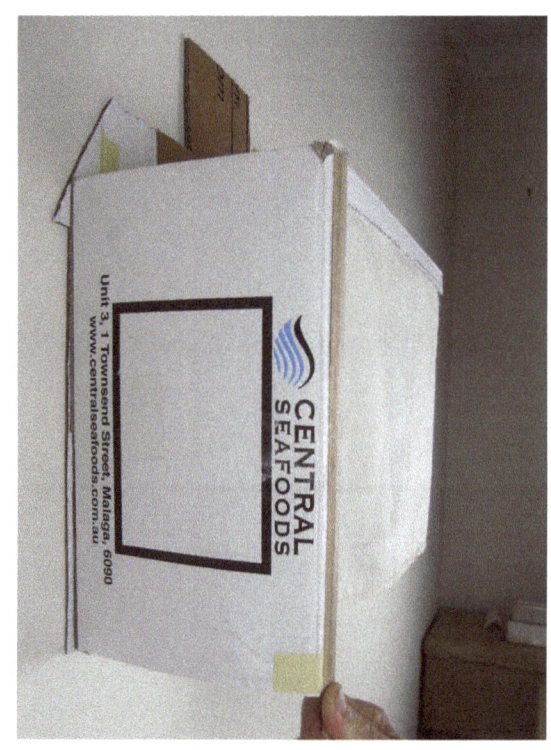

The three little pigs house songs
The tune is Baa, Baa, Black Sheep

It's very easy to maintain. (Repeat 1st 2 lines.)

Three Billy Goats Gruff.

NARR	Once upon a time in a land far away across the ocean, where there were mountains covered with lovely green pastures and bubbling brooks, there lived three billy goats.
	They were ~
BBG	*(In a very big gruff voice.)* Me Big Billy Goat Gruff, I'm the eldest and by far the largest.
MBG	*(In a middle-sized voice.)* Me Middle Billy Goat Gruff.
LBG	*(In a tiny high voice.)* Me Little Billy Goat Gruff. I'm the youngest and smallest by far.
NARR	They had been munching away on the mountain side for several days, but now it was becoming a bit bare.
BBG	I'm getting hungry. There are no big patches of grass left to eat.
MBG	Yes, I'm hungry too. I can't find any medium sized patches.
LBG	I can't even find any tiny bits and I'm very hungry. *(looking around at the ground.)*
BBG	We will have to move to a new green meadow like that one on the other side of the stream. The grass looks lush and thick over there.
MBG	Yes, it looks very tall, delicious and yummy for our tummies.
LBG	It will fill my tummy and I will get fat again.
MBG	You would indeed, Little Billy Goat. We all would.
BBG	OK, let's go then.
MBG	But Big Billy Goat we will have to cross that bridge to get there.
BBG	Yes, we will.
MBG	But a large, ugly troll with long sharp claws lives under it! He might catch us and eat us!
LBG	You're big, but we're smaller, especially me, so he is sure to catch me and eat me. How horrible and frightening. I won't cross that bridge.
MBG	Let's think about this. Little Billy Goat is the one who is most likely to get eaten, but if he says someone bigger is coming, the troll might not be interested in such a small meal.
BBG	If that works, you can go next Middle Billy Goat and see if he is so greedy that he

	lets you go across too. Then I will go.
LBG	Do you really think this will work or will he be so hungry he will just eat me, then both of you. I'm scared. I don't want to be the first to try crossing.
BBG	He won't have room to eat us all in one meal, so I'm sure he will wait for the largest. After all I am the best meal for a greedy troll!
MBG	Even though you are frightened Little Billy Goat, be brave, go and stand up to the troll. We are here.
LBG	Alright, I'm shaking but here I go. *(As he reaches the bridge he hesitates.)* Oh dear, he is coming out from under the bridge.
MBG	Keep going Little Billy Goat. *(Tripping sound as LBG goes onto the bridge.)*
TROLL	Who's that? *(He roars, hanging on to the edge of the bridge.)* Who's that tripping over my bridge?
LBG	It's only me, Little Billy Goat Gruff. I'm going across to the lovely green pasture so I can eat and grow fat.
TROLL	HO! *(Roars the Troll.)* AND I'M GOING TO EAT YOU UP!
LBG	Don't eat me, I'm sooo small and sooo thin! Why not wait for the next Billy Goat Gruff, who is much bigger and fatter?
TROLL	Hmmm. *(Thinking and scratching his head.)* Very well! Be off with you!
LBG	*(Goes tripping over the bridge - sound effects needed - and on to the green grass, takes a mouthful then looks back at the others.)*
MBG	*(Turns to BBG.)* Well that went ok. My turn now, here goes. *(MBG goes to the bridge and on to it, with sound effect of trit, trot! trit, trot!)*
TROLL	*(Coming out and looking over the bridge, he roars,)* Who's that? Who's that trotting over MY bridge?
MBG	Oh! It's me, Middle Billy Goat Gruff. I want to cross to the green field to eat and grow fat.
TROLL	HO! HO! *(He roars.)* AND I'M GOING TO EAT YOU UP!
MBG	Oh, no! Don't bother with me. I'm only middle-sized and thin. Why not wait for Big Billy Goat Gruff. He is very big and much fatter.
TROLL	*(Thinking and scratching his head again.)* Very well! *(He shouts.)* Be off with you!
MBG	*(Trots off the bridge (sound effects again and joins LBG and they both take a mouthful and turn to watch BBG.)*
BBG	*(He looks, shakes his head and walks to the bridge. Sound effects of trit, trot, tramp, trit, trot, tramp, as he walks on it.)*

BBG	Oh, no! You won't get me! I'M GOING TO GET YOU!
	(Lowers his head, stamps his feet - sound effects - tramp,tramp,tramp! tramp,tramp,tramp!)
	(They meet and fight. BBG tosses the troll who goes up in the air, turns, flails with his arms and goes backwards into the water with a big splash. Sound effects: grunting noises. Troll- Aaaah! Splash! and any more you like to put in.)
	(BBG looks over the edge, then tramps across the bridge to join the other two.)
LBG	Hurrah! The plan worked! Now we can all eat and grow fat.
NARR	That's exactly what they did and after such an adventure the grass tasted even sweeter!

Curtain closes.

THE END

The Three Billy Goats

Three frightened goats.

All their grass is gone.

Gone down their throats.

So now they're hungry blokes.

They've eaten every blade of grass.

And like it or not they have to pass

Across a bridge with a troll beneath.

Three frightened goats.

One Hungry troll

With a single goal.

Been waiting for some while,

And would like to eat in style.

His aim is to eat the biggest meal.

A big fat goat has a strong appeal.

Goat is his favourite after veal.

One hungry troll.

One little goat.

Bravely you should note.

With a scary shout

The hungry troll springs out.

He screams that he will eat him whole.

The little goat then plays his role.

Says troll could fill a bigger bowl.

One little goat.

One bigger beast

Would make a tempting feast.

He also plays his role

Tempting the greedy troll.

The troll screams out in threatening tones

That he will clean up all his bones.

Was told that later he'd spout groans,

For missing the biggest meal.

One billy goat gruff.

He's not made of fluff.

Tackled troll full on

And soon the job was done.

He biffed the troll while at full steam.

Who flew off the bridge with a piercing scream.

'Twas a great win for the billy goat team.

Three happy goats.

The tune is the Three Blind Mice

The snout for any animal

On an 8cm x 8cm piece of strong square cardboard draw and cut a hole. The size and shape of this hole depends on what you want for the snout.

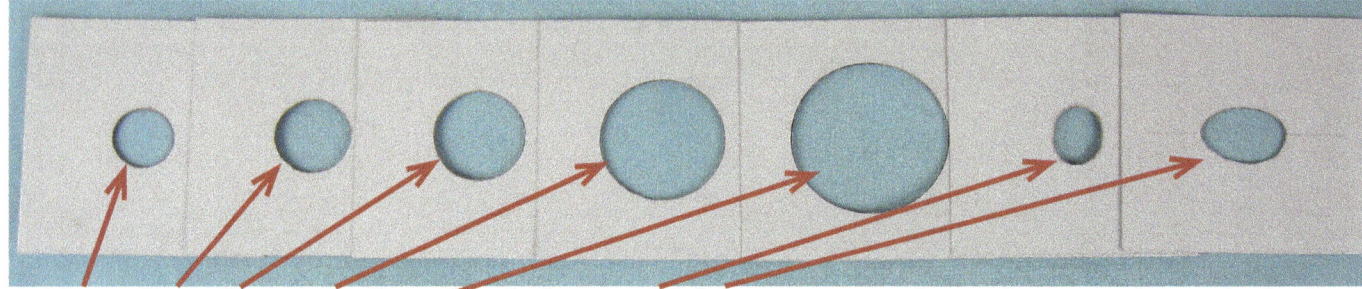

1 1/2cm, 2cm, 3cm, 4cm, 5cm etc. circle, or oval for a snout or where the snout joins the body.

Put the biggest end which joins onto the ball into the hole to check it's size. Apply glue, clamp it with a paper or hair clip and use the hole to keep that shape until it is dry.

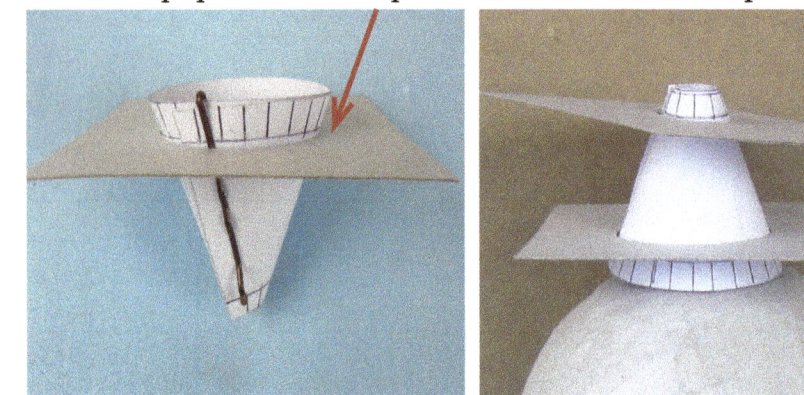

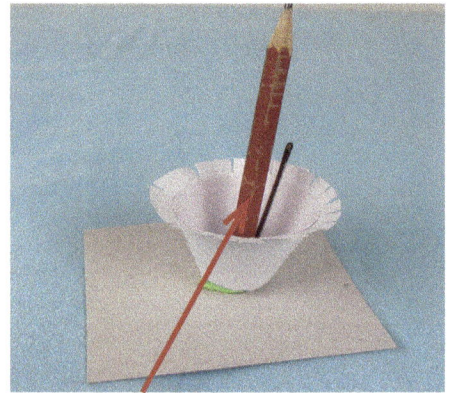

To glue on the nose end, turn snout upside down on a surface, push the inside flanges down with a pen or finger to make good contact and put it through the card hole to shape it. When dry, stick the snout onto the ball.

Making the right size circle for the snout. d1 is diameter 1, d2 is diameter2

A take away/minus sign is - ; a times/multiply sign is x, and an equal sign is =

Radius is R. Length is L. Work out what is in the ( ) brackets first.

$$R = L \times \left(\frac{d1}{d1-d2}\right) = 2.5 \times \left(\frac{3}{3-1.5}\right) = 2.5 \times \left(\frac{3}{1.5}\right) \text{ so } (3 \div 1.5) \text{ so } 2.5 \times 2 = 5\text{cm}.$$
(3 is divided by 1.5 = 2)

Draw a circle with a radius of 5cm, then another at 2.25cm.

Add the flanges like in no 2 on opposite page and cut out.

Wrap around into the diameter sizes.

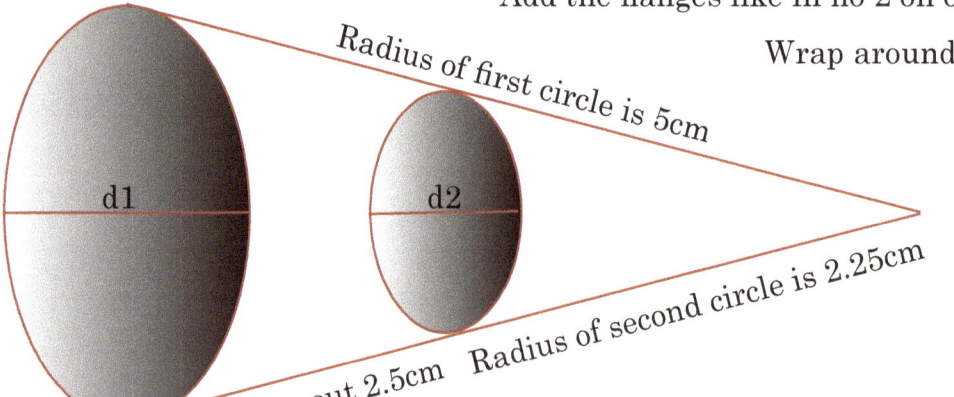

Different snouts are made by altering the length and fatness of the cone.

Small snouts eg. fox are near the point of the cone, big bear ones are away from the point.

Goat - paper head.

1. Cut out the snout. It will go round twice to make the snout stronger, so cut off half of each flange just inside the line, then the card does not get in the way.

A diagram and formula are on the previous page if you want to make a different sized snout. Draw enough of the circle to go round twice for strength.

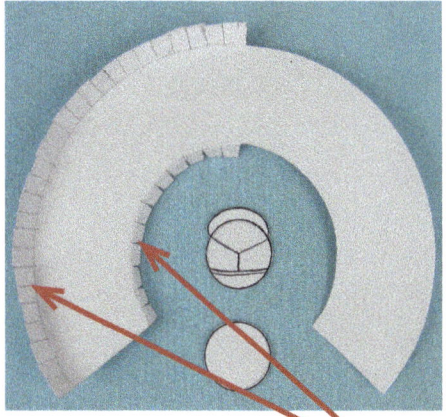

2. Cut out the snout, nick the edges, bend opposite ways.
3. Circle it round twice and glue the overlap together.

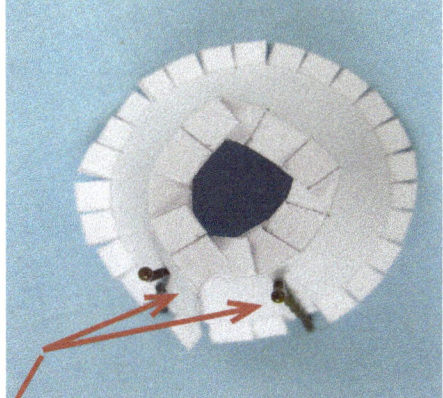

4. Cut out the 2 snout fronts.
5. Glue on one snout front to the inward bending card.

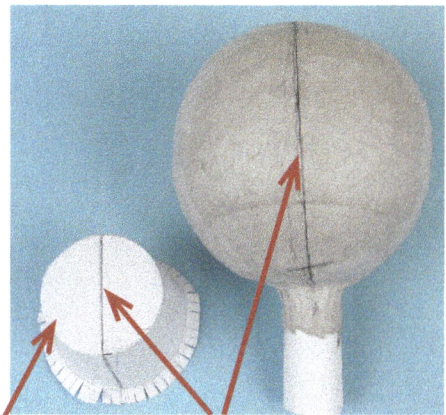

6. Mark the centre of head and snout.

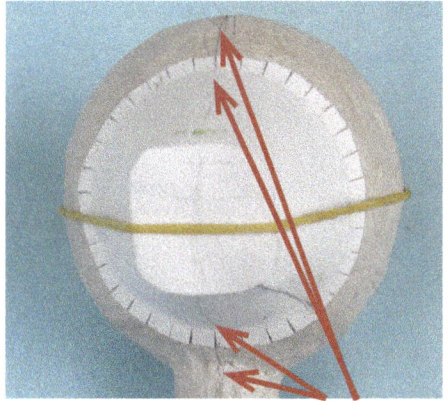

7. Glue the snout on, lining up on the centre.
It can be held there with an elastic band until dry.

8. Cut out 4 ears, join the 2 pairs, bend bottoms to front and back, then shape ears.

9. Mark where the ears go, check them in place, then glue them on.

10. Paint the head and neck white, then with colour. Finally paint inner ear.

11. Draw and colour in 2nd snout front. Glue in place.
12. Draw or paint a mouth.

13. Colour and cut out eyes, glue them on.
14. Make a beard if wanted.

Little billy goat

Snout

Cut off this half of the flange.

Make these small cuts so the flange can be bent out to sit firmly on the ball when glued on.

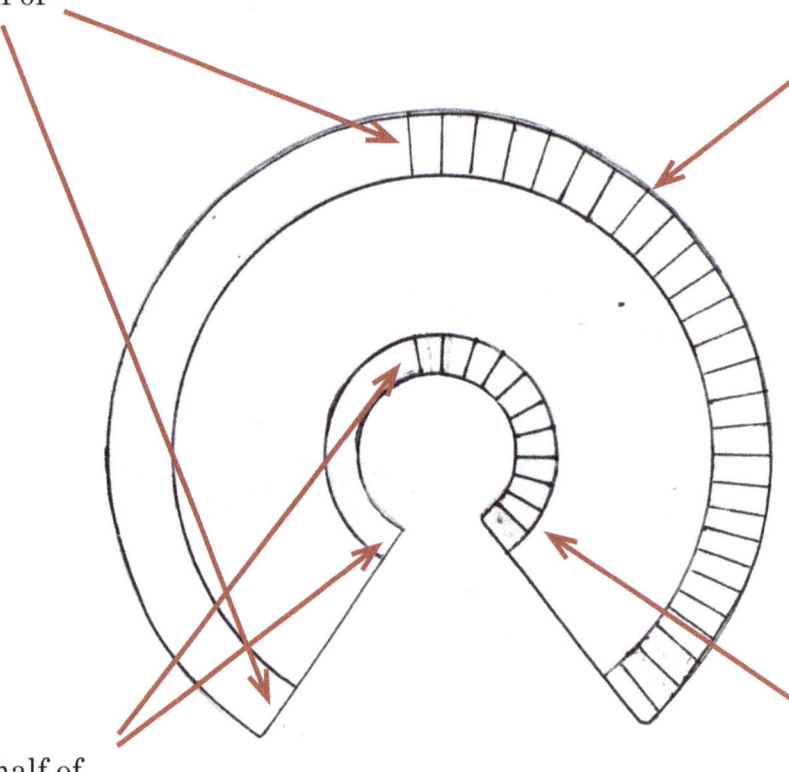

Cut off this half of the inside flange. There is not room for it in the small nose end.

Make these inside cuts so the end of the snout can be bent inwards and the first snout cover glued on to it.

Nose

1. First snout end/cover.
2. Colour in, glue onto cover and bend over top edge of snout.

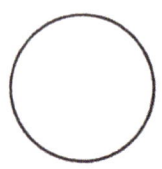 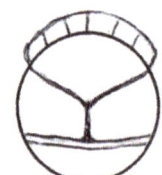

Ears

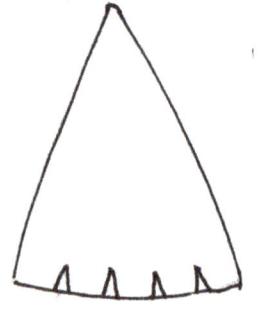 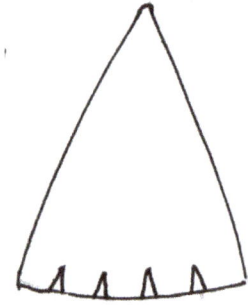

1. Cut out 4, glue the 2 pairs together.
2. Curve, bend flanges to back and front.
3. Glue the ears onto the head.

Eyes

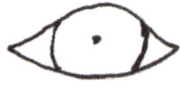 

Colour in or cut out colour paper irises.

Beard - if wanted.

Middle billy goat

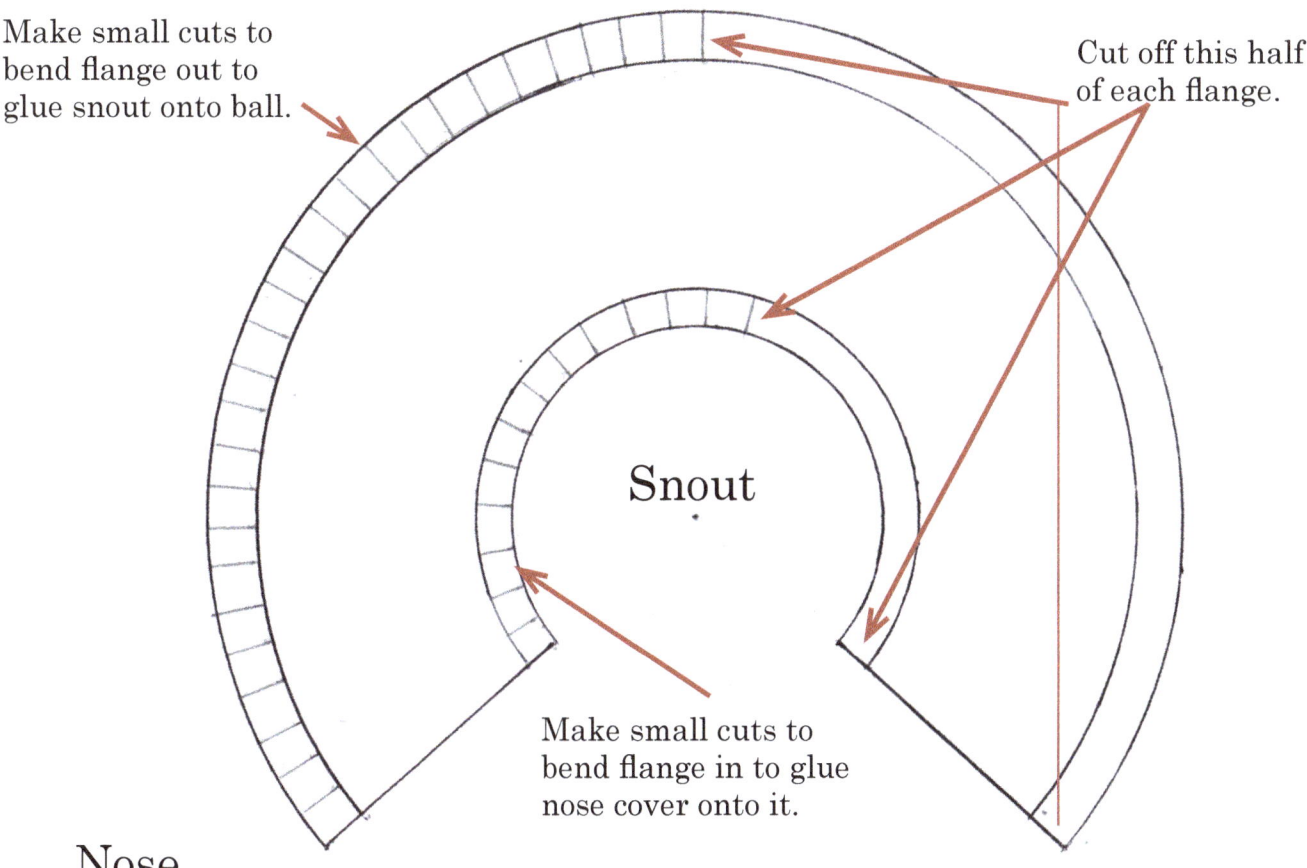

Make small cuts to bend flange out to glue snout onto ball.

Cut off this half of each flange.

Snout

Make small cuts to bend flange in to glue nose cover onto it.

Nose

1. Cover for front end of the snout.
2. Colour in. Glue onto cover and bend over the top edge of snout.

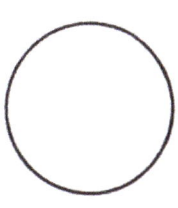 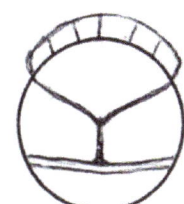

Ears

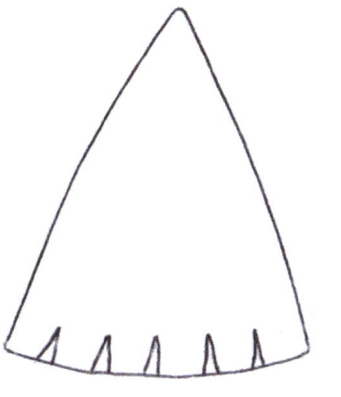 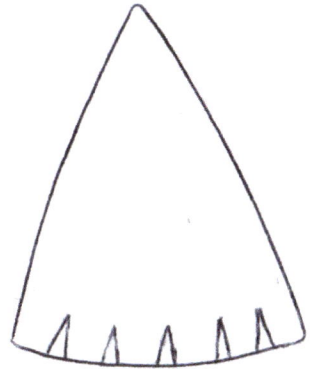

1. Cut out 4. Glue the 2 pairs together.
2. Curve the ear. Bend flanges to front and back.
3. Glue the ears onto the head.

Beard

1. Cut out one of each. 2. Glue 1 on top of 2, 'x' onto 'x'. 3. Glue on under the chin.

Eyes

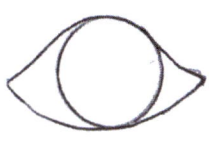 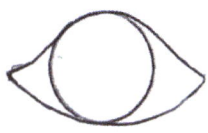

Colour in or cut out colour paper irises.

Big billy goat

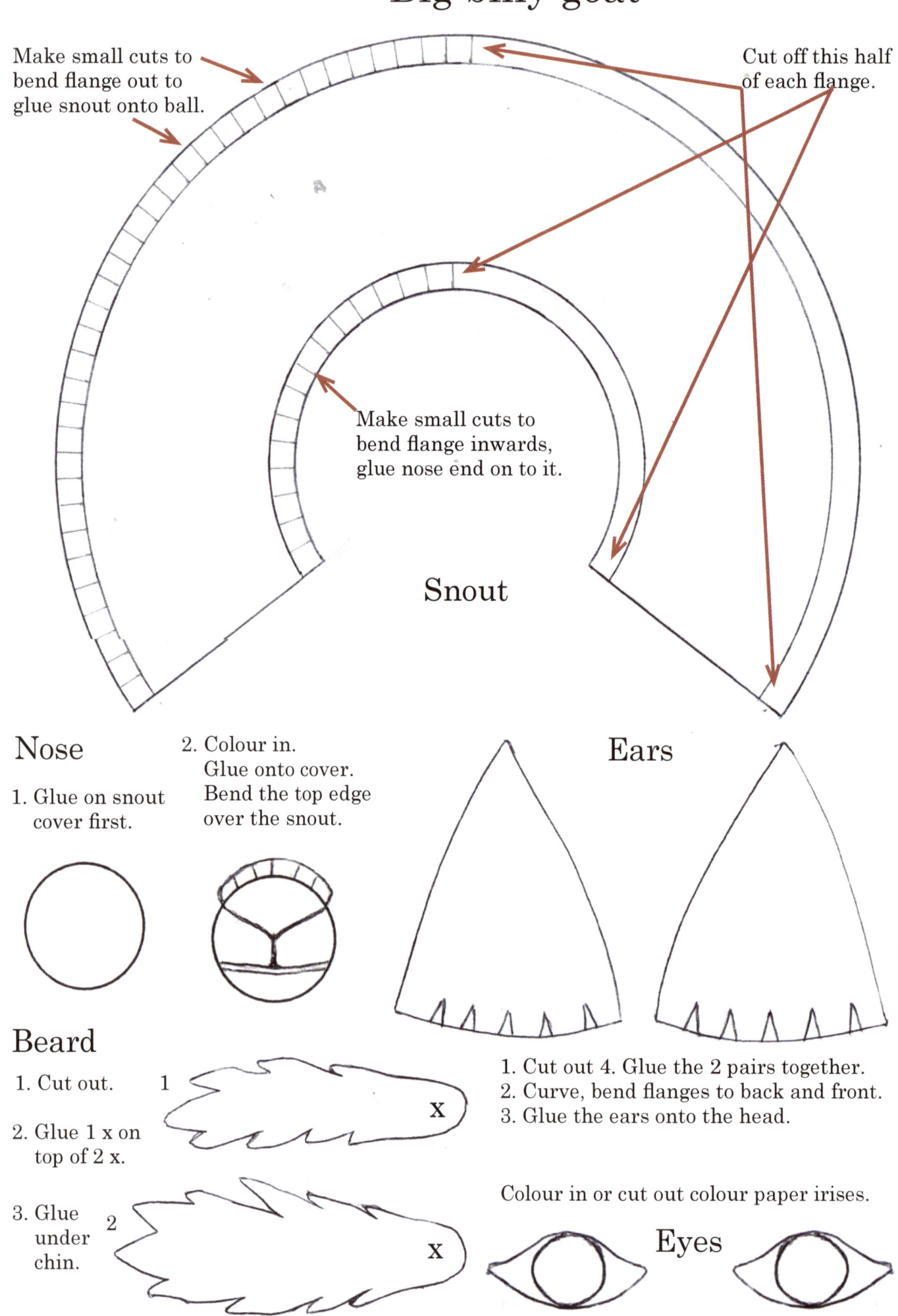

Make small cuts to bend flange out to glue snout onto ball.

Cut off this half of each flange.

Make small cuts to bend flange inwards, glue nose end on to it.

Snout

Nose
1. Glue on snout cover first.
2. Colour in. Glue onto cover. Bend the top edge over the snout.

Ears
1. Cut out 4. Glue the 2 pairs together.
2. Curve, bend flanges to back and front.
3. Glue the ears onto the head.

Beard
1. Cut out.
2. Glue 1 x on top of 2 x.
3. Glue under chin.

Colour in or cut out colour paper irises.

Eyes

77

Goat horns

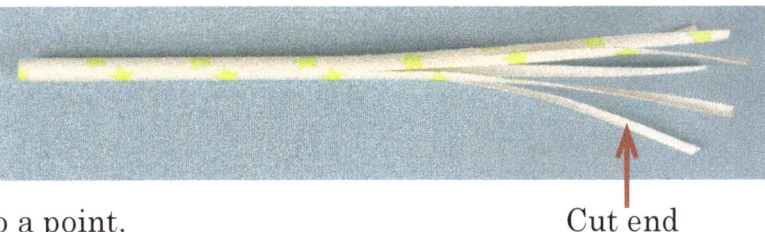

1. Use 1/2 or 3/4 of a paper straw.
2. Cut 1/3 of its length into strips.
3. Soak it in water for a few minutes.
4. Gently bend it overlapping cut ends to a point.
5. Cover with glue.
6. Wrap paper strips around it adding glue all the time.
7. Do 4 layers ending with plain paper.

Cut end

News paper   Plain paper

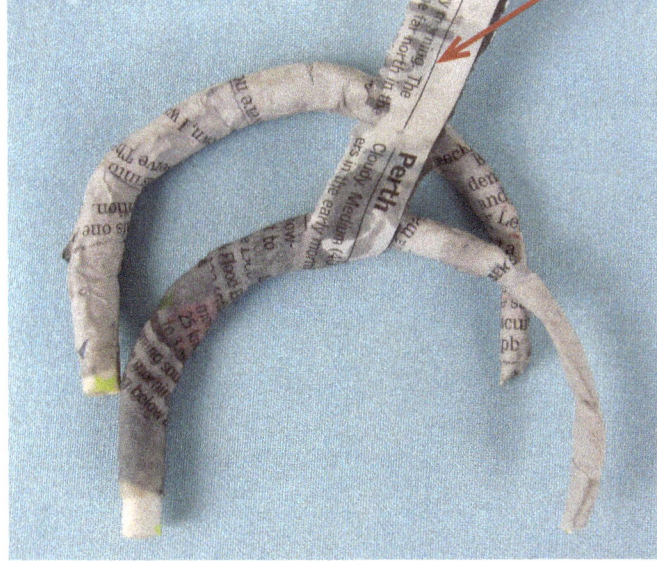
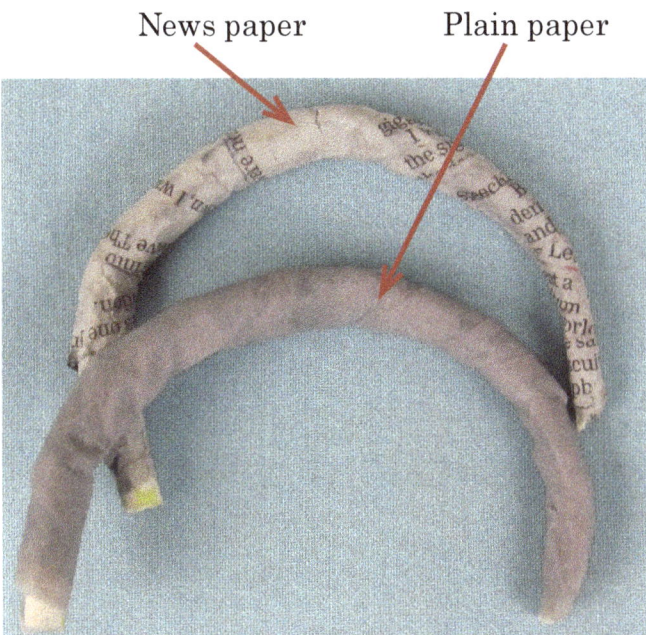

8. Undercoat with white paint then colour.

Cut a paper straw in half to make her horns.

3/4 of a straw for each of his horns.

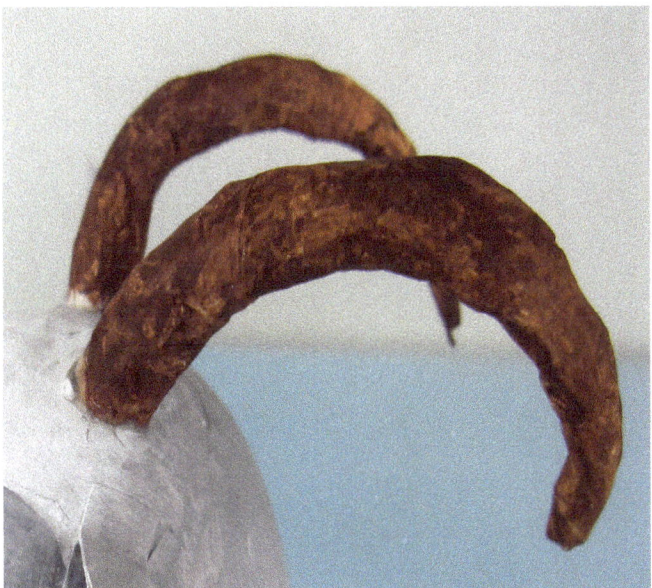
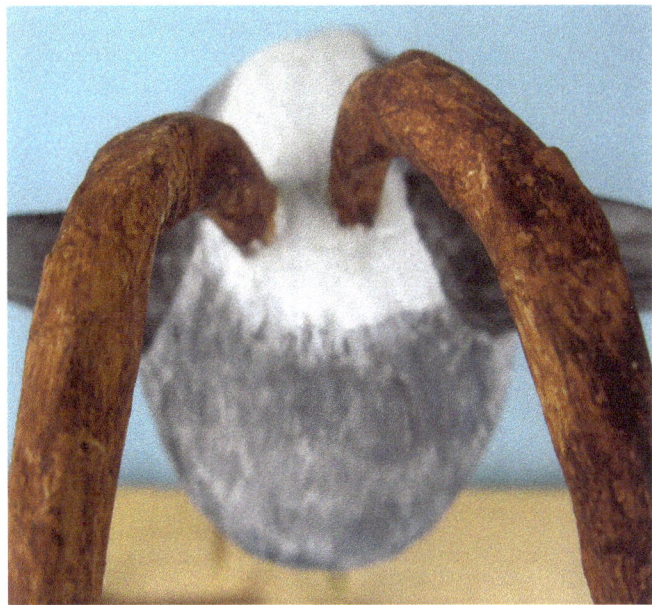

Troll

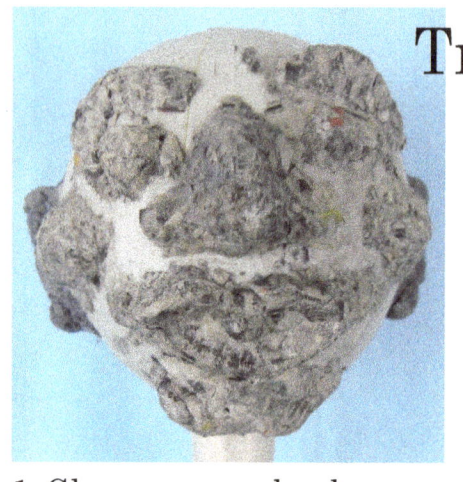
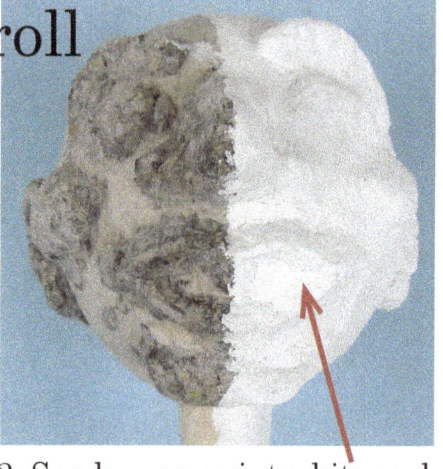

1. Glue paper mache shapes onto the head. Let it dry.
2. Sandpaper, paint white and then skin colour.
3. Glue on long hair, make part pom poms. 4 on next page.

These pictures vary slightly because 2 trolls were made - one for illustration purposes.
The pieces of wool can be pulled through the pom pom to different lengths for a wilder look.

The paper heads were easier to make with the templates than shaping the polystyrene.
They were also easier to paint.
Made properly like this they are sturdy and will last a long time.

Paper heads

Big billy goat

Middle billy goat

Little billy goat

Troll

4. Piece of red wool between 2 card discs. Wind green out centre round edge.

5. Keep winding round card. When enough cut the wool round circle edge.

6. Tie the piece of red wool pulling the green ones into centre.

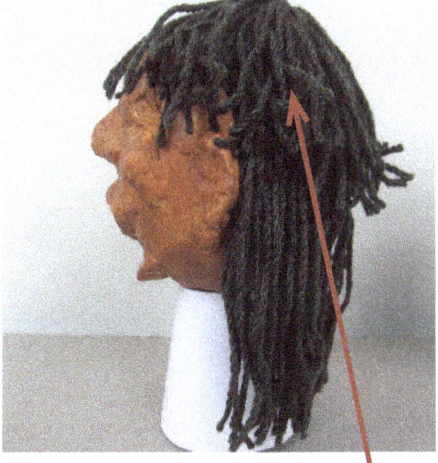
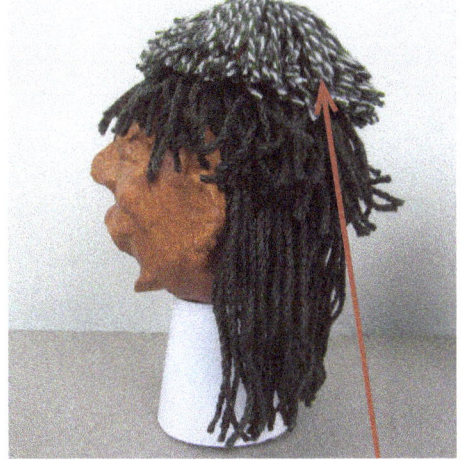
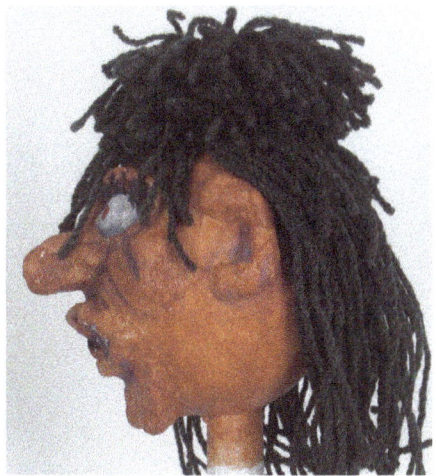

7. Glue flattened large pom pom onto the head.

8. Glue flattened small pom pom on top of the large one.

9. Paint eyes, mouth, nose, ears and shadows.

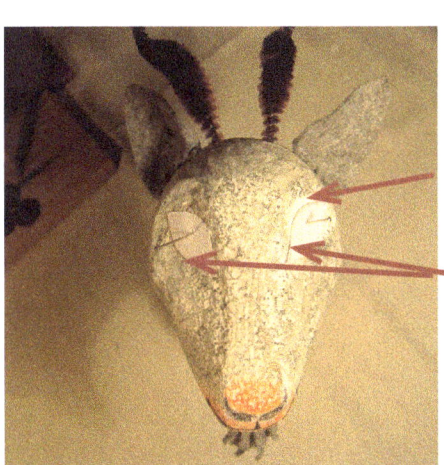

Polystyrene heads

Heads were sandpapered, undercoated with white paint then coloured with crayons.

Middle billy goat with eyes pinned on.

Below
Eyes, beards, neck frills glued on and horns added.
MBG   LBG   BBG

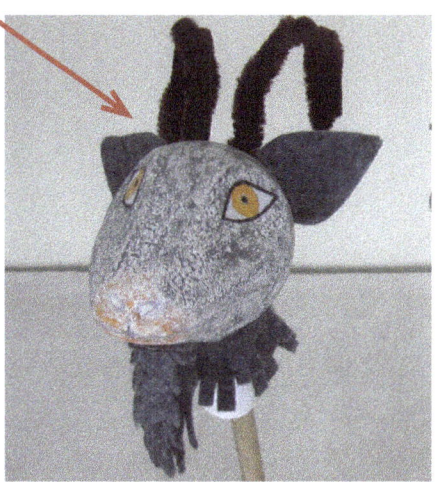

Little Billy Goat

Middle Billy Goat

Paper heads

Big Billy Goat

Troll

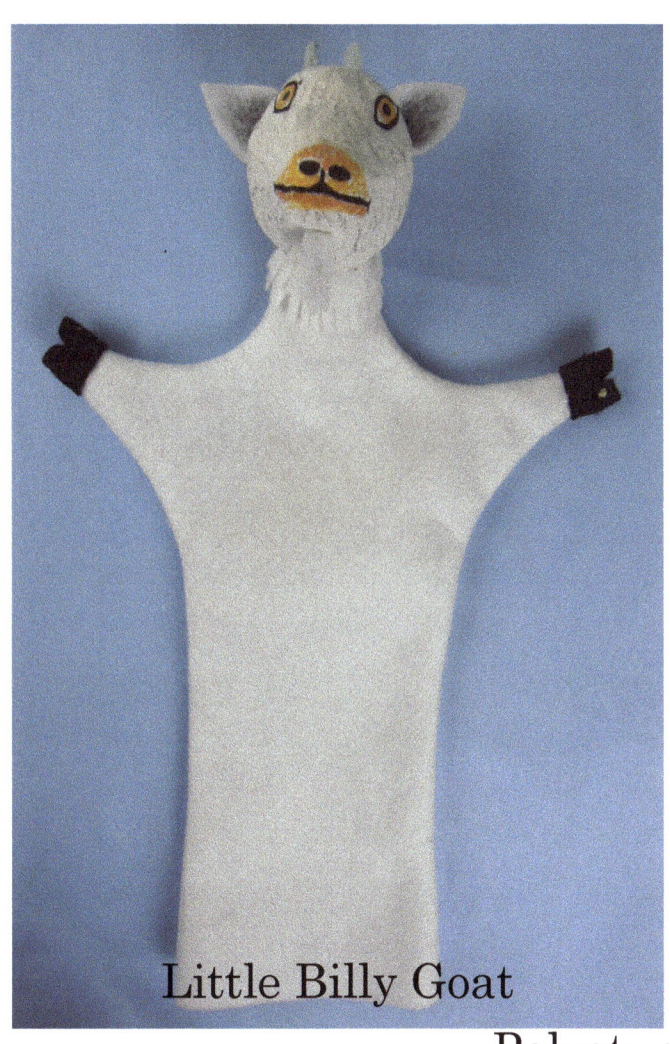
Little Billy Goat

Middle Billy Goat

Polystyrene heads

Big Billy Goat

Troll

The bridge

The backing board was 110cm long, 18cm high, top centre 50cm, two side ramps 35cm each.
1. Score and bend a 50cm x 15cm strip and two 35cm x 15cm strips into 'u' channels.

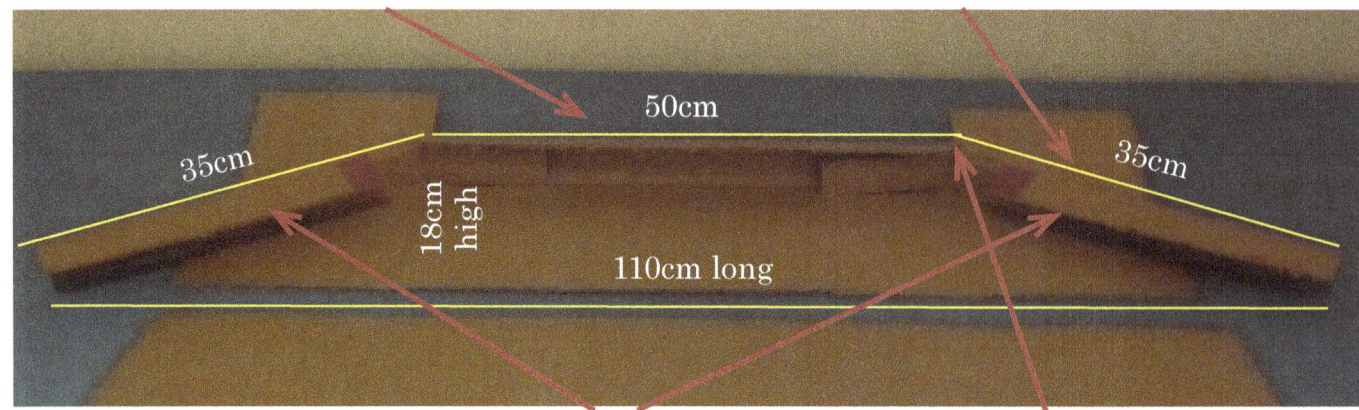

2. Glue these 2 'u' channels onto the backing. Join and strengthen the two top bends.

Bridge is upside down with rocks on the it while gluing the top 'u' channels together at the corners .

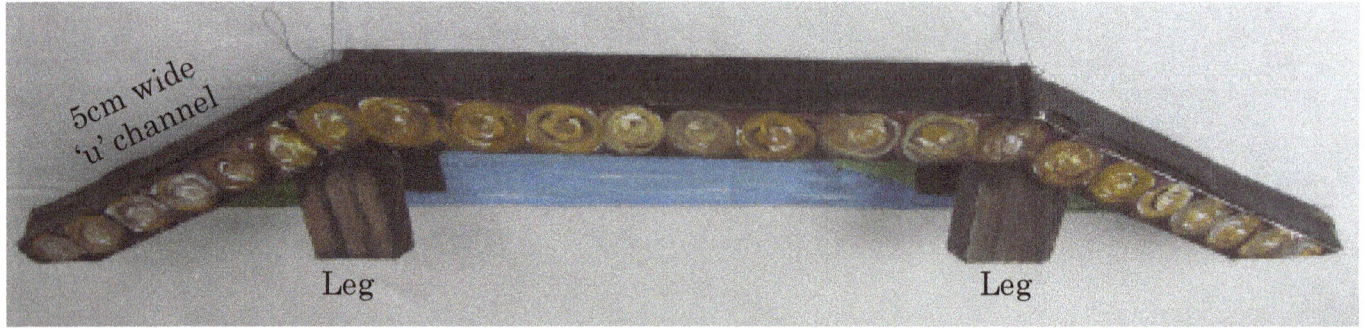

3. Make two front legs and glue them in under the front bridge flap or paint all four legs on the bridge backing.

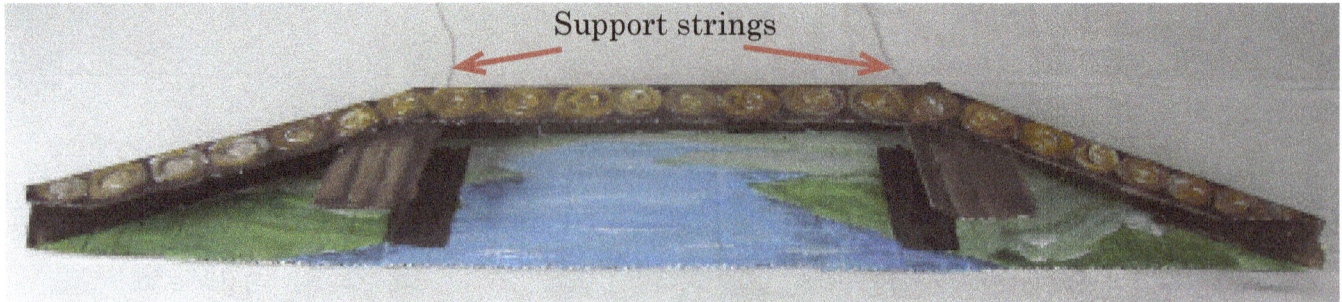

The bridge needs its own scene with 4 bridge legs to hide the puppeteers arms as their puppet goes over it.

Paint in the water it crosses and grass or rocks on the banks below it.

A simple bridge can be painted on flat cardboard bent over along the top to keep it ridged and straight.

The hills are painted to fit in with the bridge and kept low so the puppeteers are able to see their puppets over them.

The bridge hangs from a rod half way between the back drop and the front proscenium so the Troll can go in front of it and the goat puppeteers can go behind it.

The bridge also hangs in the middle between the two stage wings so the goats can all fit at each end before and after crossing it. As in the photo below.

The three billy goats talking about crossing the bridge. Hanging on black twine.

Little billy goat meeting the Troll when crossing the bridge.

Middle billy goat crossing the bridge and meeting the Troll.

Big billy goat crossing and meeting the Troll.

Big billy goat butting the Troll and pushing him down into the water.

Goldilocks and the Three Bears

(Inside the house scene, kitchen or living room).

NARR	Once upon a time there were three bears - a father bear, a mother bear and a baby bear - who lived in a house in a wood. One day Mother Bear made the porridge as usual and they all sat down to eat.
B BEAR	*(Tasting his porridge)* Ouch, mine is too hot.
M BEAR	*(Tasting hers.)* Oh dear, so is mine.
F BEAR	I think we should go for a little walk in the woods while it cools and then baby bear won't burn his mouth.
M BEAR	Ok. Come on. Out we go.
NARR	They weren't the only ones walking in the woods that morning. Goldilocks, a little girl with long golden hair, wandered near the cottage. She knocked on the door. Nobody answered, so she turned the handle and walked in.
G-LOCKS	(Comes in and goes to the table.) Yum! Porridge. (Puts her hand to the largest bowl of porridge and then to her mouth.) Ouch, that is too hot!
	(Tries the middle size one.) Yuck! That one is too cold.
	(Tries the small one.) Yummy! This is just right. It is delicious. (Eats it up.)
	Oh, it's all gone and I'm tired. I will just sit down for a minute.
.	(Sits on the big chair.) Oh, this is too hard, I'll try the next one.
	(And she does) No, this one is far too soft. Perhaps that one will be alright.
	(She sits on the little one and wriggles around.) Ooh this one is just right. Lovely! She wriggles then pauses. (It breaks) Oh! It's broken.
NARR	Goldilocks was still tired so she went into the next room which proved to be a bedroom with three beds in it.
	Bedroom scene
G-LOCKS	My, what a big bed. I'll just lie down on it. Oh! This a bit of a climb. Made it. *(Flops down.)* How uncomfortable and so hard. I'll try that one. *(And she slides off the bed and goes to the next one and lies down.)* Oh dear, this is too soft. It swallows me up. I'll try the small one. *(She goes over to it and falls onto it saying...)* That's better. This is my size and soooo comfortable. Yes. Very comfortable.
NARR	It was so comfortable she fell fast asleep straight away. Soon the three bears arrived home from their walk.

Living room scene or kitchen.

F BEAR	*(Arriving at the table first, growls.)* Who has been eating my porridge!
M BEAR	(Comes to her place and exclaims.) Someone has been eating my porridge!
B BEAR	*(Looking in his bowl.)* And someone has been eating my porridge. AND they've eaten it all up!
F BEAR	*(Turning around he notices his chair.)* Who has been sitting on my chair?
M BEAR	*(Standing next to her chair.)* Who has been sitting on my chair?
B BEAR	*(Beside his chair, cries.)* Who has been sitting on my chair AND BROKEN IT?
F BEAR	Someone has been in here, we will check the rest of the house. Come! *(They exit, the scene changes and they enter the bedroom.)*

Bedroom scene.

F BEAR	*(Growling)* Who has been lying on my bed?
M BEAR	*(Looking at her bed growls.)* Who has been lying on my bed?
B BEAR	*(Next to his bed, cries out.)* Someone has been lying on my bed AND SHE IS STILL HERE! LOOK!
G-LOCKS	*(Sits up, jumps out of the bed and runs out.)*
3 BEARS	*(The three bears stare after her.)*
M BEAR	Well, come on, I will make some more porridge and we will have breakfast.
NARR	Goldilocks learnt her lesson and never went into someone else's house again unless invited.

The curtain closes.

THE END

The tune is Twinkle, Twinkle Little Star.

Goldilocks, Goldilocks, you silly girl

Be a little more careful.

What made you think you could enter their house

Softly, softly as a mouse?

What made you think you could try their chairs?

Don't you know they're grizzly bears?

What made you want to eat their food?

Don't you know that's very rude?

On top of it all to find a bed

After you had been well fed.

And then lie down and go to sleep.
Is sillier even than little Bo Peep.
The bears came home and soon found you.
This time you knew just what to do.
The bears could have had you for their lunch.
Luckily they were a kindly bunch.
You ran away as fast as you could
And learnt it was best to try and be good.

Goldilocks

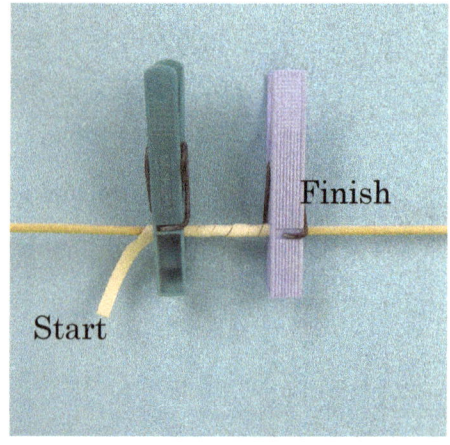

Hair painted on	Rectangle of painted card / Card cut into narrow strips	A card strip round a stick.

Small head

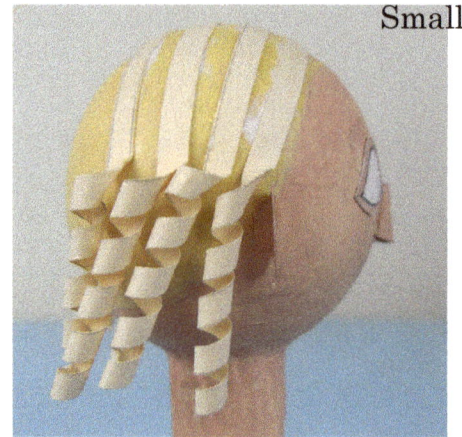
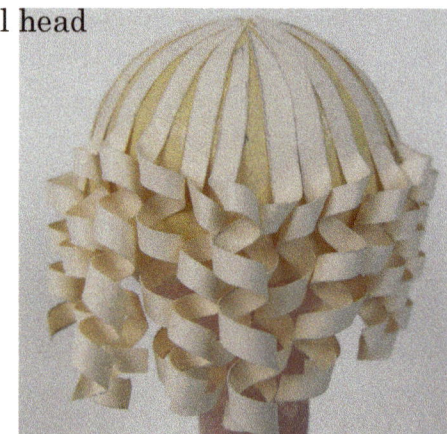

5mm x 8cm curled locks going in opposite directions.

Back view of short curls starting lower down.

Completed view of curls going in opposite directions.

Large head

Glued on longer curls starting higher up and stretched out.

Side view of curls glued on and painted.

1cm strips of card painted and curled. Side view is opposite.

1.5cm wide curls - front view.

Side view of 5mm curls,

5mm curls all over the head.

Finished small ball puppet head

Finished large puppet head.

Side view of 1cm curls on previous page.

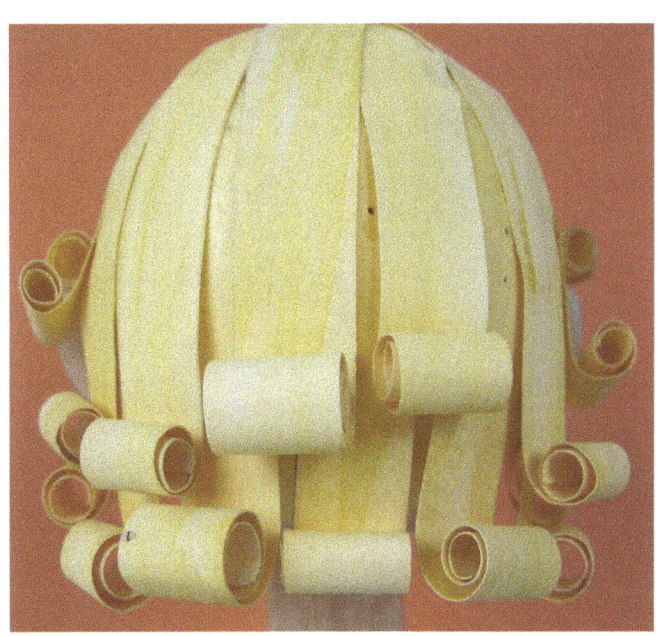
Back view of 1.5cm curls on previous page.

Polystyrene head

A 75cm ball undercoated and painted.

A foam nose, cardboard eyes, mouth and ears.

Unravelled wool for hair with a babies head band around it.

Paper heads

These heads are paper machie made on a ball, cut in half, rejoined by more paper strips then undercoated with white paint.
The 4 cardboard ears are joined together into 2 pairs and shaped.
Next they are painted with colour and the template nose and eyes glued on.
They can be left like this, really detailed and made more life-like or characterised.

Working out a different size snout template

Making the right size circle for the snout. d1 is diameter 1, d2 is diameter 2

Take away/minus sign is - , a times/multiply sign is 'x' , and an equal sign is =

Radius is R. Length is L. Work out what is in the ( ) brackets first.

Father Bear Work out the bottom line then divide 6 (on top) by 1.5 (on bottom)

Father Bears snout diameter 1 is 6cm and diameter 2 is 4.5cm.

$$R = L \times \left(\frac{d1}{d1-d2}\right) = 4 \times \left(\frac{6}{6-4.5}\right) = 4 \times \left(\frac{6}{1.5}\right) = 4 \times (6 \text{ divided by } 1.5 = 4)$$

So 4 x 4 = 16cm

Draw part of a circle with a radius of 16cm, then an inner circle of 12cm (16 - 4).

Add the outside and inside flanges like the template in no. 3 on the next page.

Draw enough of the circle to wrap round twice. No. 3 and 4 on next page.

Cut it out and follow the instructions.

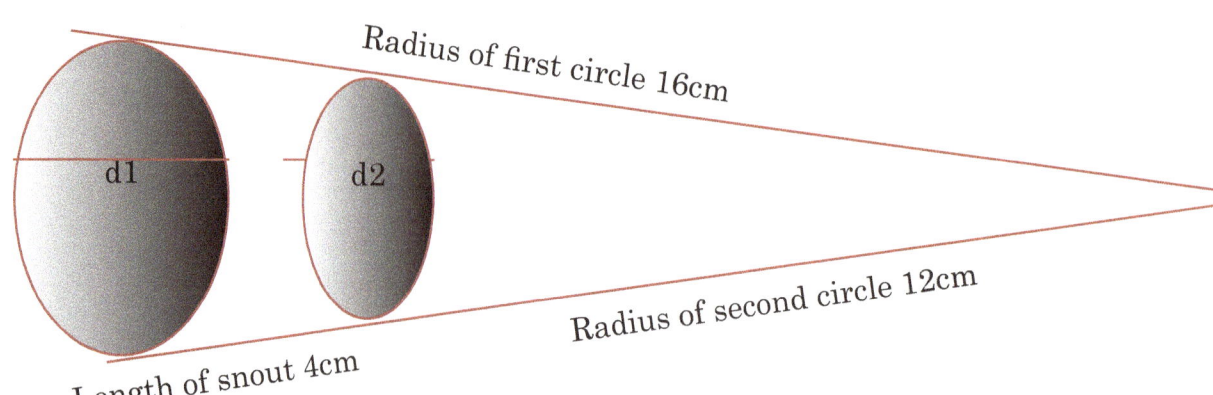

Instruction for making a bear

A diagram and formula are on the previous page if you want to make a different size of snout.
Draw enough of the circle to go round twice for strength.
There is a snout template for each animal on their template page.

1. Cut out the snout.
2. Cut off half of each flange just inside the line, so it does not get in the way.

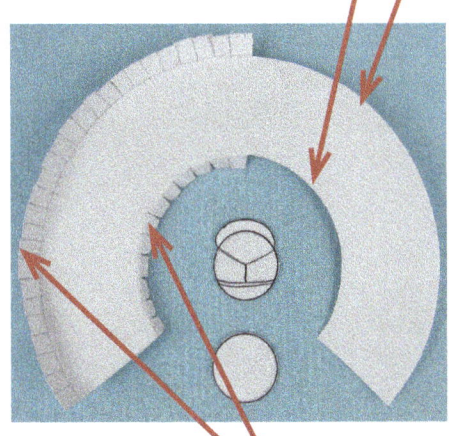

3. Nick the remaining half and bend them opposite ways.

4. Circle round 2x with small circle flanges inwards, glue the overlap together.

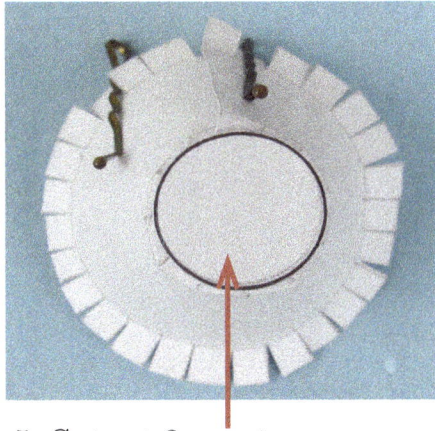

5. Cut out 2 snout covers.
6. Glue plain snout front to the inward bending card.

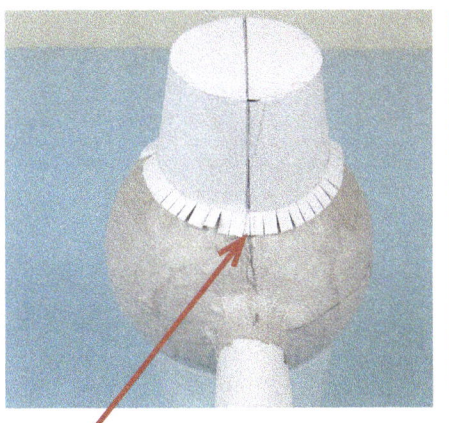

7. Mark the centre of the head and snout, glue the snout on, lining up the centre.

8. Cut out 4 ears, join the 2 pairs, shape the ears, bend flanges to back and front.

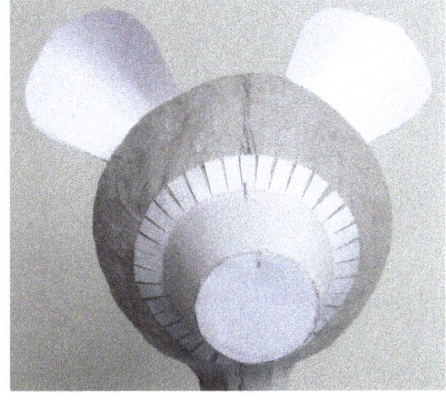

9. Mark where the ears go, check them in place then glue them on.

10. Paint the head and neck white, then with colour, finally paint inner ear.

11. Colour and cut out eyes, try them in place then glue them on.

12. Colour in 2nd snout front. Glue in place.
13. Draw or paint a mouth.

Baby bear

Instructions for making a bear head are on p 90.

Snout

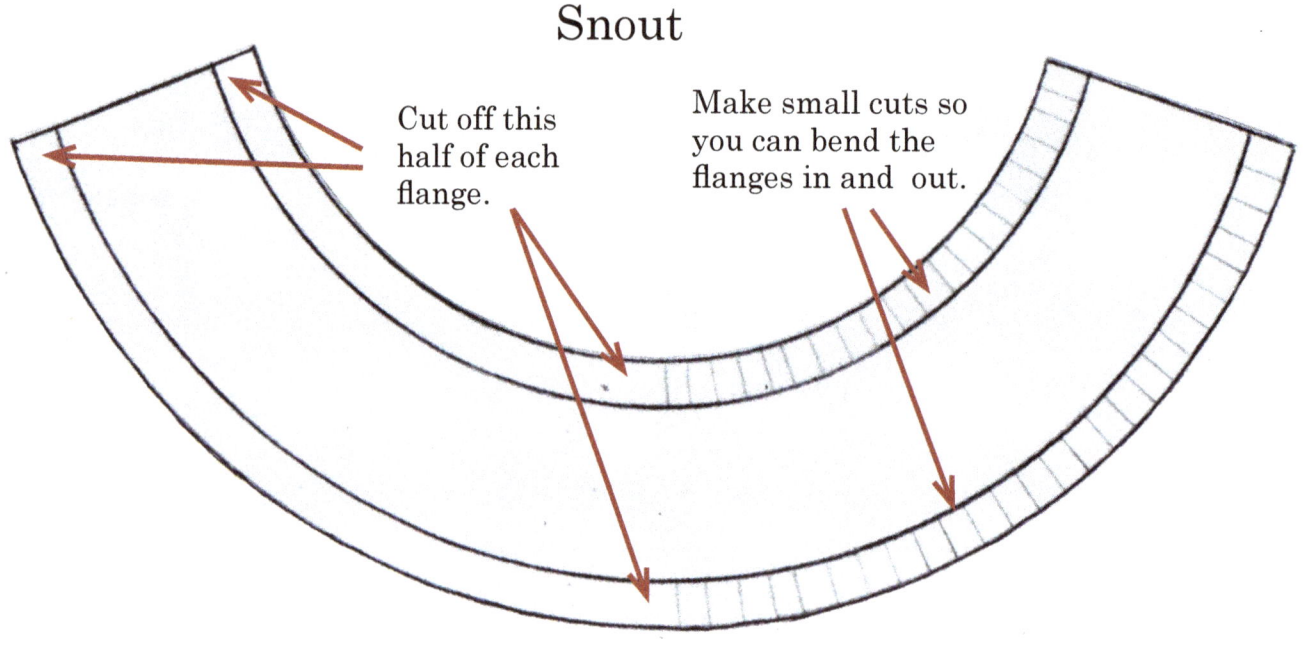

Cut off this half of each flange.

Make small cuts so you can bend the flanges in and out.

Nose

1. The snout cover that goes on first.

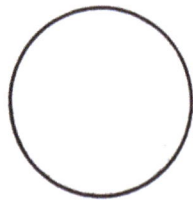

2. Colour in and glue onto the first one. Bend it over the top edge of the snout.

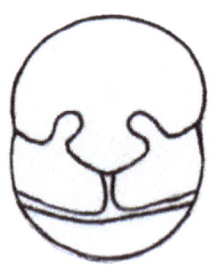

Ears

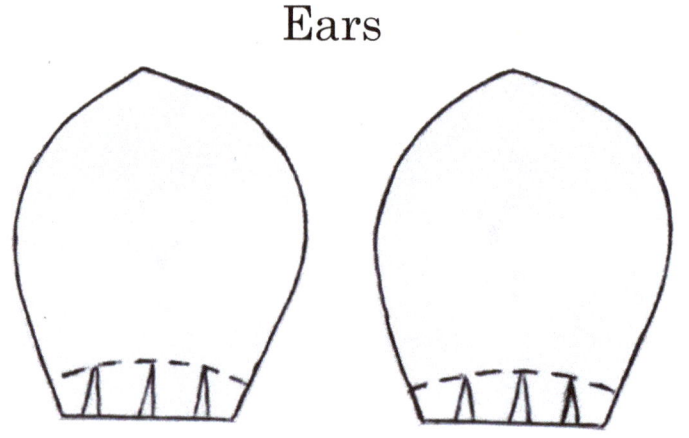

1. Cut out 4, glue the 2 pairs together for strength.
2. Curve, bend flanges to back and front.
3. Glue the ears onto the head.

Eyes

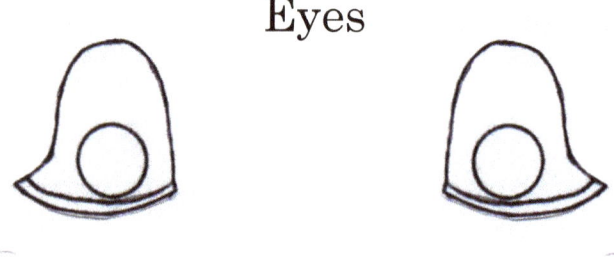

The irises can be coloured in or cut out from coloured paper and glued on for a stronger effect.

Mother bear

Instructions for making a bear snout are on p 90.

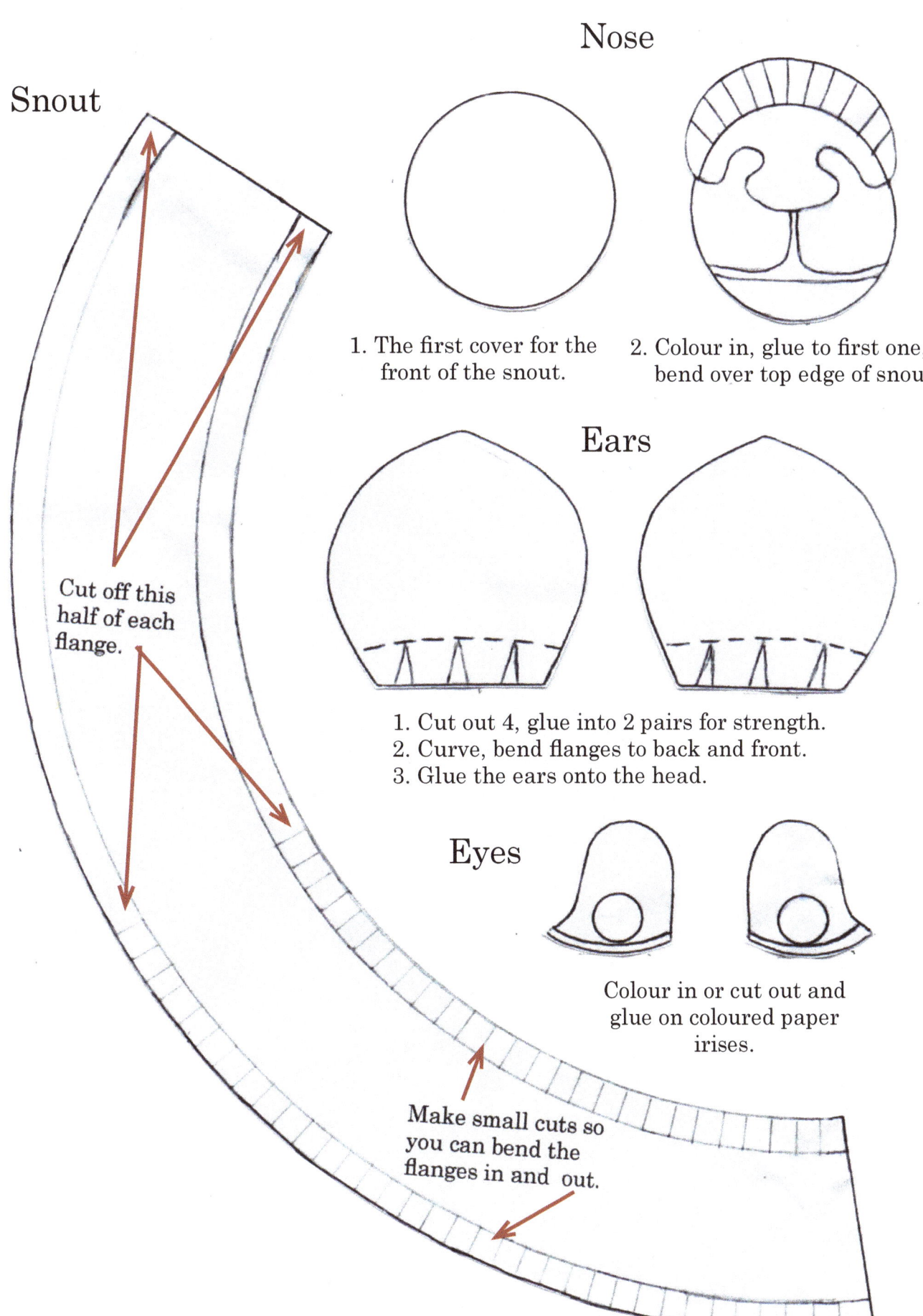

Snout

Cut off this half of each flange.

Make small cuts so you can bend the flanges in and out.

Nose

1. The first cover for the front of the snout.
2. Colour in, glue to first one, bend over top edge of snout.

Ears

1. Cut out 4, glue into 2 pairs for strength.
2. Curve, bend flanges to back and front.
3. Glue the ears onto the head.

Eyes

Colour in or cut out and glue on coloured paper irises.

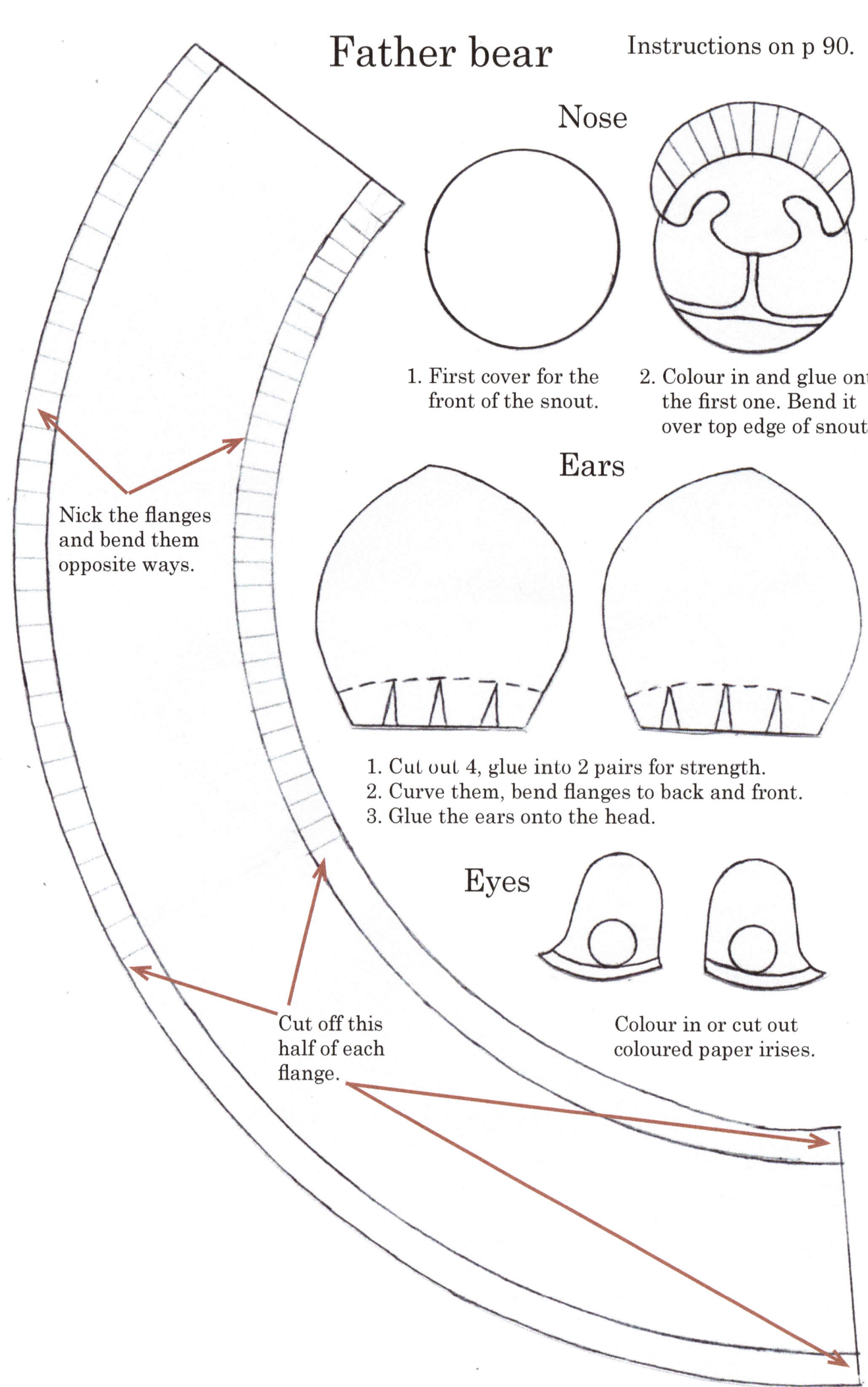

Polystyrene heads

 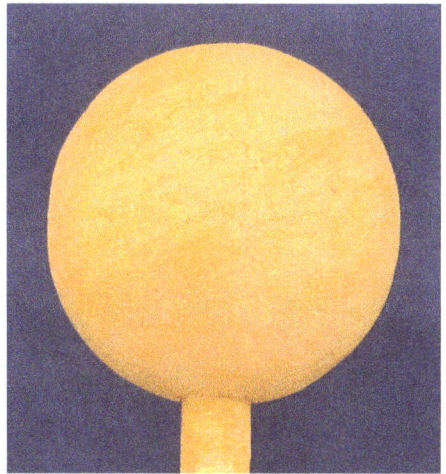 

1. Join a neck into the ball as shown on p 26.
2. Join a section of a poly drink cup onto the front with paper strips and glue.
3. Paint the whole head the colour of the puppet glove.
4. Make the felt ears, eyes. and nose to go on the head.
5. Try ears, eyes and nose on.
6. When right, glue them on, bending the top over the snout.

Neck frill

These make them look more like a bear. There are 3 strips of felt.
The inside one, 5cm x 10cm, is glued around 5mm out from the neck.
The next is 3cm x 13cm and and is glued around the outside of the first.
The outside one is 2.5cm x 20cm and is glued around the outside of the 2nd one.

Strip of felt

	Leave the top 5cm uncut so it can be bent and glued to the head.
	Parallel cuts all the way along.

The glove fits into that 5mm gap that is around the neck under the frills.
They can be left the plain colour of the head and glove or the head and neck all painted as in the illustration below.

Mother   Baby   Father

Baby Bear

Paper/cardboard is not suitable for frills, so they have none.

They can have felt ones like the second set of bears if wanted.

The instructions are on p 94.

The irises on the paper heads are coloured paper cut out and glued on.

The polystyrene heads have button irises glued on.

Both types are nice and strong to draw the audiences attention.

On the second set of bears, the head with the felt ears and neck have all been painted.

The two paper Goldilocks puppets are back on p 87 with more examples of hair.

Paper puppets

Mother Bear

Father Bear

Goldilocks

Baby Bear

Polystyrene puppets

Mother Bear

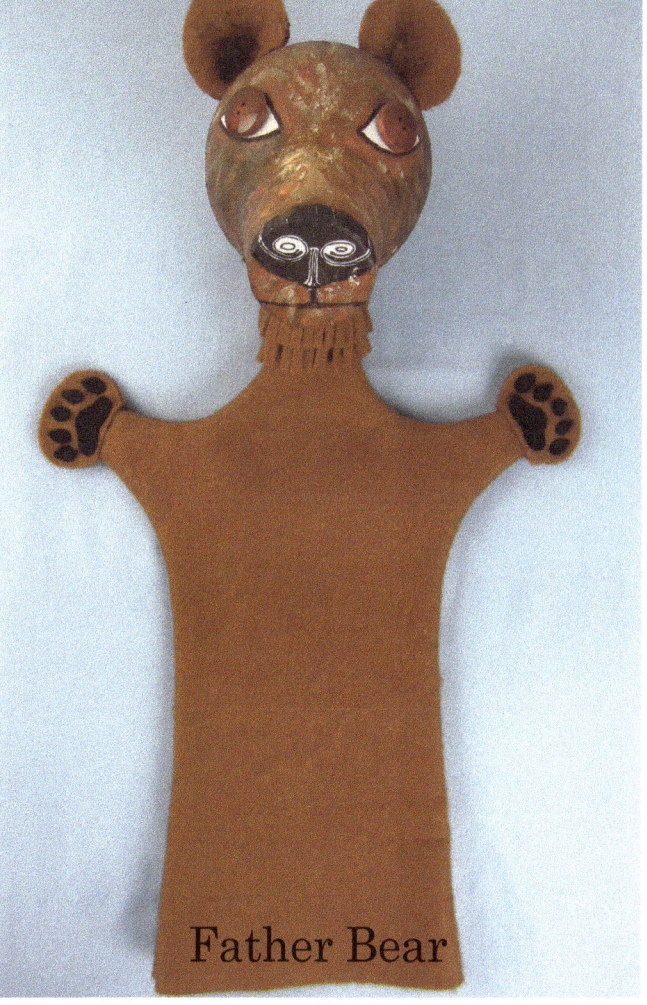
Father Bear

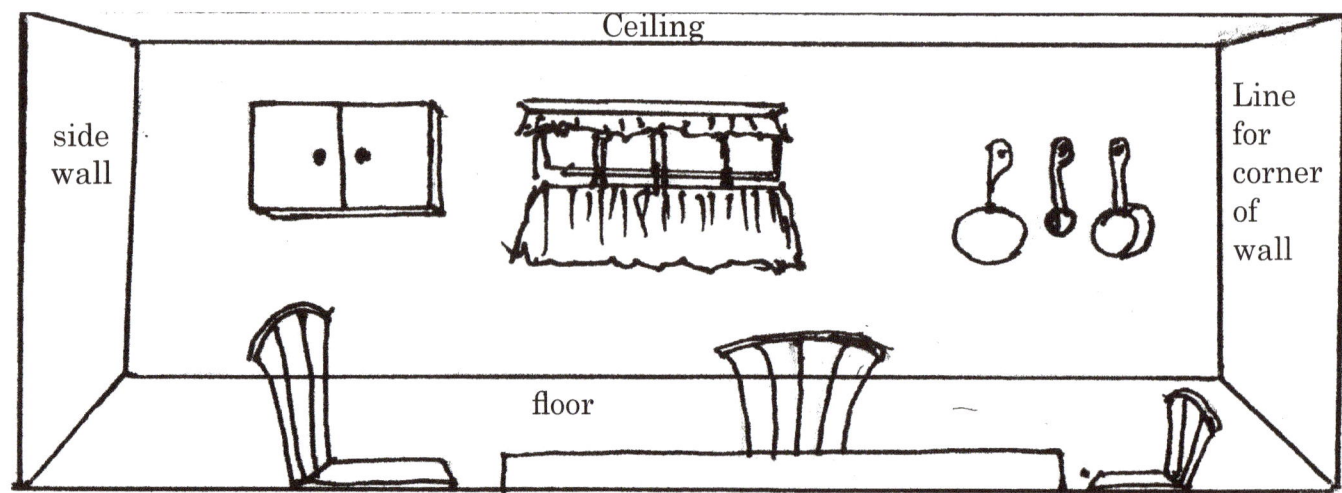

Floor and ceiling were painted on white blockout and sewn onto the backdrop fabric for 3D.

Backdrop features are drawn on the fabric but not outlined as in the scenery photos. They can be paper cut outs pinned on.

The door and bed ends are made from cardboard boxes undercoated white so the colour paints come up better and less paint is used. Sewn-on floor with corner lines drawn on wall.

Front

Door is 25cm x 45cm

Back

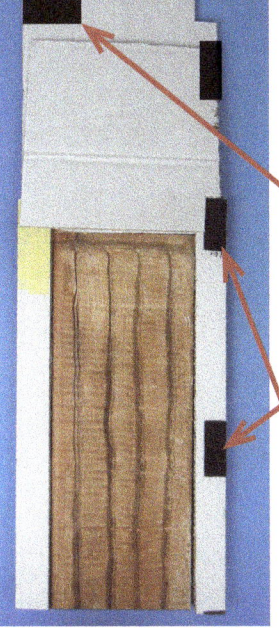

Box ends for chairs.

Door opens forward so you can see the puppet entering.

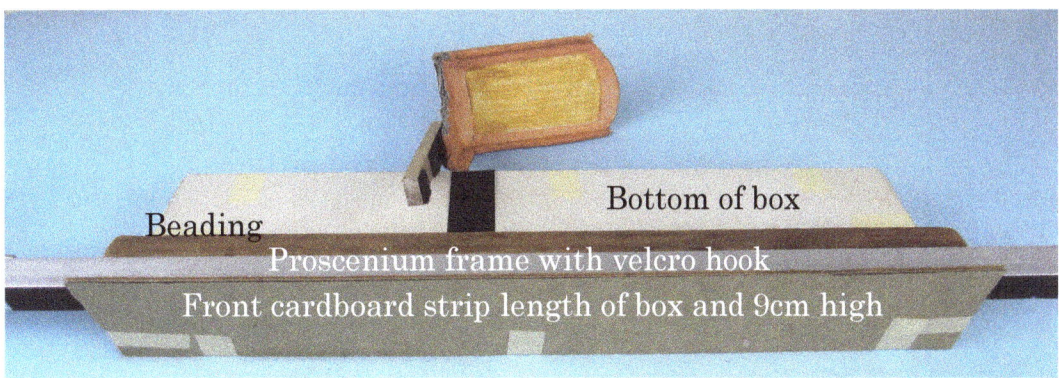

16 x 15 x 12cm   14 x 13 x 10cm   12 x 10 x 8cm

Velcro loop for attachment to proscenium

Father and baby opposite sides.

Make a hole in the side of the chair seat away from the audience. The puppet can go in and look as if it is sitting on the chair.

Beading   Bottom of box

Proscenium frame with velcro hook
Front cardboard strip length of box and 9cm high

A strip of strong cardboard glued on one side of box to hang down over the front the of proscenium. The table cloth hangs down over this.

Leave a 30cm gap for aluminium and velcro hook and loop.
A piece/s of beading glued to box to go behind proscenium frame.

A box glued together so it is rigid.

Piece of velcro across the box

Chair support

Vecro on strong card or wood.

Velcro to join to the curtain support rod.

Velcro to join to the side frame.

Small box ends make good beds.

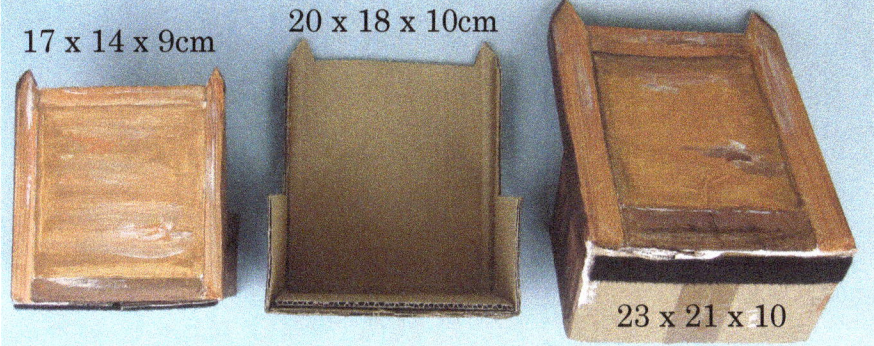

17 x 14 x 9cm   20 x 18 x 10cm

23 x 21 x 10

A small side and base makes them strong, look real, and keeps them upright.

These scenes are far more clear and vibrant because the windows, cupboards, etc have been outlined with strong colours. What did they do and say as they came to the table?

How did they get up and leave? Did they have a family discussion as it happened?

Does she peek in first, bounce in excitement, look around, commenting. She can say how full each bowl is and what it taste like, etc.

How does she act when breaking the chair? Fall over? Exclaim "Oh dear!"

How does she climb onto each bed and bounce, lie down, sit up, etc and chatter away about it?

How do they enter? Look at each bed? Little bear gets ahead and sees Goldie. What happens?

The Gingerbread Man

NARR There was a little old man and a little old woman who lived very happily in their house on a farm except for the fact that they had no children. One day the little old woman was baking gingerbread. She made one in the shape of a little boy with currants for eyes and a piece of orange peel for a smile on his face. Down his front she put cherries for buttons and then she popped him in the oven to cook. After a while she could smell the hot gingerbread and opened the oven door to look in. The Gingerbread Man jumped out and began to run away.

OLD Woman Stop!

OLD Man Stop!

(*The door opens, GBM runs out the door with the old woman and old man following.*)

G B MAN Run, run, as fast as you can.

You can't catch me.

I'm the Gingerbread Man!

(*He runs right across the stage and round the back with them following. An apple tree appears from the left. A boy and girl can be heard off stage playing chasey or something.*)

BOY Caught you.

GIRL I'm thirsty and hungry. Let's go and get an apple.

BOY Yes. Beat/race you.

A boy and girl enter from the right and pick an apple. Add extra dialogue .)

NARR The Gingerbread Man ran on until he came to a boy and a girl under an apple tree. (*He runs in and starts bouncing on the spot near them.*)

GIRL Hello! What are you doing?

BOY Yes! What are you up to little man?

G B MAN I've run away from a little old woman, a little old man and I can run away from you I can!

(He sings as he runs off.)

Run, run, run as fast as you can!

You can't catch me.

I'm the Gingerbread Man!

GIRL He's gingerbread?

BOY That's what he said! Let's catch him. Stop!

(*GBM runs across the stage. The girl and boy run after him. The little old woman and man run through. while the tree goes off in the opposite direction. Another tree appears from the left, then a dog chases a cat in from the right. The cat climbs the tree and the dog sits by the roots. Again, work out how they enter, - woof, meow, and interact. The GBM runs in and shows off.*)

CAT	What are you so purrrky about?
Dog	Yes, and what are you? You smell mighty good. A bit like my dog bisuits.
GBM	How insulting. I'm not a dog biscuit.
CAT	Then what are you?
GBM	I'm a gingerbread man.
Dog	So I could eat you?
GBM	Oh no you can't.
G B MAN	I've run away from a little old woman, a little old man, a boy and girl and I can run away from you I can. (He sings and runs.)
	Run, run, run, as fast as you can.
	You can't catch me.
	I'm the Gingerbread Man!
DOG & CAT	Woof woof! Meow, meow! We will see about that? *(And they chase after him.)*

(He runs across the stage, the cat and dog following. The little old man, woman, boy and girl appear and hurry across the stage. The tree slowly moves off as they leave the stage.

A hay stack comes from the left to the middle. The cow and horse can moo and neigh in the back ground on either side. The horse looks around as it wasnders to the hay and noses around the stack. Moo and neigh. Cow may even lie down chewing its cud.

NARR	GBM ran on until he came upon a horse and cow in a paddock. (*He runs on stage, stops still, looks up at the big horse then around at the cow.*)
H & C	(Together) What a little fellow you are. Where are you off to in such a rush?
G B MAN	I'm running away.
H & C	Running away? Why?
GBM	They all want to eat me.
H & C	To eat you? Why?
G B MAN	Because I'm a gingerbread man. I've run away from a little old woman, a little old man, a boy and a girl, a dog and a cat, and I can run away from you, I can! *(He runs off as he says this)*
	Run, run, run as fast as you can!
	You can't catch me.
	I'm the Gingerbread Man!
HORSE	*(Neighs and raises it's head up.)* We'll see about that. I'm much bigger than you.
GBM	But not faster.

(Again GBM runs across the stage. The horse and cow take off after him. And the little old man and old woman, boy, girl, cat and dog go across the stage. The hay stack moves off to the right as they leave the stage.
A river appears on the proscenium. The GBM comes running in and stops with room behind him for the fox to come in.)

NARR	The little Gingerbread Man ran until he came to a river.
GBM	*(He cries out)* Help! How can I get across the river?
FOX	*(Appears behind him from the side.)* I'll help you.
G B MAN	*(The GBM jumps with fright and turns his head around. He looks at the fox over his shoulder.)* You can?
FOX	Yes. Jump on my back and I will carry you across.
G B MAN	But don't you want to eat me up? Everyone else does.
FOX	Whoever heard of a fox eating gingerbread? I'm a good swimmer, hop on my back. I'll have you across in no time.

(The GBM jumps on his tail, if he has one, or on his back. They start to cross the river.)

(All the others start arriving and gather around that side as the fox carries GBM across the river. Choose your order and the little old woman might become more and more upset. What do the others do? The GBM can turn his head and move around on the fox, laughing at them, etc. as he goes across the water. He is a very cheeky fellow.)

G B MAN	My feet are getting wet.
FOX	Well, jump on my back/head. *(These depend on the fox having a tail, etc.)*
G B MAN	My feet are still getting wet.
FOX	Well, jump on my head/nose. *(He jumps on his head/nose.)(He cries out)*
G B MAN	I'm still getting wet.
FOX	Well, jump onto my nose. *(He does. The fox tosses him into the air, catches him and slowly eats him. Or he can keep tossing him if he likes and then eat him.)*
FOX	<div align="center">"Delicious!"</div>

All of them *(except the fox)* say or sing and dance, this verse.

We ran ran ran as fast as we could
But couldn't catch him, like we thought we should.
He was so sly, while we were quite dim.
How we wish we'd been able to catch him.
The Gingerbread Man was very dim too.
Trusting foxes is not what you do.
Old fox didn't use his legs but his head
To get a mouthful of nice gingerbread.

The End.

Extending fingers

Puppeteers can extend their pointer and thumb so that the glove puppet has longer arms or legs.
Measure the distance from the end joint to where you want to extend it to.
Cut a rectangle that length by at least 3 times the distance around the finger.
Roll it up until it is tight on the finger, then tape or glue it. Put it on and place hand in glove.

Large props

The props introduced in this story can be made and acted by one or 2 people.
They have to bring it on stage, take it to its position, step back to let puppeteers use it or go past it and then remove it off stage.
A gentle, quiet object that adds interest and meaning to the play.

How to make a straw

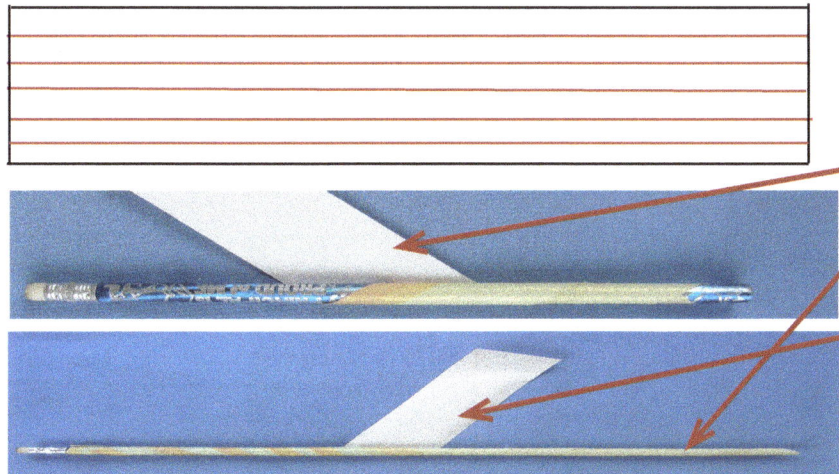

1. Cut 6 strips (30cm x 3.5cm) from an A4 sheet of paper.
2. Glue 2 together to be longer.
3. Put glue along the edge where it will overlap only the paper.
4. Wind it round 2 pencils diagonally (for length) as shown.
5. Wind a 2nd long strip around it in opposite direction. Put glue on all the strip for strength.
6. Remove pencil and let it dry.

How to lengthen a kebab

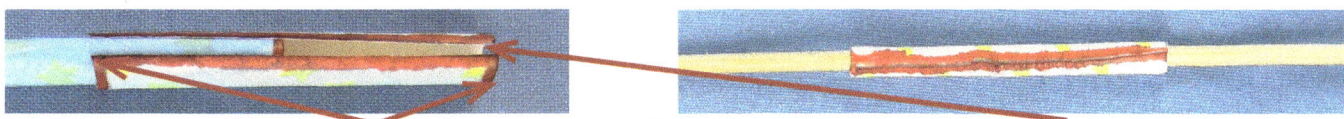

1. Cut a drink straw in half lengthwise.   2. Cut one down the middle, remove a 3mm strip.
3. Push one side in under the other. Keep pinching it together until it is tight on kebab stick.
4. Glue the head stick and the extension piece into it and make them meet in the middle.

Gingerbread Man's head

1. Glue a kebab stick across the middle of GBM's head.
2. When dry. Glue the back piece onto it. 3. Bend both to meet on the side edges.

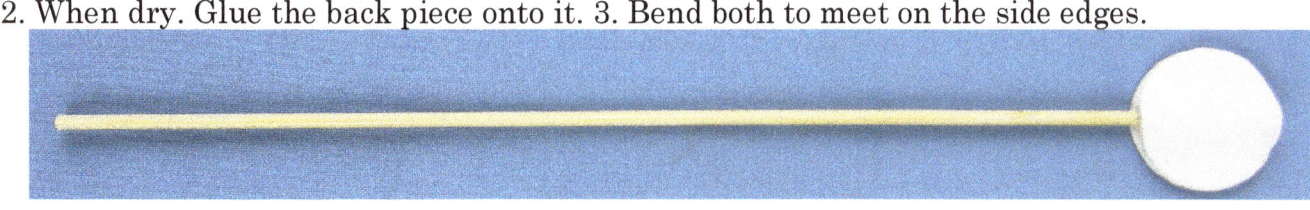

2. Lengthen the kebab so it sticks out the bottom of the straw for 2 or 3cm.
   Hold this and use it to turn his head.

Little old woman

1. Paint the hair with brush strokes in hair direction.
2. Mark where features will go.
3. Glue the ears on.
4. Paint the skin colour.

Making plaits

1. Choose white or coloured paper for hair.
2. Paint same colour on the head and card if white.
3. Paper grain or creases run down the plait.
4. Fold a 9cm x 20cm rectangle of crepe paper in half, then into overlapping thirds.

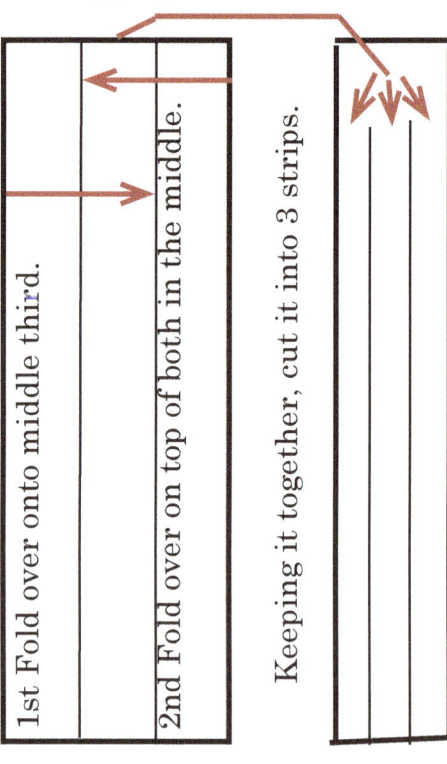

5. Clamp across top. Fold right over middle strip.
6. Fold left over middle, keep alternating sides.
7. Keep folding strip each time.

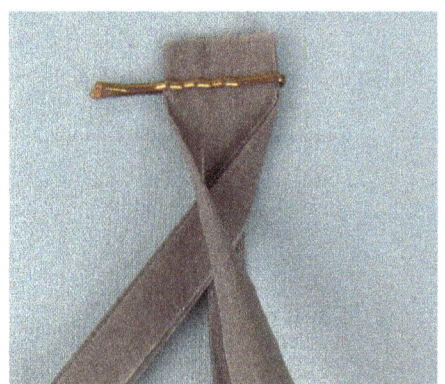

Little old man

Cut more crepe beards between these sizes. Cut into strips, as drawn in red. Glue beard layers on under the mouth.

Beard

Eyebrow

Hair

No 1 is card. Fold under bottom edge, glue along above eye.
No 2 put on folded crepe, cut out. Fold bottom edge under and glue it along above the eye.

1. Cut 2, 3cm pieces of crepe.
2. Hold together, fold in half, put template on it. Cut it out.
3. Cut hair strips up from the bottom edge.

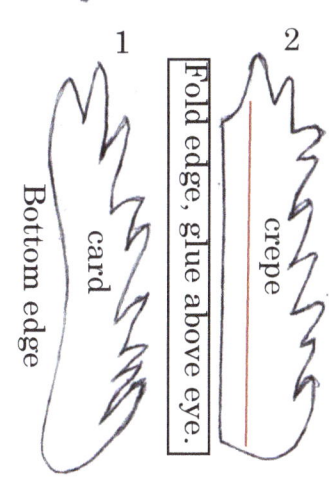

Eyebrow

Girl

Girl with the template card hair on p 106.

The hair can have more vertical (up and down) cuts.

Hair

Boy

Brown card cut like template on the next page so hair can overlap and be shaped to the head.

The overlapping is more visible in this view. It can be streaked with paint as well.

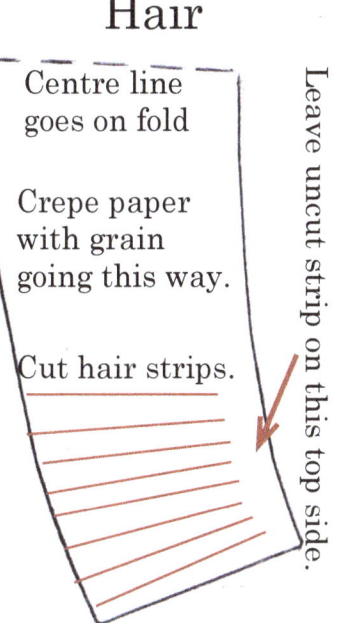

Centre line goes on fold

Crepe paper with grain going this way.

Cut hair strips.

Leave uncut strip on this top side.

108

Boy's hair

It can be coloured cardboard and paint.

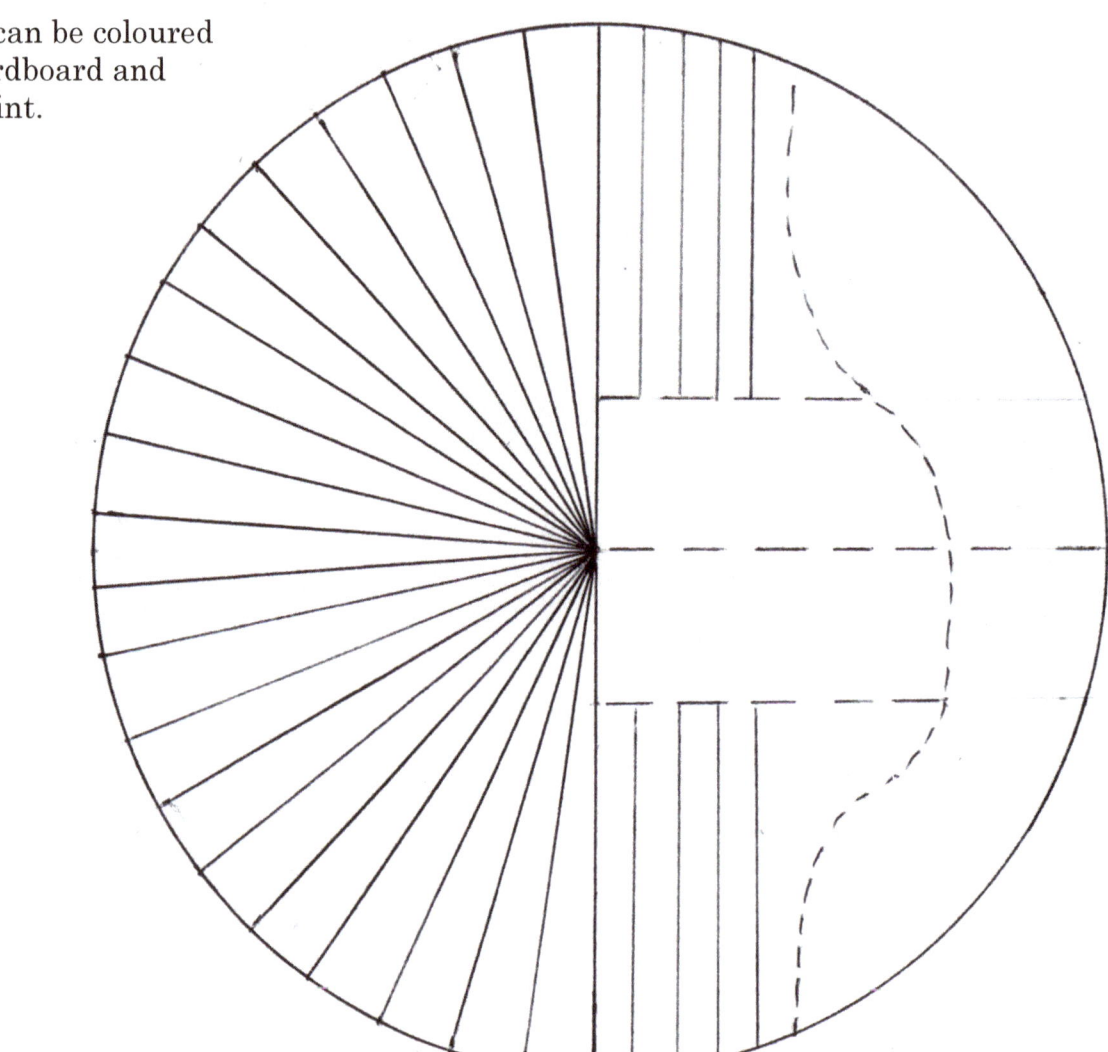

1. This paper pattern is a basic hair cut for a male puppet. It can be added to or some of it can be removed. Place it on a piece of paper, alter it, try it on the head.

2. Cut it out in paper or cardboard (can be coloured).

3. Glue the ears on before the hair, then the hair will go around them. Gently curve cardboard over a pencil.

4. Glue on centre then the sides.

5. Hold in place with pins and elastic bands until dry.

6. Trim. Paint if needed.

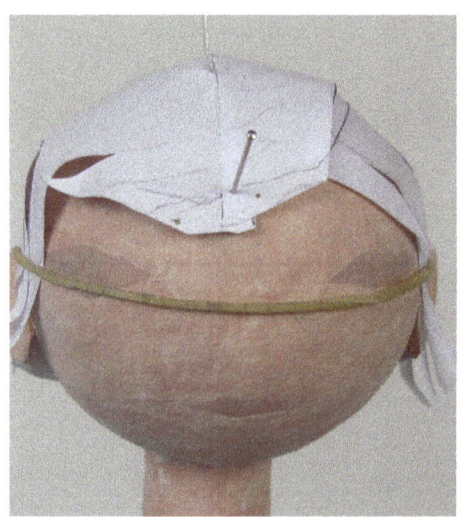
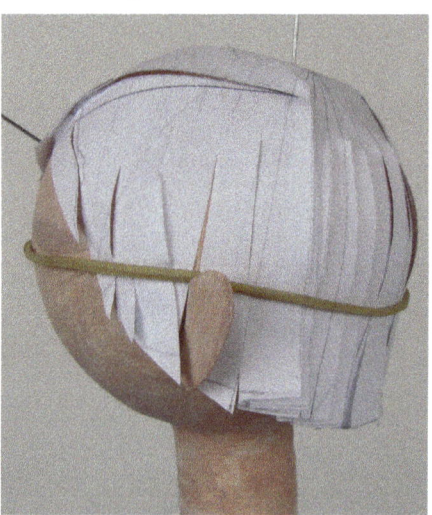
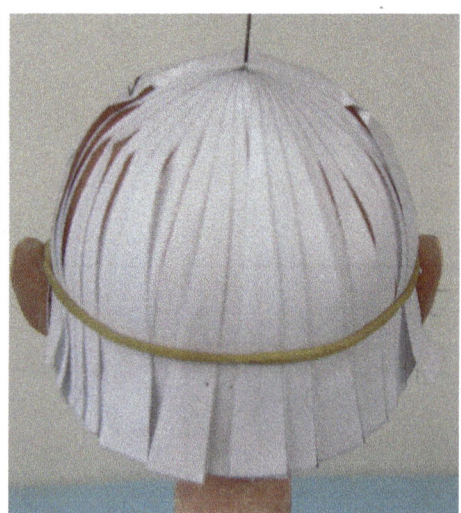

Girls' hair

Can use coloured cardboard and paint.

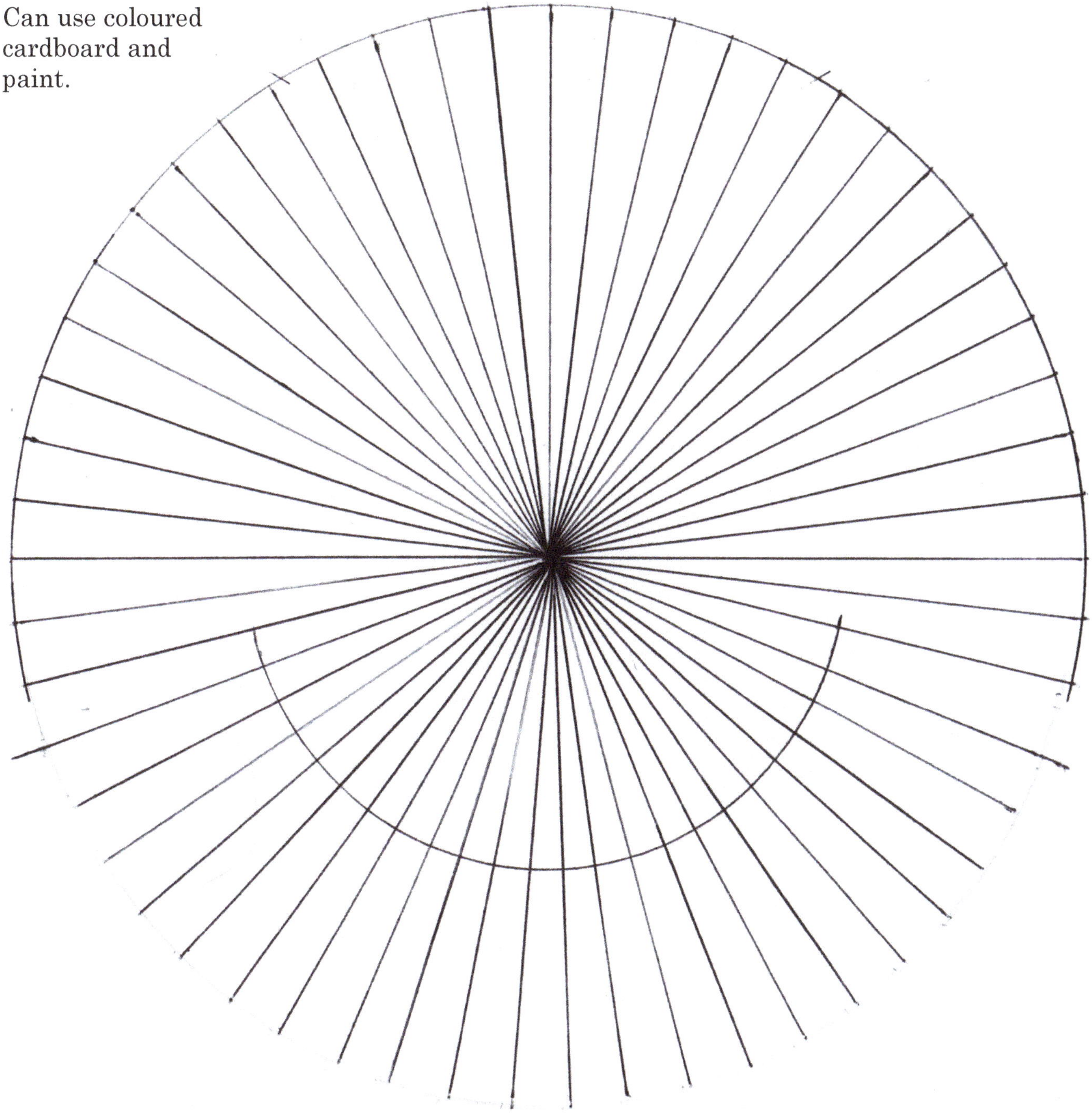

1. Draw round the template.
2. Cut it out and paint it.
3. Bend hair where needed.
4. Stick middle onto head. Overlap the hair.
5. Hold in place with pins and elastic bands.
6. Glue rest of hair down, trim, paint or decorate with ribbons, etc.

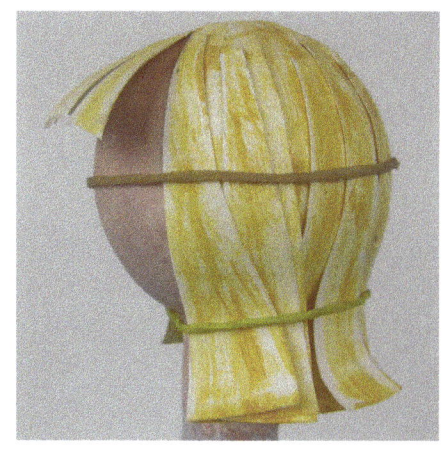

Cow

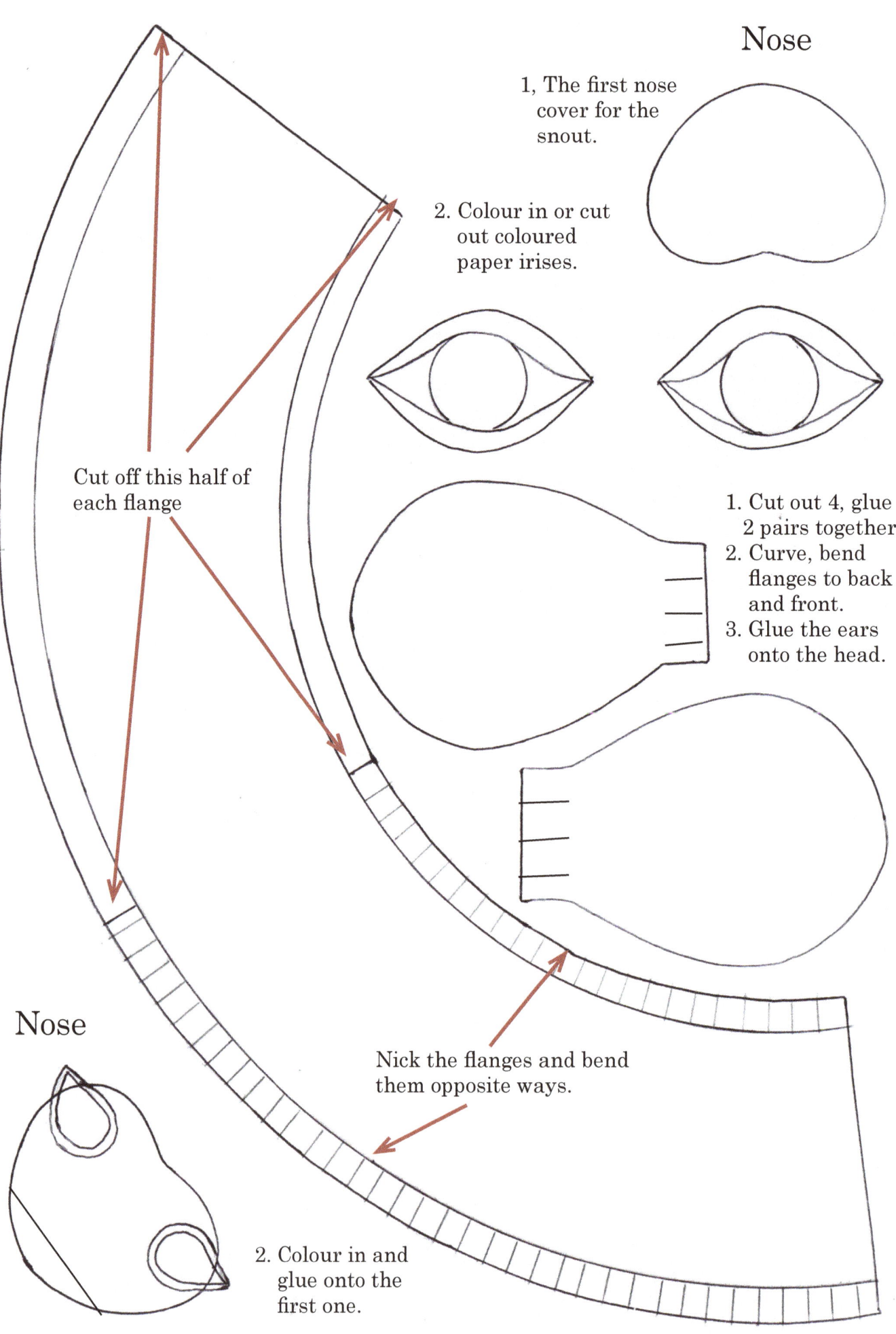

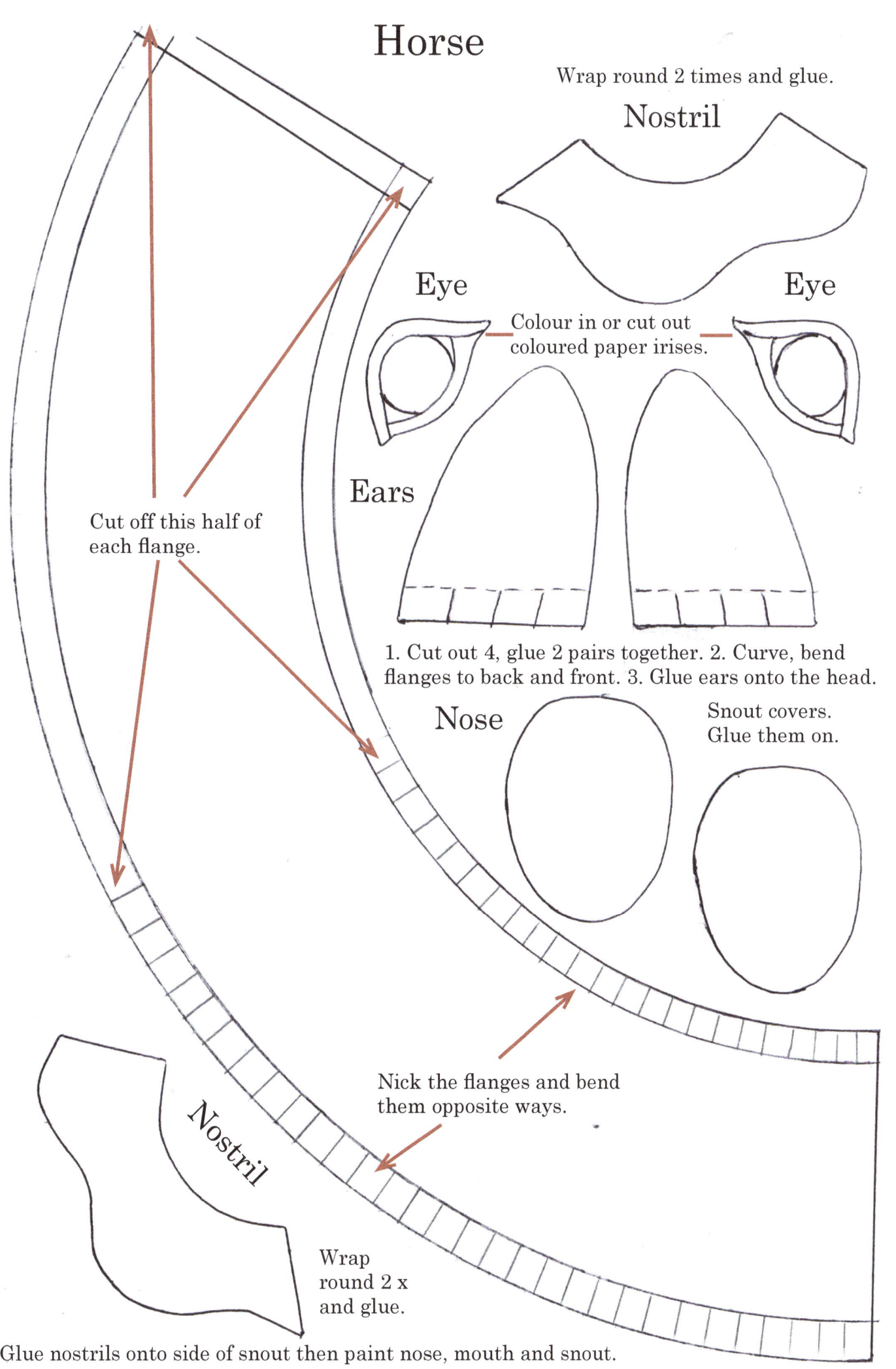

Cow

Cow's snout cards ~ ball and nose end.

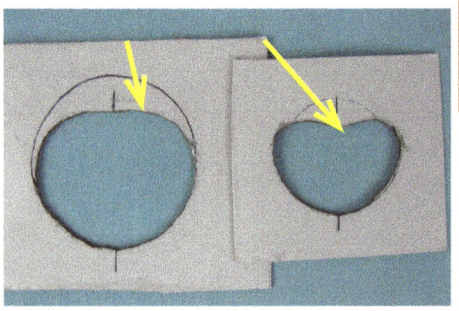

Back view with some cow patches on the head.

Nose end
Ball end

Horse

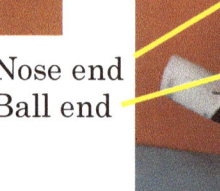

Horse's ball and nose snout cards

Mane

1. Cut 2 x 12cm crepe squares.

2. Fold in half across grain - now it's 4 thickness of paper.

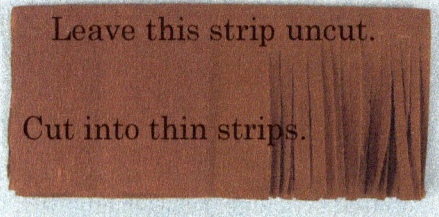

Leave this strip uncut.

Cut into thin strips.

3. Glue uncut part to the head then fold cut mane over it.

Fringe

Make a narrow fringe the same way for on top.

Nostril

Roll and glue on this way up.

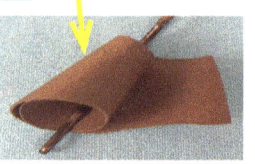 

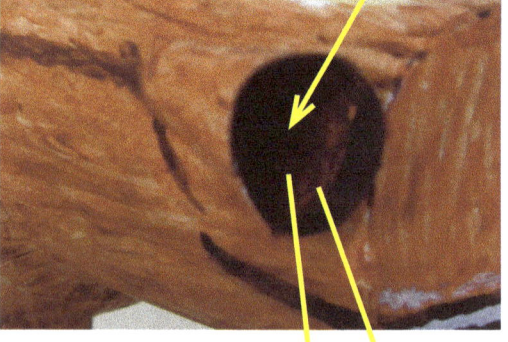

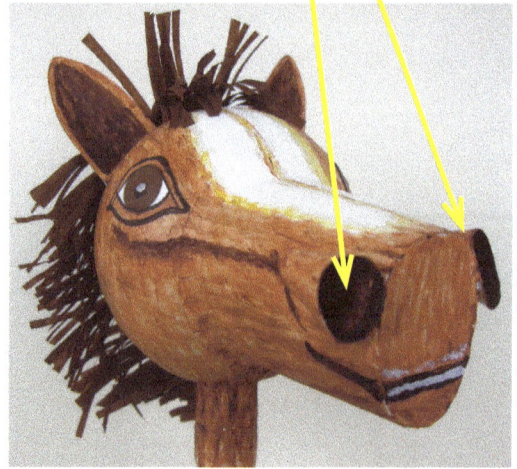

113

Cat

Ears

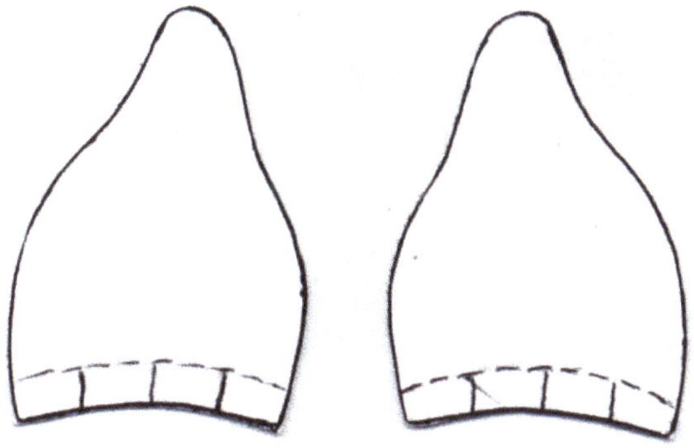

Eyes

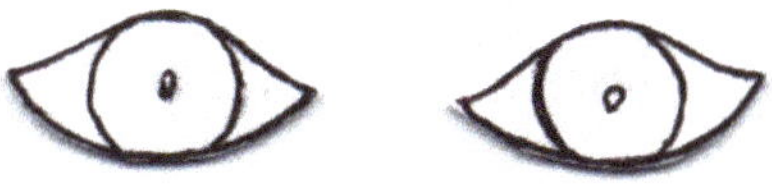

Colour in or cut out and stick on coloured paper irises.

Nose

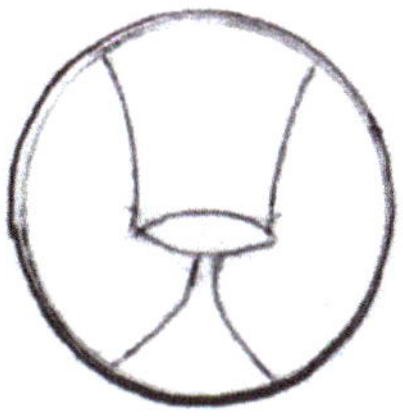

Colour in and glue this nose on or do the suggestion below.

1. Cut out 4, glue 2 pairs together.
2. Curve, bend flanges to back and front.
3. Glue the ears onto the head.

A small part of a polystyrene ball/bead or a blob of paper mache can be stuck on for the cat's snout.
Whiskers can be broom hair, etc.

Dog

Nose

1. The first nose cover for the snout. 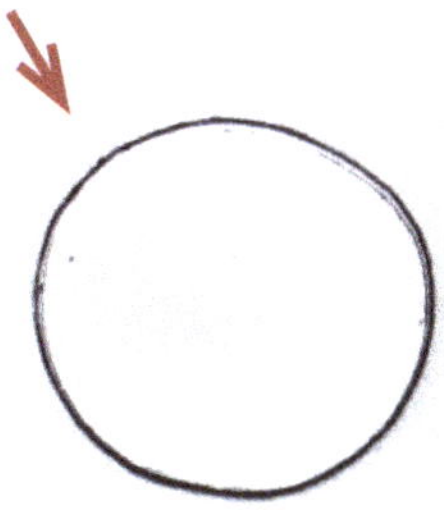
2. Colour in, glue onto the first one, Bend it over the top of the snout.

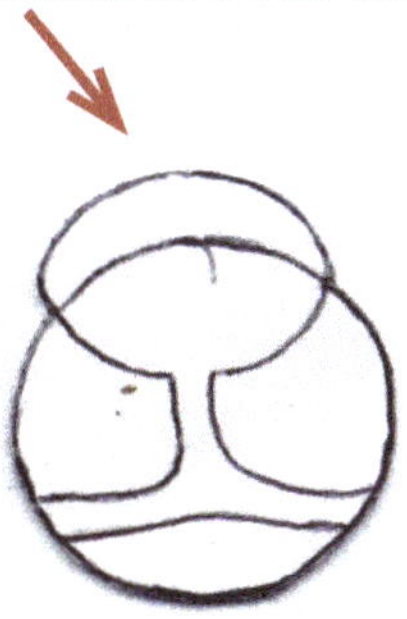

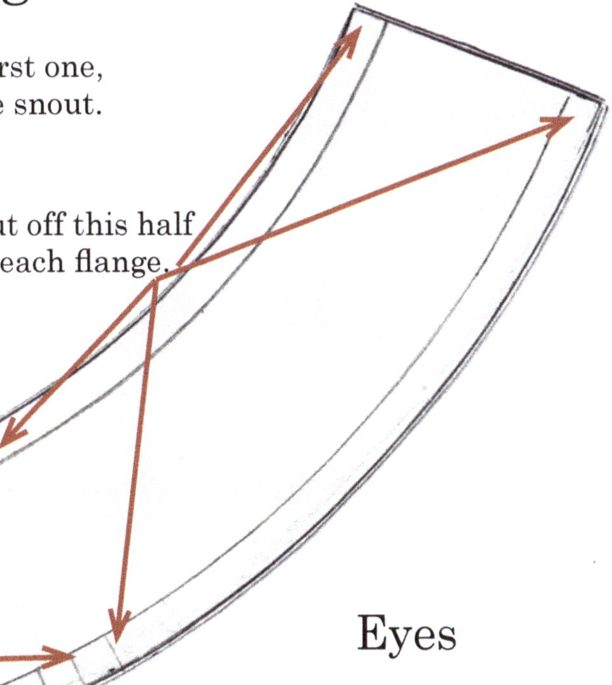

Cut off this half of each flange.

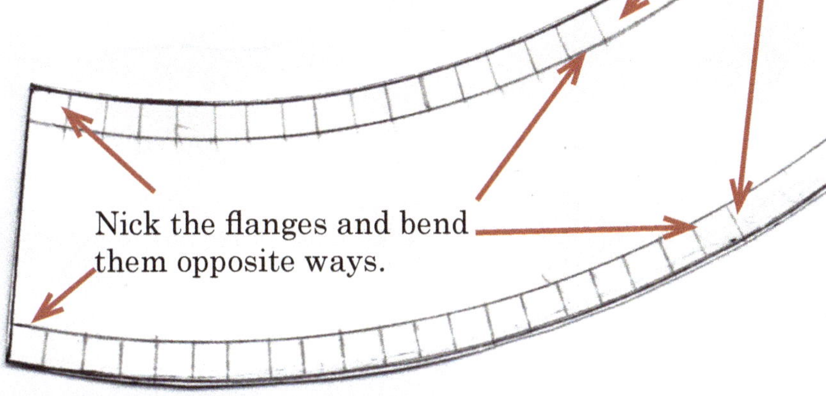

Nick the flanges and bend them opposite ways.

Eyes

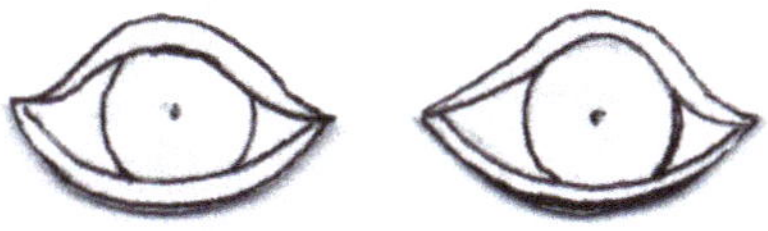

Colour in or cut out and stick on coloured paper irises.

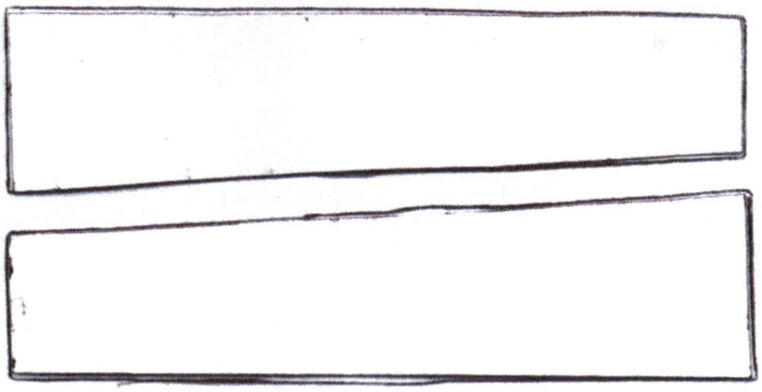

Ears

1. Cut out 4.
2. Glue together in 2 pairs and shape them while they are damp.
3. Glue the ears onto the head.

114

Fox

Instructions p 72

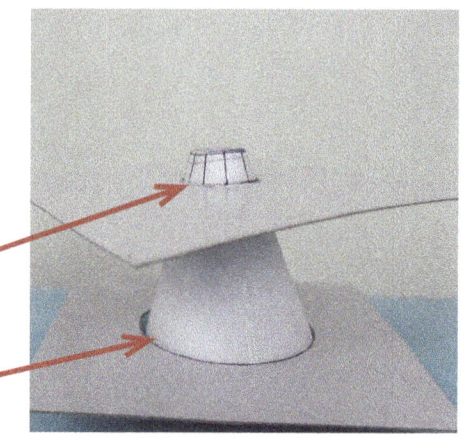

A hole in the cardboard the shape and size of the nose.

Another one for where it is glued onto the head.

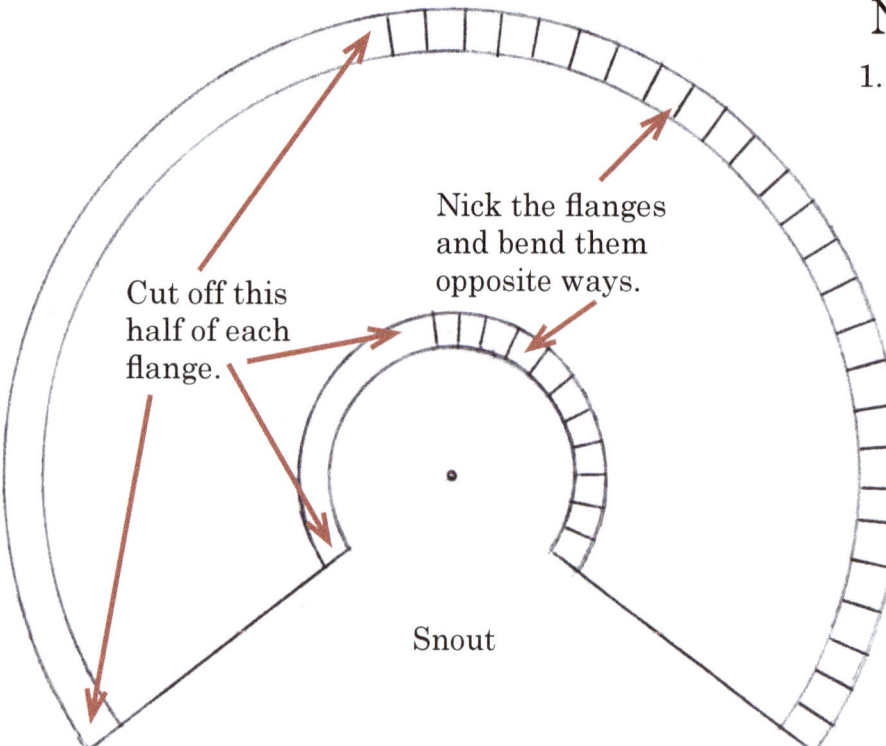

Cut off this half of each flange.

Nick the flanges and bend them opposite ways.

Snout

Nose

1. 1st snout cover. Glue it on.

2. Colour it in, cut it out. Glue on, bend over top.

Eyes

Colour in or cut out coloured paper irises.

Ears

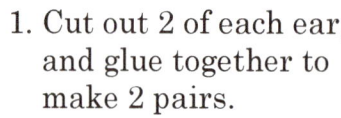

1. Cut out 2 of each ear, and glue together to make 2 pairs.

2. Curve ears and bend flanges opposite ways.

3. Glue the ears onto the head.

Painted neck frill

Piece/s of felt cut and glued around the neck.

Glove fits in under them.

It can be a 13cm x 5mm frill, or two frills with another 15cm x 3.5mm around the outside.

13/15cm x 5mm strip

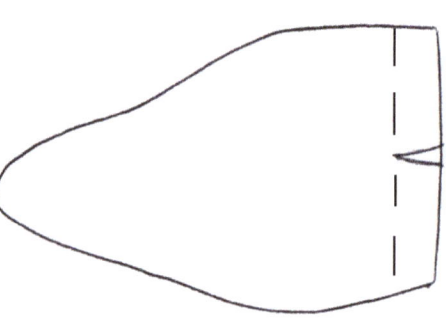

Cut 5mm strips along the length.

Glue frill onto the head 5mm out from the neck.

Cat

Nose is part of a polystyrene ball. Pieces of material glued on the front and back of the head.
Not enough to make the whole glove so strips of material were glued onto the glove.
Tried realistic sizing so cat and dog have very small heads.

Dog

Dog nose and snout cards

Dog ears and snouts can be all shapes and sizes. These are long ears for fun. This dog looks cute and shaggy painted all over. The felt glove can be painted or use shaggy material.

Fox

Fox nose and snout cards

The eyes make this fox look friendly and mischievous.

Brushed brown hair would make the fox more interesting, but it is okay to keep it plain.
The round snout where it joins the head ball could have been shaped more like the nose end.
Exaggerated shapes on the animals distinguish them and give them character.
The paper head was slightly smaller than the polystyrene one.

Gingerbread man

Can be a card front, kebab stick glued down the middle, a few divided cards glued either side for packing and a back card glued over them.

or

Have full movement or just move head, legs or both.

Have one puppeteer,
or
2 puppeteers to pass him around other puppets,
or
Have different puppeteers in each scene.

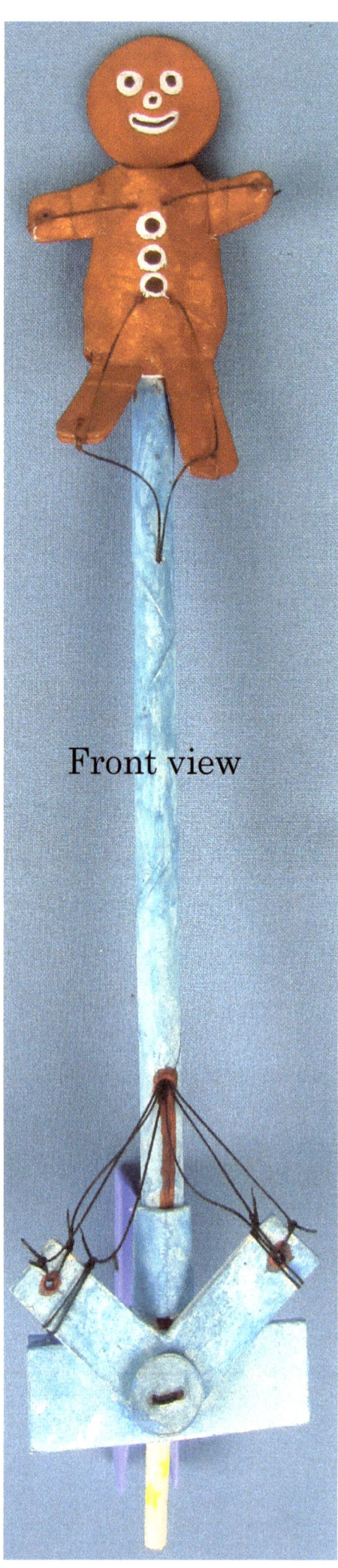

Front view

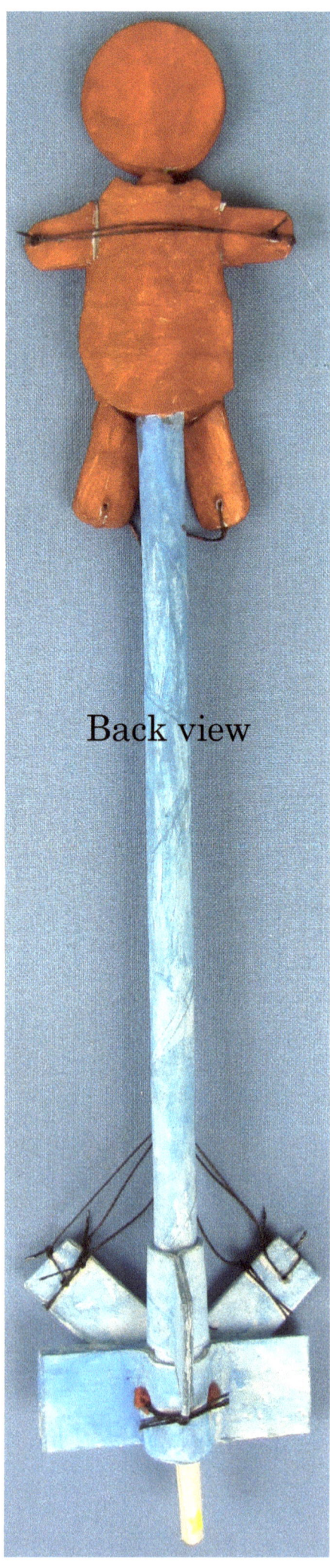

Back view

Gingerbread Man

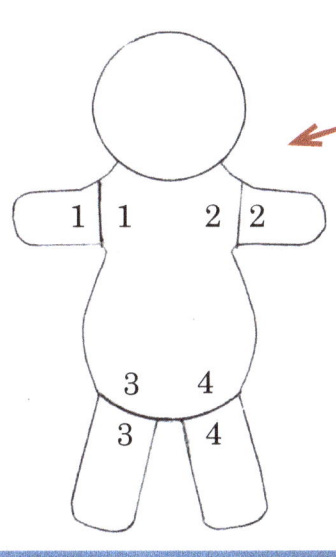
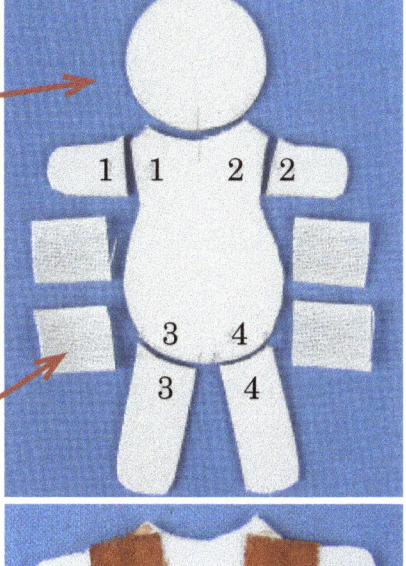

1. Number parts for rematching.

2. Using template from p 115 cut out in thick card ~
   2 heads,
   2 bodies - cutting across the limbs,
   2 lots of limbs.
   Keep each body together and label parts 1,2,3,4 and a,b,c,d.

3. Cut out four 1cm x 1cm pieces of tape or lightweight material for hinges.

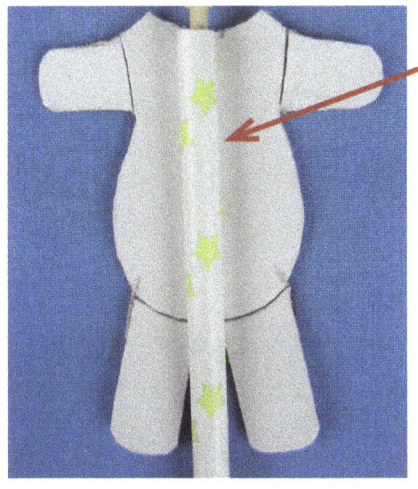
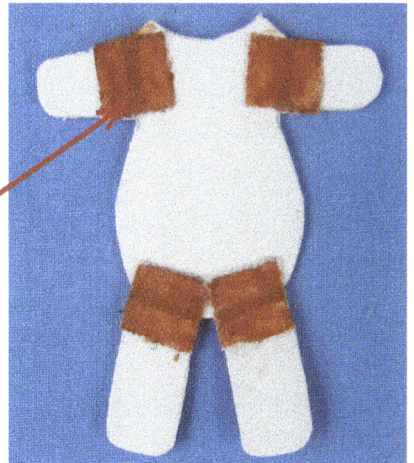

4. Glue tape to limbs.

5. Put no glue in join line.

6. Glue limbs to body.

7. Trim tape to shape

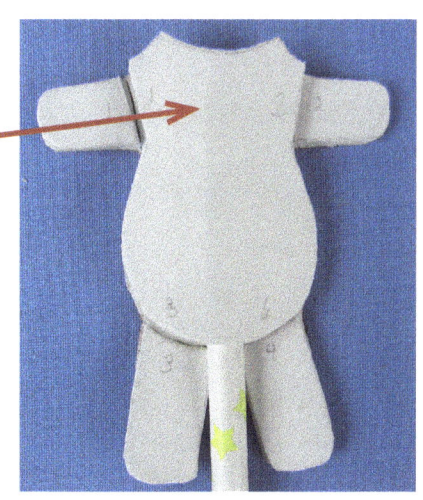

8. Glue straw down back.

9. Glue the back on.

10. Glue the 2nd arm piece onto the back of each arm.

11. Glue the 2nd leg piece onto the back of each leg.

12. Glue strips of white paper across side join and over the shoulder join.

13. Do 3 layers round the body

Front   Back   Front   Back

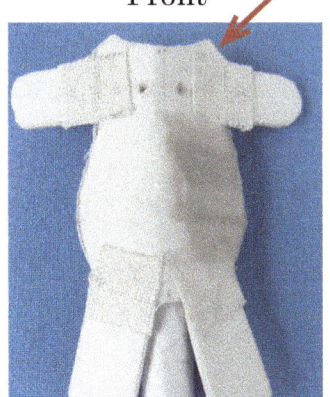
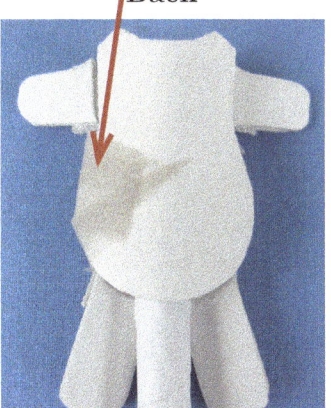
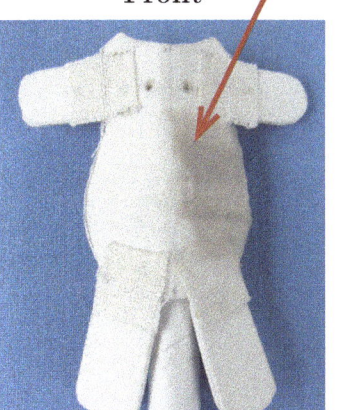
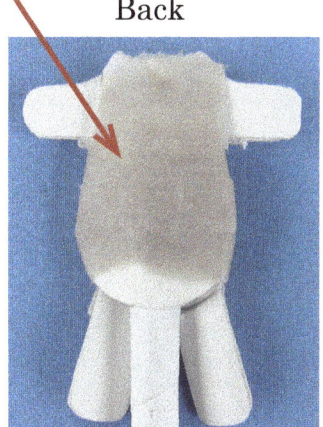

118

Puppet strings

1. Make string holes in the hands, feet, body and straw.

2. Cut up straw to bottom hole.

3. Tie thread to a hand. Cross the back to other hand, tie it.

4. Thread it into the body, then down straw, out the bottom. Pull it up the split and out the bottom hole.

5. Thread twine into leg body hole and out bottom of the straw, pull up to bottom hole, let 10cm hang out.

6. Measure distance from body hole to foot down the straw and out the bottom hole with 10cm extra. Cut it off.

7. Tie it at the foot, thread it down straw and out hole.

8. Cut out control pieces in strong card.

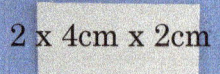
Cards

2 x 4cm x 2cm

4 x 6cm x 2cm

9. Make holes in lever and cardboard button.

Button

Lever

10. Put a hole in middle of one 6cm card, and 2 in another to go past each side of straw.

Puppet control lever

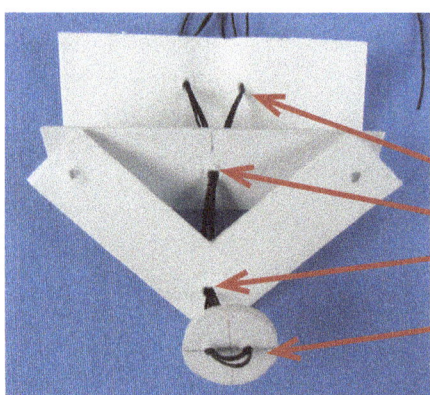

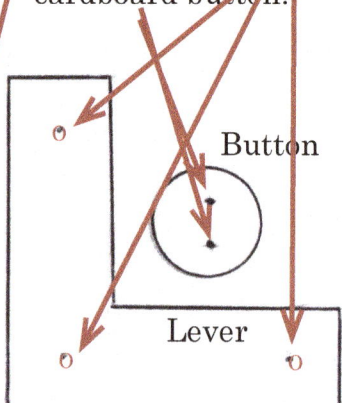

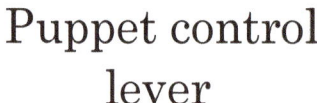

11. Put thread through back, front, lever, button, then back through button, etc.

12. Glue in place on the straw. Keep front card straight and bend back over straw.

13. Tie threads off tight behind the straw at the back. Glue the knot. Trim ends off.

14. Tie puppet threads to the lever. If correct glue them and trim them off.

16. Paint everything.

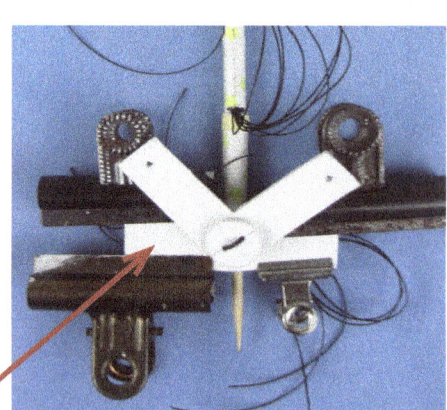

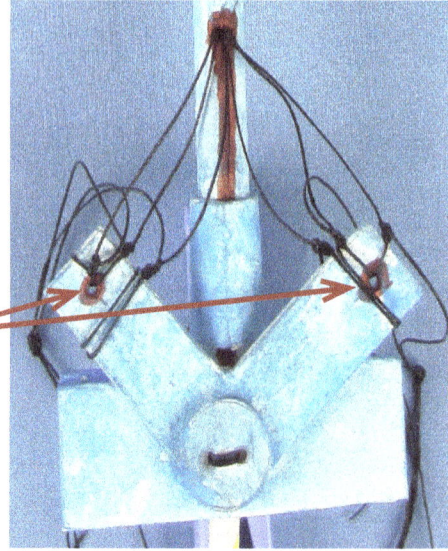

Polystyrene heads

The old woman has a piece of foam for her nose, button irises and grey wool for her hair.

The hair needs to be fine wool for making the plaits.

Glue the hair on all over the head down to the bottom then plait the extra long back hair.

His mouth and ears are cut out of felt and stuck on.

The old man's nose is half a wood bead and his irises are buttons.

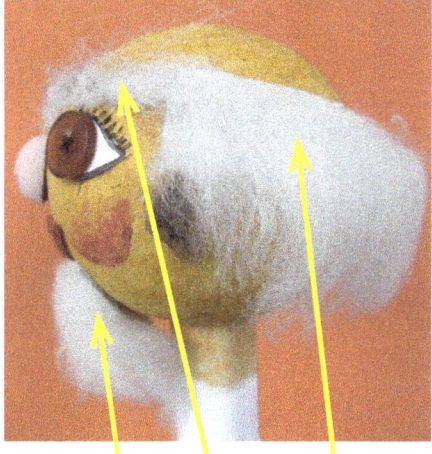

Fine sheeps wool still on the sheep's skin are his eye brows, hair and beard.

The fox has painted eyes, nose, mouth, felt ears and neck frills.

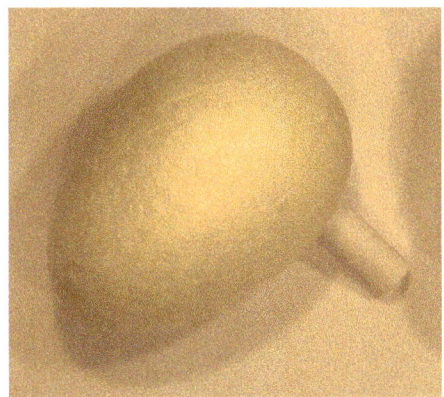

Polystyrene egg with cardboard neck.

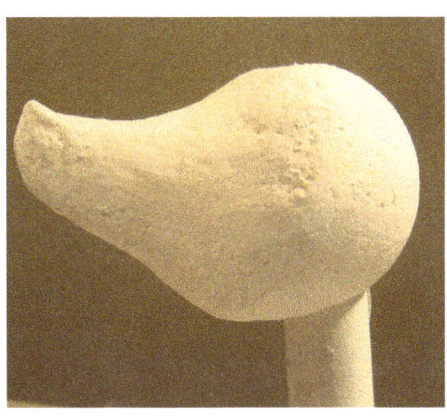

Shaped using a saw, rasp and sandpaper, then undercoated.

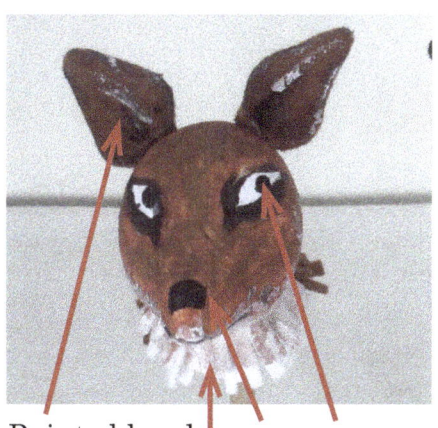

Painted head, nose, eyes, ears, and neck frill.

Little Old Woman

Little Old Man

Paper Heads

Boy

Girl

Cat

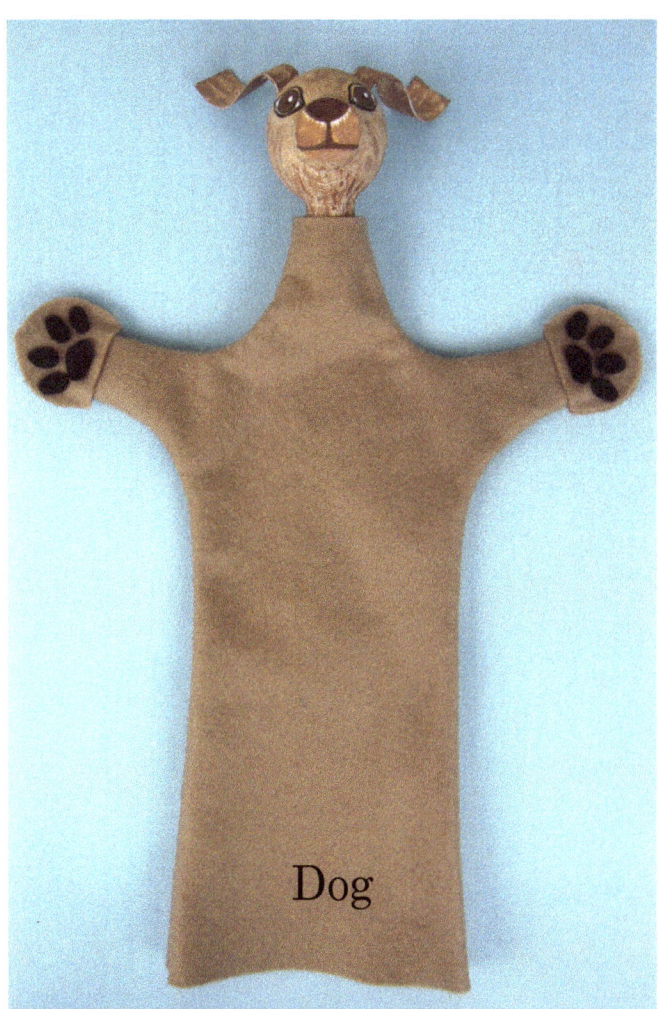
Dog

Polystyrene heads

Cow

Horse

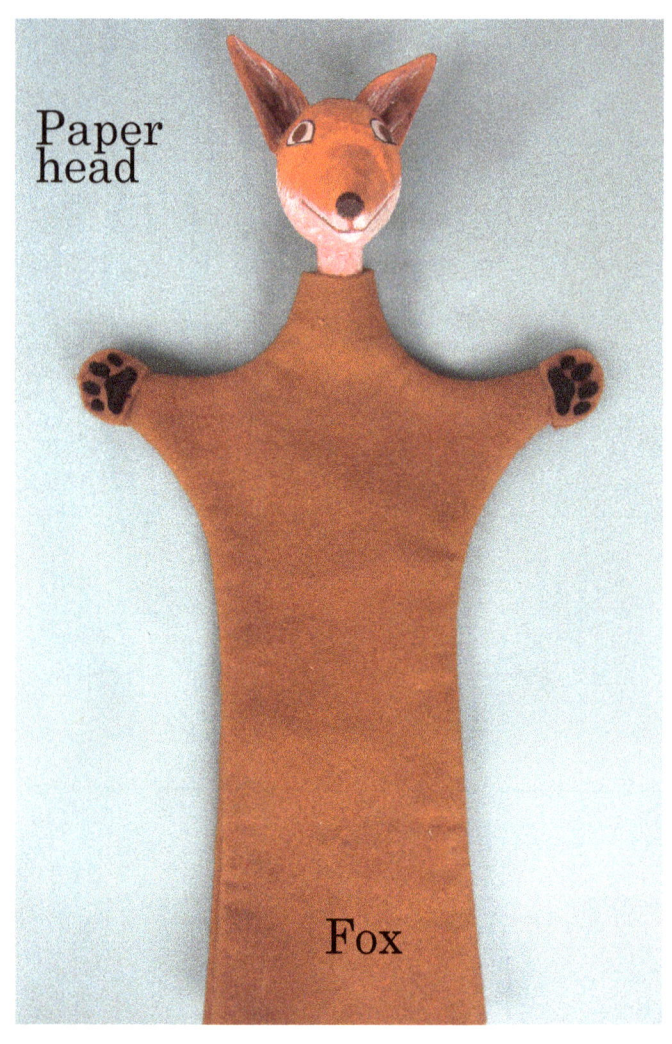

Paper head

Fox

Fox

Polystyrene heads

Old woman

Old man

Large props

The next two plays provide the opportunity to make and use larger props to increase drama, acting, scenery depth and more script possibilities.

Glove puppets are acted from below so scenery in the middle of the stage area needs to hang. The scenery needs to hang from a Qubelok rail placed across the top of the theatre. Qubelok is best because it is square so will velcro well to the curtain support Qubelok. Scenery will hang straight on it and not swing.

Position it across the middle between the front and the back scenery drop. However it can be placed above wherever your actors need it
The rail enables the prop to be moved smoothly, kept at the same height all the time and also hang by itself while the puppeteers act around it.

Moving the props across the stage improves the flow of the story.

Hanging the props

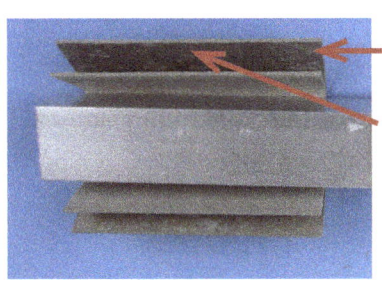

1. Bend a 10cm long thick piece of card board around 3 sides of the Quebelok.
2. Then bend a second 10cm piece around on top of it.
3. Glue them together. Make sure it fits the Qubelok well but slips on and off easily.
4. Clamp in place until dry.

Top view

Inside

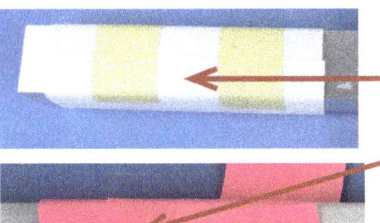

If no cardboard is available,
1. Wrap a piece of paper round the Quelok 3 times as a spacer.
2. Wrap and glue long strips of paper round it 6 times like doing the straw.
3. Dry it.
4. Remove and cut out one side.

Top

Inside

If thin card.
Glue 6+ layers together.

or glue 4 layers of thin card and then paper around it like a straw.
Leave it to dry.
Remove and cut one side off carefully.

Top

Inside

The 'U' can be strengthened by adding more card or paper layers.

If needed remove them carefully off the metal to finish drying inside.

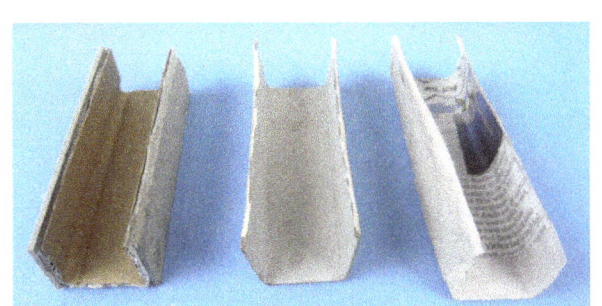

The 'U' must be loose enough to slip over the Qubelok easily.

10cm is long enough, it allows the prop to be on stage as long as possible.

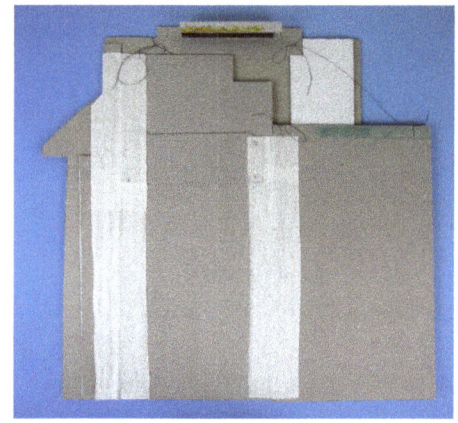 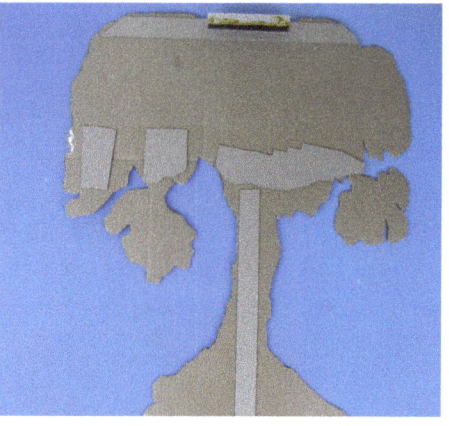 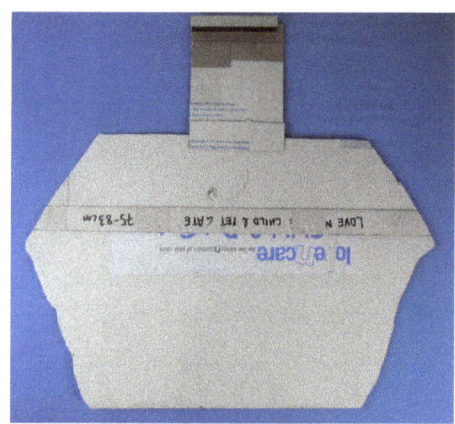

Glue the tube at the top, in the centre of the back, so the prop is balanced and hangs straight. Keep the tube short so that the prop can travel for the maximum distance on the rail.

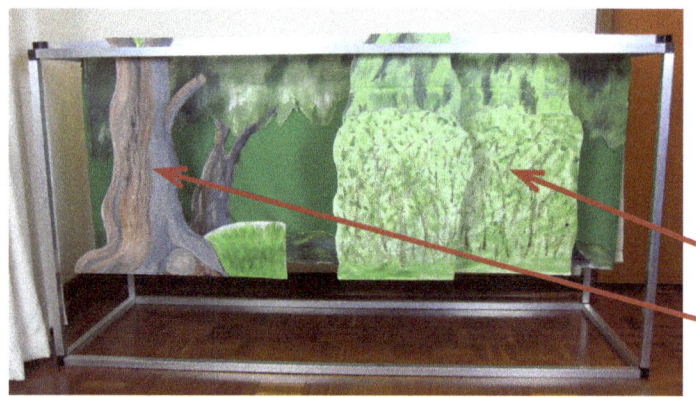 

Scenery on the Qubelok rails.

Scenery hanging over the scene it belongs to.

This rack is for the large or small proscenium scenery.

These large props can be stored hanging over their scene or on their own Qubelok rails in the scenery rack.

This prop needs to be held when the door is open.

Attachment points

The props can be velcroed anywhere on the proscenium.

Leaves, etc. can hang attached along the top of the proscenium.

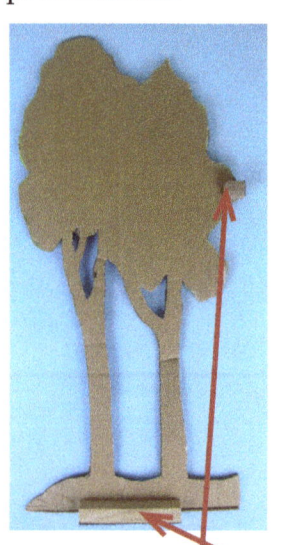   

This tree attaches at the bottom and side.
61cm x 30cm

This shrub attaches on the bottom and side.
41cm x 28cm

Cottage
H68cm x W66cm

These are big for the puppets to use.

Keep them on the rod.

Move from left to right for motion.

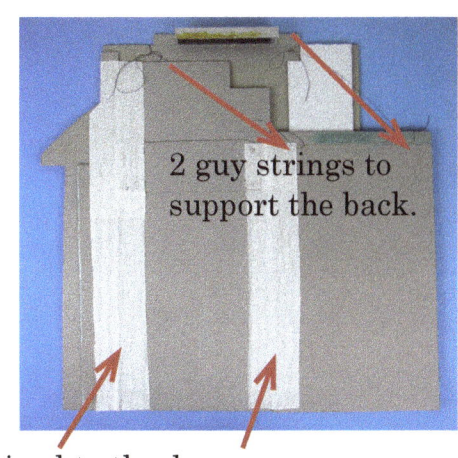

2 guy strings to support the back.

The door is hinged to the front door post. The inside scene is joined to the door.
When the door is opened the scene becomes visible through the doorway.

Apple tree
H70cm x W65cm

A piece of aluminium 'u' is glued on the top edge.

Intructions for making a paper or card tube are on p122.

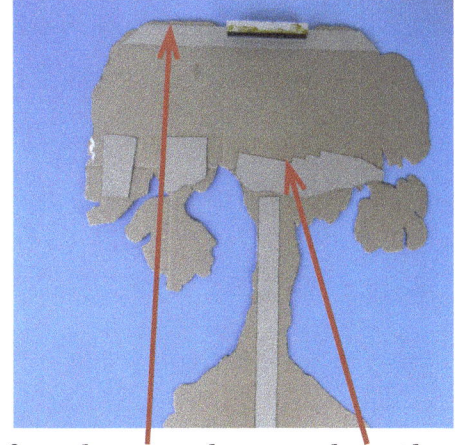

They can reach the apples and also sit under the tree. It is reinforced across the top, along the box fold line in the cardboard and down the middle of the trunk.

Tree
H73cm x W72cm

Lift the prop onto the rod placed across the theatre.

Hold the bottom of the prop when moving it to centre stage.

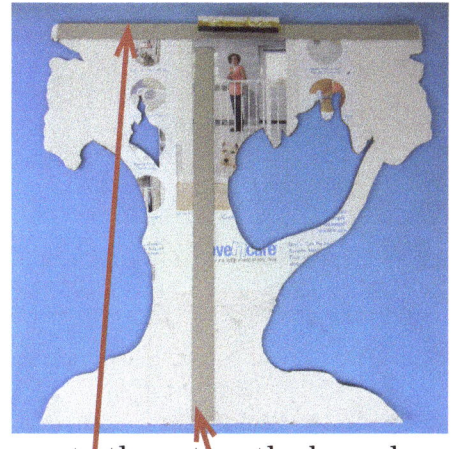

The tree trunk is wide enough to hide the puppeteers arm going up to the cat on the branch.
There is a root hollow for the dog to sit in. It is reinforced along the top and down the middle.

Hay stack
H70cm x W45cm

Then after all the puppets go through move the prop on across the stage until it reaches the curtain support rod. Lift it off.

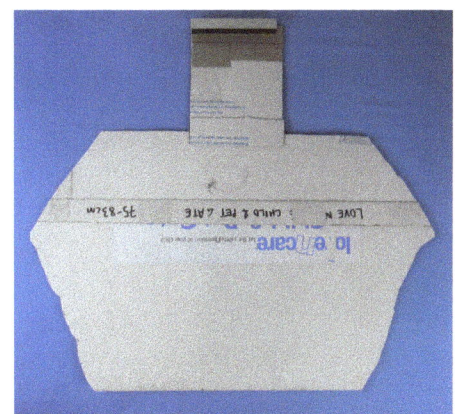

The hay stack can be round. Make sure it is bigger than a small pile of hay.

Water and a piece of land velcroed along the front proscenium frame.

Back view of 180cm x 14cm prop. Cardboard glued to a 1cm x 2cm wood beading. Two blocks with velcro on their bottoms are glued to it. These attach it to the proscenium frame.

The back drop was just low hills and it was used for the three pigs as well.

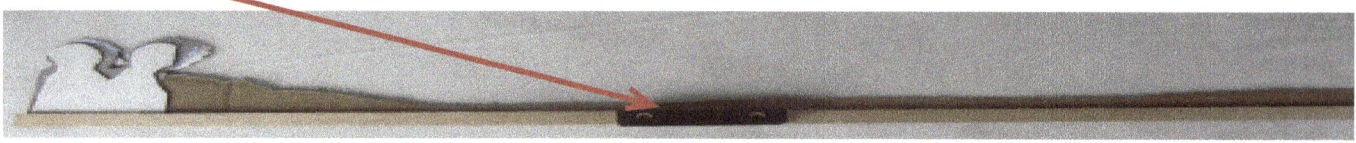

The cottage door allows the story to begin in the kitchen.

This small bush balances the scene.

Boy and girl at the apple tree.
The GBM comes in and after their discussion they run after him off stage.

The tree is left hanging while the little old man and woman come through with care.
The boy and girl fall in behind them when they are back stage and they stay in that order.

The dog chases the cat up the tree where it sits and cleans it's self. The dog barks.
GBM comes along, they interact and he goes off followed by them. Can add in lots more.
The cat and dog drop back behind the girl and boy when they get around the back.

All the puppets going across the stage in front of a prop, The little old man and woman, boy and girl, cross the stage in front of this tree. It goes off in the opposite direction as they leave.

The horse and cow come to eat some hay. GBM runs in, chats and leaves chased by them. The little old man and woman, boy, girl, cat, dog come through as the cat and dog leave. The hay stack slowly moves off this side after they have passed it.

GBM arrives at the river. How is he going to get across? Fox comes in behind and scares him. He jumps and looks over his shoulder at the fox who invites him to get on board.

All the others arrive at the river, they bunch up together talking and watching as the GBM moves up the foxes body. They can be very excited, say a lot and suddenly go silent when the fox eats the GBM. Then they can sing their song.

Little old woman gets very upset as she watches GBM going away across the water.
He reaches the foxes nose, is thrown in the air by the fox, caught and eaten.

A final wave from the fox.
The group sing or say their verse about their adventure.

TROLL	*(Appearing.)* Who's that! *(roars louder than ever.)* Who's that tramping over MY bridge?
BBG	Ah! *(In his biggest, gruffest voice.)* I'm the Biggest Billy Goat Gruff…AND I'M TRAMPING OVER THIS BRIDGE!
TROLL	*(Roaring loudly.)* THEN I'M GOING TO GET YOU! *(Moves up more onto the bridge.)*

Little Red Riding Hood

A Forest Scene

NARR	Once upon a time there lived a girl named Little Red Riding Hood. She was called that because she loved to wear a bright red cape with a hood. One day she was playing outside when her mother came out and called her.
MOTHER	*(Mother comes out onto the porch and calls-)* Little Red Riding Hood.
LRRH	*(Gets up and comes running.)* Yes, Mother.
MOTHER	Grandma is not feeling well.
LRRH	Oh, poor Grandma.
MOTHER	Yes. I have just baked some bread and wondered if you would be happy to stop playing and take some bread and cheese to her?
LRRH	Yes, Mother.
MOTHER	Come inside and get your cape. I've put the bread and cheese in a basket for you.
LRRH	Oh, it will be fun. *(They talk inside as she puts on her cape.)*
MOTHER	Here is a basket with the bread and cheese in it. *(The basket is put on her arm. Then they come out onto the porch again.)*
MOTHER	Remember to go straight there and stay on the path through the wood. Do not wander off it.
LRRH	Yes. Goodbye Mother. *(Crosses the stage, turns to wave. She and the mother disappear. The porch is removed.)*
NARR	So Little Red Riding Hood set off to her grandmother's house on the other side of the woods.
	(She circles around the back of the stage. A thicket is hung on the rail and slid towards stage centre. A woodsman comes in and starts to look for wood. He is talking to himself).
W-MAN	Yes, there should be some good wood on the other side of this thicket. Hello! Someone is coming and I think I know who it is. It's small, red and skipping along.
W-MAN	Good morning, Little Red Riding Hood.
LRRH	Good morning. *(She comes towards him.)*
W-MAN	What are you doing in the woods today?

LRRH	I'm going to visit my grandma who is not well. I am taking her some fresh bread Mother has just baked and cheese to go with it.
W-MAN	Is that so? I think she will be very glad to see you. I'm going through this thicket to gather some wood. Just make sure you stay on the path and I hope she is better soon. Goodbye LRRH.

(He goes through the centre of the thicket and drops do

LRRH	Yes, I will stay on the path and not wander off.

(LRRH skips on across the stage. The thicket moves off. A tree trunk is hung on the rail and slid towards stage centre.

WOLF	*(Enters from the left, stops and looks ahead, then says.)* What a lovely little girl is coming. She could be a very tasty meal.
LRRH	*(Comes on from the right and meets the Wolf at the tree).*
WOLF	Good day, little maid. Where are you off to on such a fine day?
LRRH	I am going to see my grandmother. She isn't well so I am taking her this bread and cheese.
WOLF	What a nice idea. Where does she live?
LRRH	Her cottage is just at the end of this path on the other side of the wood.
WOLF	Hum. See how pretty the flowers are just over there? I am sure your grandma would love to have some.
LRRH	*(Looks across at the flowers.)* Oh yes she would. They are pretty. I shall pick some and take them to her.

(The wolf moves behind the tree and drops out so she can move across in front of the tree. She goes to the flowers. The wolf pops his head around the tree to look at LRRH and says.)

WOLF	Yes, that's a lovely idea. Take your time and pick the nicest ones. I will be off. *(As he goes he says to the audience.)*
WOLF	And I will get to that cottage before her.

(She bends down at the flowers and adds some to her basket. Turn some drawn ones up in her basket. Then she gets up and walks on saying.)

LRRH	She'll be so pleased and I will still get there in good time.
NARR	Meanwhile, the wolf has run as fast as he could along another path to the grandma's house where she is in bed.

Bedroom scene

(Bedroom scene with the porch doorway placed so that the audience can see the wolf come to the door).

WOLF	*(The wolf knocks on the door.)*
GRAN	Who's there?
WOLF	*(imitating RRH's voice)*. Little Red Riding Hood. I've brought you some bread and

	cheese.
GRAN	Come in dear. I am too weak to come to the door.
WOLF	*(The wolf comes in)*
GRAN	(Alarmed) You're not Little Red Riding Hood!
WOLF	No! I am not and I am going to eat you up. *(He eats her, puts on a nightcap then gets into the bed.)* Now I will wait for Little Red Riding Hood. What a feast I am having today.
NARR	Little Red Riding Hood has gathered her posy of flowers and arrives at the house.
LRRH	*(She knocks at the door).*
WOLF	Who's there?
LRRH	Little Red Riding Hood, Grandma. I've come to see you and I've brought some fresh bread with cheese.
WOLF	Come in. I am too weak to come to the door.
	(RRH comes in the door.)
WOLF	How nice to see you. Come over and sit with me. *(She puts the basket down.)*
LRRH	*(Comes towards the bed, pauses and says)* Oh Grandma, what big ears you have!
WOLF	All the better to hear you with.
LRRH	*(Coming forward one step.)* Oh Grandma, what big arms you have!
WOLF	All the better to hug you with.
LRRH	*(Another step closer.)* Oh Grandma, what big eyes you have!
WOLF	All the better to see you with.
LRRH	*(Beside the bed.)* Oh Grandma, what big teeth you have!
WOLF	All the better to eat you with! *(Jumps out of bed and eats LRRH in one mouthful.)*
WOLF	Now I am full and very sleepy. What a feast. *(Turn up the body shape he lies down in the bed and starts to snore.)*
NARR	Just then the huntsman/woodsman who lived nearby was passing the house.
H-MAN	*(Off stage he says)* Goodness, how loudly the old woman is snoring. She sounds very unwell. I will just pop in and see if she is all right. *(He comes to the porch and pops his head in the door. He goes over to the bed and looks.)*
	A wolf fast asleep and just look at that full belly. *(Raises his gun to shoot it).*
	Hang on a minute, perhaps it has eaten the old woman and she might be saved.
	(Takes out his hunting knife and cuts open the wolf's stomach. LRRH jumps out.)
LRRH	Oh! It was so dark in there.

H-MAN	LRRH! Goodness gracious! Where's your grandma?
GRAN	Coming. Give me a hand young man please. Oh, how terrible that was!
	(Then Grandmother slowly climbs out, shaky but alive.)
GRAN	Thank you so much. You have saved us. How did you know we were in there?
H-MAN	When I was going past your cottage I heard loud snoring and thought you must be unwell. I looked in to check and saw the wolf sound asleep in your bed with a very full belly. I went to shoot him but suddenly thought you might be alive so I cut him open and out you came. I am glad. Go and get me some stones Red Riding Hood. *(She does)*
H-MAN	Put them in here. *(She does)*
	Now, Grandma sew the wolf up. *(And grandma does)*
WOLF	*(Waking up, moves and rattles).*
H-MAN	Now everyone can hear you coming. *(Laughs.)*
WOLF	Woe is me. *(exits)*
H-MAN	Good bye Little Red Riding Hood. Leave wolves alone next time. They are dangerous.
LRRH	Grandma, I brought you some bread and cheese, also these flowers I gathered on the way.
GRAN	Oh, how lovely. Thank you dear. Now you must be off home.
LRRH	Yes. Goodbye, Grandma. I must hurry before it gets dark. I will be sure to go straight home along the path and not wander into the wood or talk to a wolf. *(Runs off out the door. Grandma goes to the door and watches her from the porch. LRRH calls goodbye from off stage and Grandma waves from the porch.)*

The curtain closes.

Little Red Riding Hood

I won't wander through the woods,

Through the woods,

Through the woods.

I won't wander through the woods.

I'll do what mother told me.

I will stay just on the path,

On the path,

On the path.

I will stay just on the path.

I'll do what mother told me.

Then I won't meet a big bad wolf,

A big bad wolf,

A big bad wolf.

Then I won't meet a big bad wolf

Cause I've done what mother told me.

Depending on the age and ability of the puppeteers here are further possibilities to include.
Large porch, tree and thicket to encourage more creativity, puppetry skills and drama.
Small basket for developing puppet control and mob cap to enhance the character.
The porch, four poster bed, and thicket each need 2 people to manouvre them (team work).
The last play so give yourselves and the audience an unforgetable glove puppetry experience.

Mob cap on Grandma and Wolf

1. A 30cm x 10cm piece of material for this head

2. Turn ends and tack a hem.

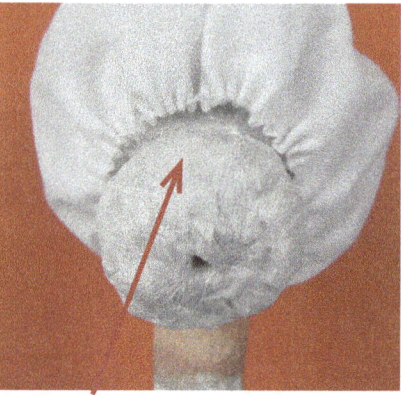

4. Gather it round the bun,
5. Oversew together, tie off.

6. Put ribbon through holes or tack along and gather.

7. Adjust, tie off under chin.

33cm of edging

Piece is 14cm wide and long

30cm x 3cm strip

1. Tack edging to material.
2. Turn it out, sew round it.

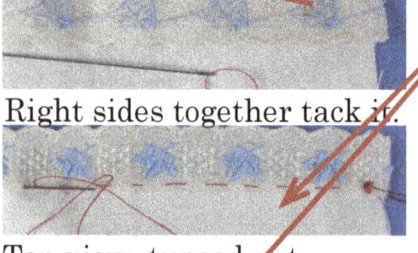

Right sides together tack it.

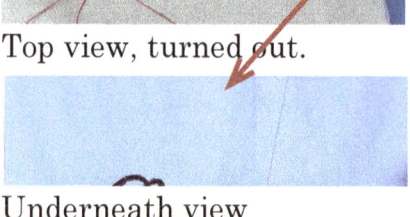

Top view, turned out.

Underneath view

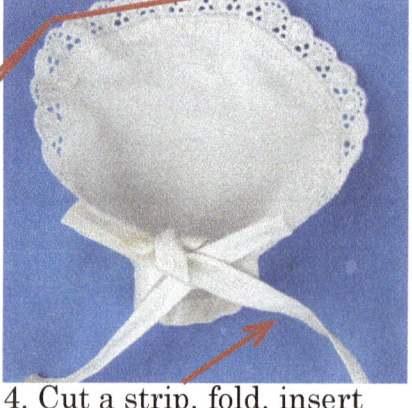

4. Cut a strip, fold, insert shape, machine strip

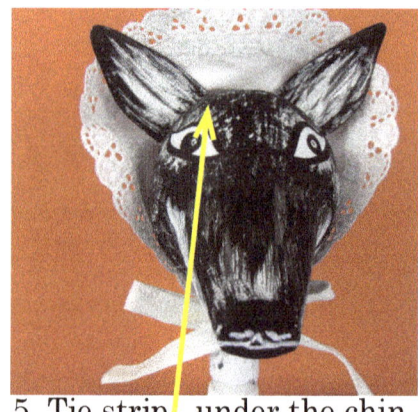

5. Tie strip under the chin.
6. Blu-tak cap to head.

The wolf's mob cap needs to be made to go on very quickly and easily. A bit of blu-tak on the forehead will make the cap sit forward between the ears.
Grandma's cap can have coloured ribbon and the material wider than 10cm to poof up more.

Little Red Riding Hood

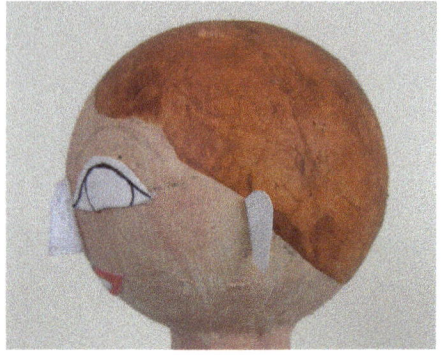

1. Paint with brush strokes going the way of the hair.
2. Fold a square in half, cut in strips to this point.
3. Roll up, glue a strip of crepe round the uncut bit.

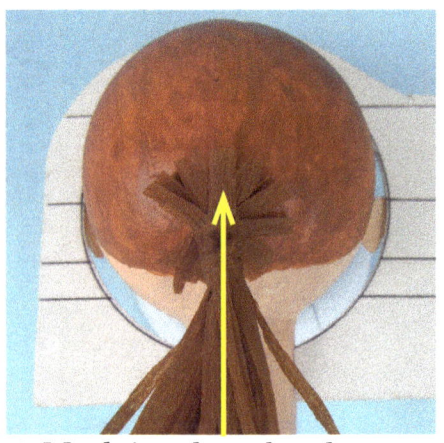
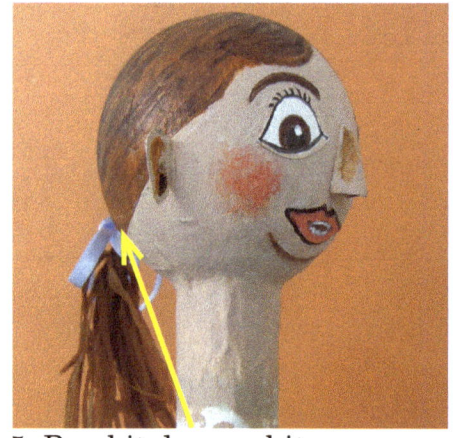

4. Mark its place, bend out top strips, glue it on.
5. Bend it down a bit. Tie a ribbon round it.
6. Paint streaks on the hair.
7. Do the face and ears.

Mother

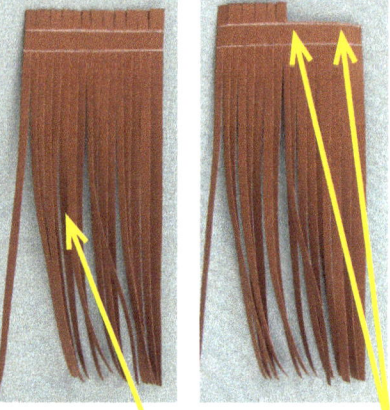

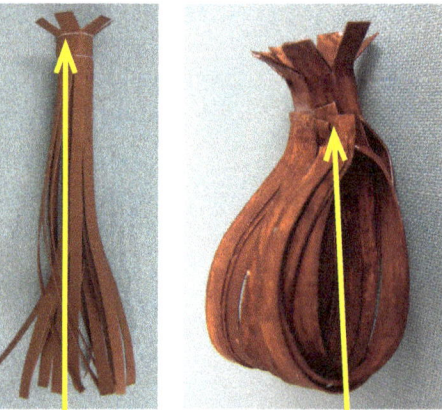

1. Paint with brush strokes going the way of the hair.
2. Cut strips in a painted card.
3. Cut off 1/2 of these.
4. Roll up and glue.
5. Bend up and glue long strips.

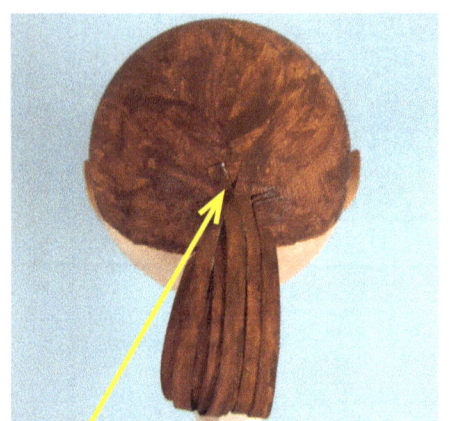
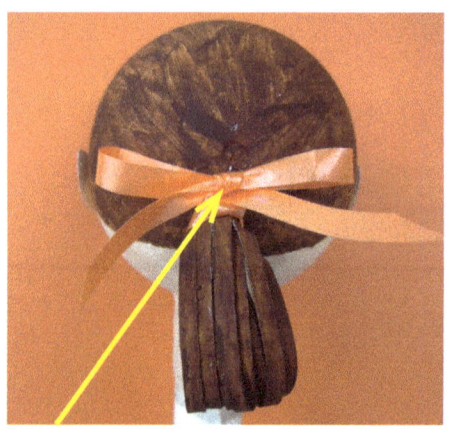

4. Bend top strips out then glue it onto the head.
5. Tie a ribbon around it. Streak the hair if not done.
6. Colour and glue on mouth, eyes, nose, eyebrows, ears.

Grandmother

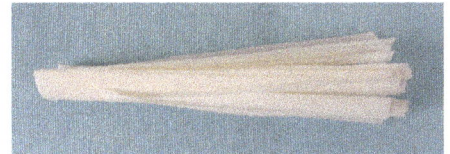

1. Paint the hair on the head with the brush strokes going the way the hair would go.
2. Cut 12cm square of crepe.
3. Fold in half across grain.
4. Cut into strips leaving 10mm uncut along the fold.
5. Put glue along fold, roll up.
6. On the diagonal roll up a square of paper.
7. Make it into a doughnut.
8. Glue the roll from no. 5 into the hole.

Paper puppets are simpler looking characters when finished. Photos do not do them justice. The white bun is 2x the size of the grey one and grey streaks are darker than in these photos.

Woodsman

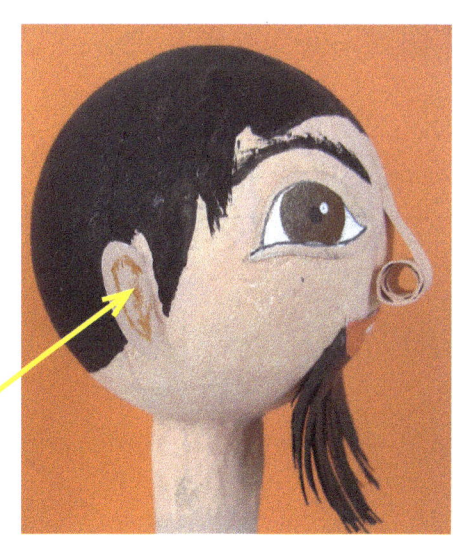

Painted hair

Painted cardboard eyes

Rolled cardboard nose

Painted cardboard mouth

Painted cardboard ears

Black cardboard beard

Beard

Beard templates

Both together, can be different sizes and more in number.

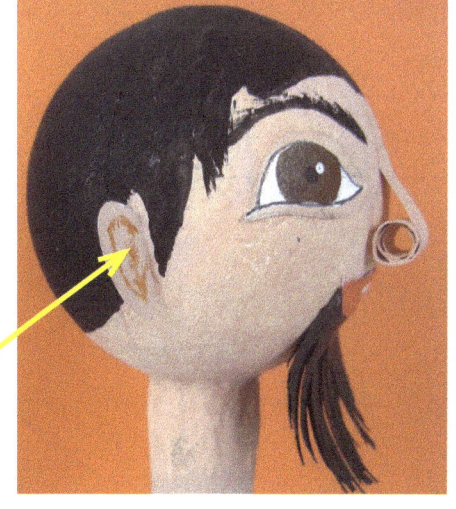

Making a bun

Crepe paper is soft, has an up and down grain, stretches across the grain and needs to be handled carefully.

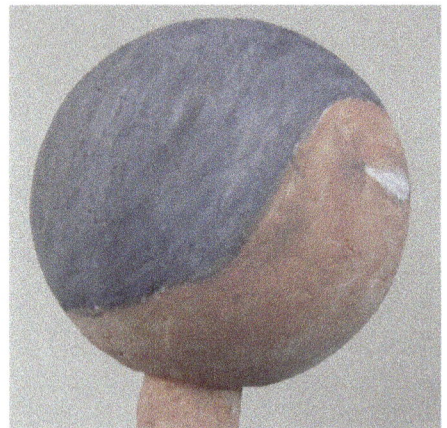

1. Paint the hair on the head with the brush strokes going the way the hair would go.

2. Cut 12cm square of crepe paper.
3. Fold in half across grain.
4. Cut into narrow strips leaving 10mm uncut along the fold.

5. Put glue along the uncut strip at the fold and roll it up.

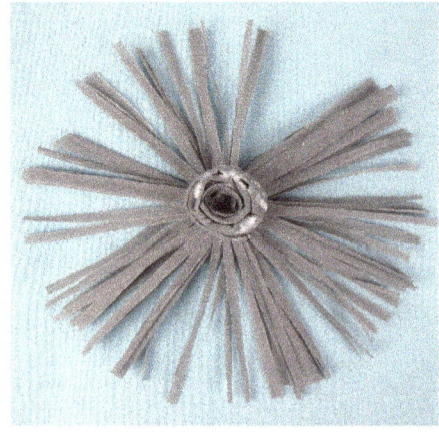

This is the bottom view with the strips bent out around it. The hole in the doughnut must be big enough for this centre core to fit in.

6. On the diagonal, roll up a square of crepe paper.
7. Wrap it round to form a doughnut. Glue it.
8. Glue the roll into the hole.

9. Take one outside strip at a time, bend it over the doughnut and glue it underneath.

Bottom view of them bent over and glued.

Top view of bun.

The bun glued onto the head. Needs paint to match hair.

Polystyrene heads

Red Riding Hood

- Wool hair
- Cardboard eyes, button irises glued on
- Shaped balsa wood nose
- Cut out red felt mouth with the white painted on

Mother

- Wool hair
- Painted cardboard eyes
- Small piece of foam painted for the nose
- Painted cardboard mouth
- Cardboard ears
- 2 pieces of wool, one for each eyebrow

Grandmother

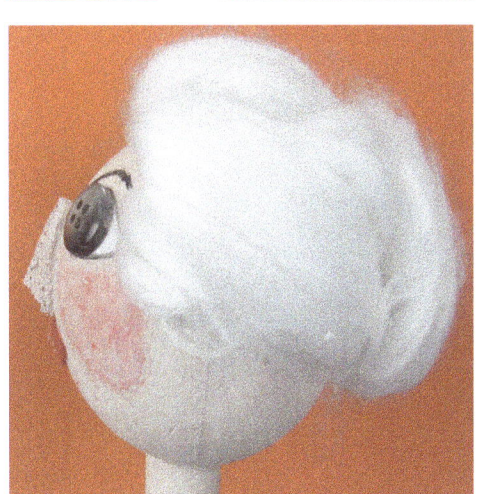

- Father Christmas beard for hair
- Cardboard eyes with button irises
- Foam nose
- Red felt mouth

Woodsman

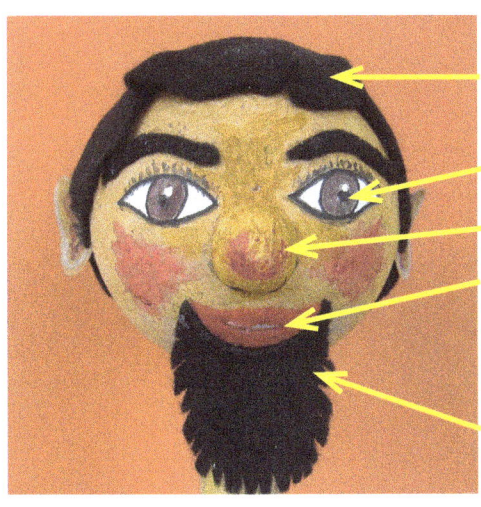

- Black felt hair
- Painted cardboard eyes
- Half a wood bead nose
- Red felt mouth
- Cardboard ears
- Black felt beard
- Black felt eyebrows

Wolf

Basic head instructions are on p 37.
Also there are very full instructions on p71 and p72 for a snout and the goat head which is similar to the wolf.

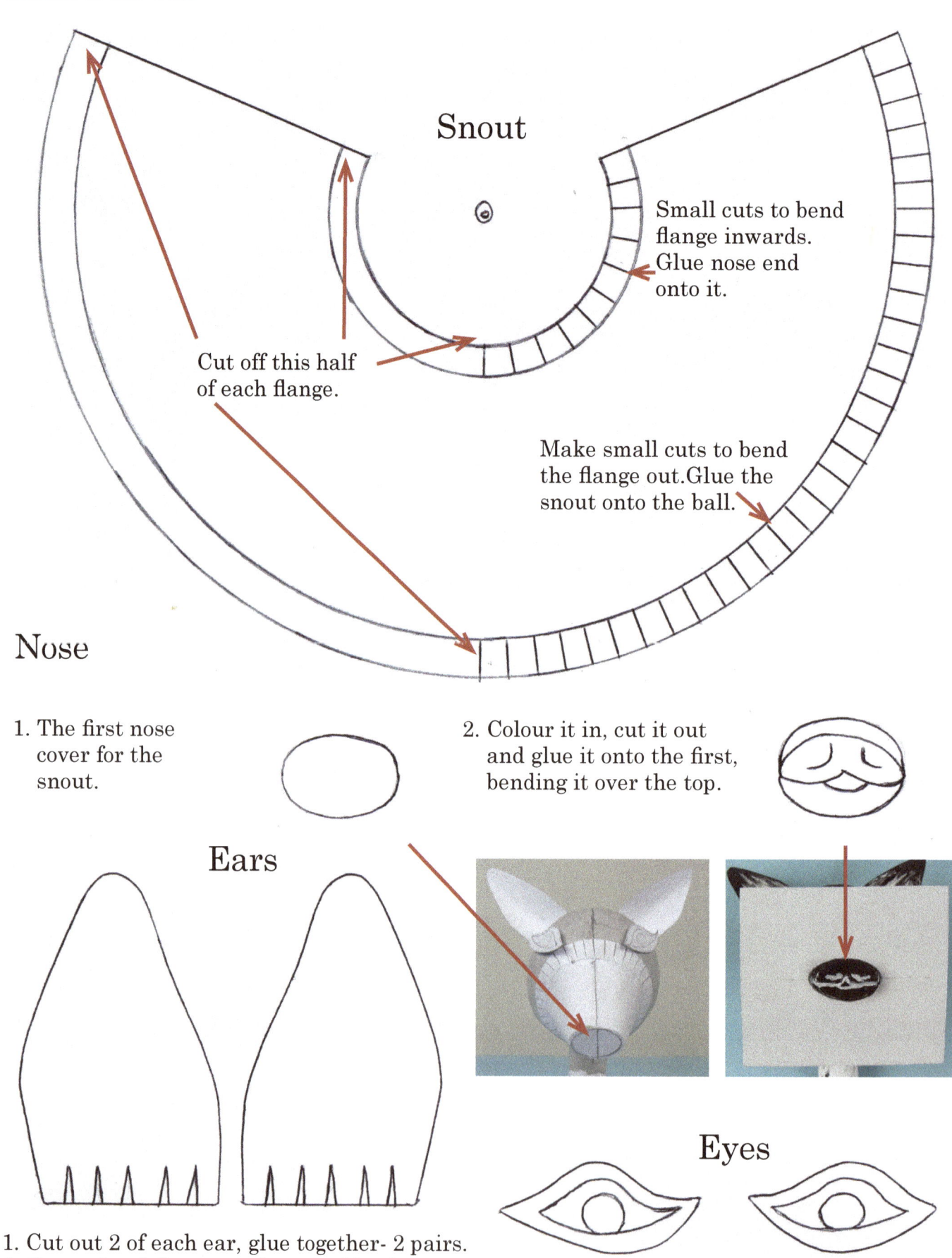

Snout

Small cuts to bend flange inwards. Glue nose end onto it.

Cut off this half of each flange.

Make small cuts to bend the flange out. Glue the snout onto the ball.

Nose

1. The first nose cover for the snout.
2. Colour it in, cut it out and glue it onto the first, bending it over the top.

Ears

1. Cut out 2 of each ear, glue together- 2 pairs.
2. Curve, bend flanges to front and back.
3. Glue ears onto the head.

Eyes

Colour in or cut out coloured paper irises.

Polystyrene head

1. A cardboard neck glued into a polystyrene egg.

2. The centre and shapes drawn, on then cut off.

3. Sandpapered to gentle curves.

A folded piece of felt stuck on. Cut like hair around the head. A piece of felt cut and glued around the neck.

The painted felt makes him different to the paper one at the bottom of p 59 which has no trims.

The felt to go around the neck. is below.

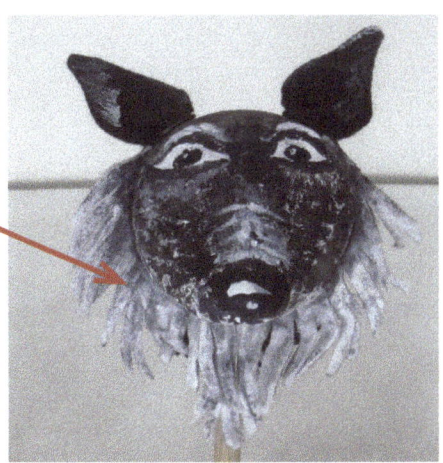

Cut a 14cm x 5cm strip. Glue it onto the head 5mm out from the neck. Glove fits in under it.

 Continue all the way along.

White chest and paw trims below that can be sewn or glued on before or after making the glove.

Cap p133 must go on and off easily.

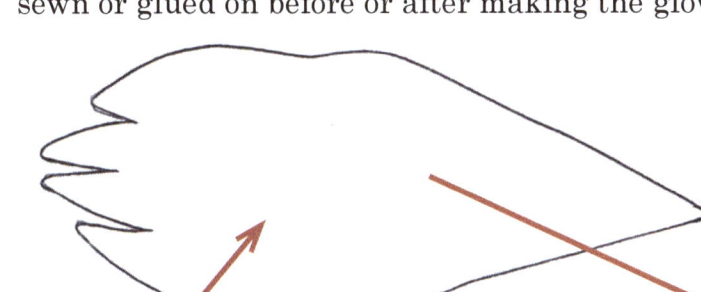

The white felt top for the back of the paw.

Front/bottom of the paw, made with felt or painted.

Red Riding Hood

Mother

Paper puppets

Grandma

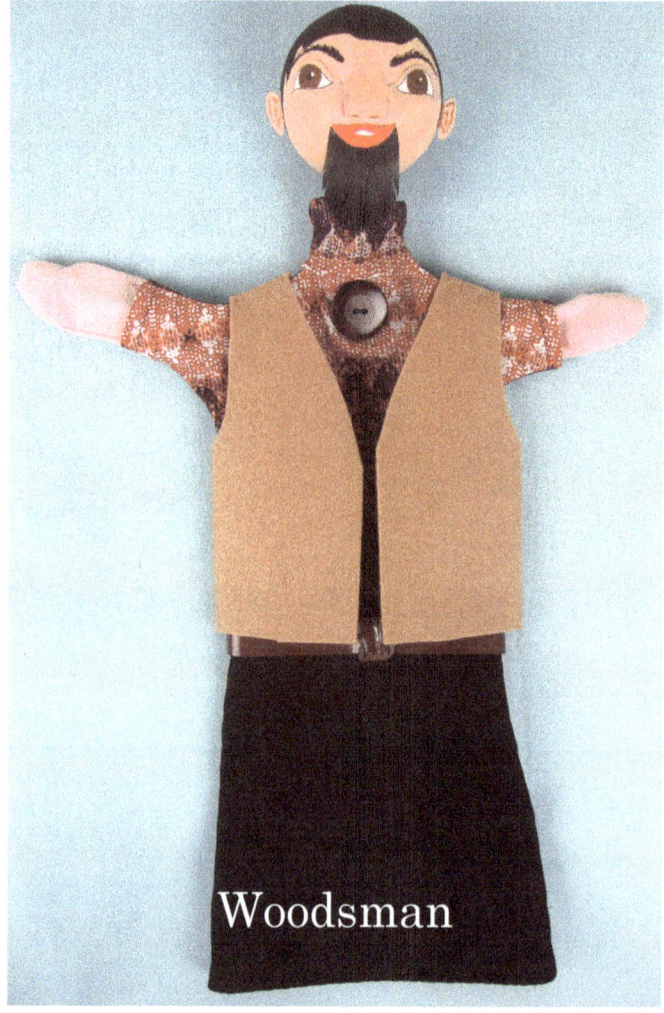
Woodsman

Red Riding Hood

Mother

Polystyrene puppets

Grandma

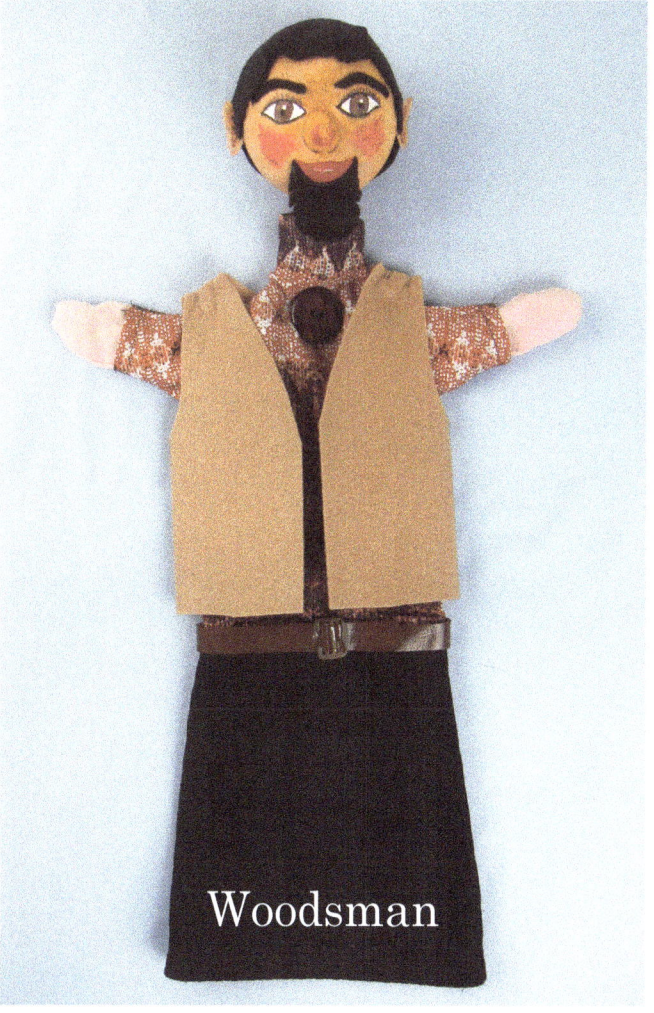
Woodsman

This was the sketch for Grandma's bedroom but it was changed, then changed some more. An old-fashioned wash stand was drawn instead. No ceiling, floor or side walls in this design.

The porch sits on an angle so actors are seen when they come knocking at the door.

The 4 poster bed attaches here and here.

The porch makes a very interesting door.

The middle of the bed sits on the rail.

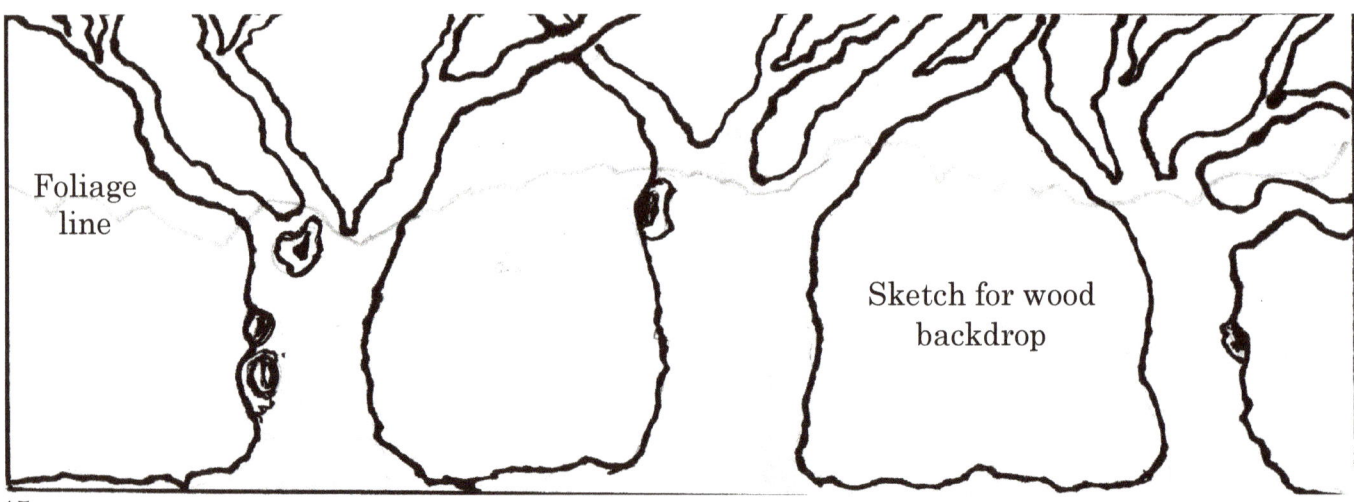

Foliage line

Sketch for wood backdrop

Children draw, paint tree trunks and canopy then cut out and attach them to the material.
For this one
White blockout was undercoated. Trees, canopy and ground were painted on it.
This was cut out and sewn onto see-through material. A lot more work but very effective.

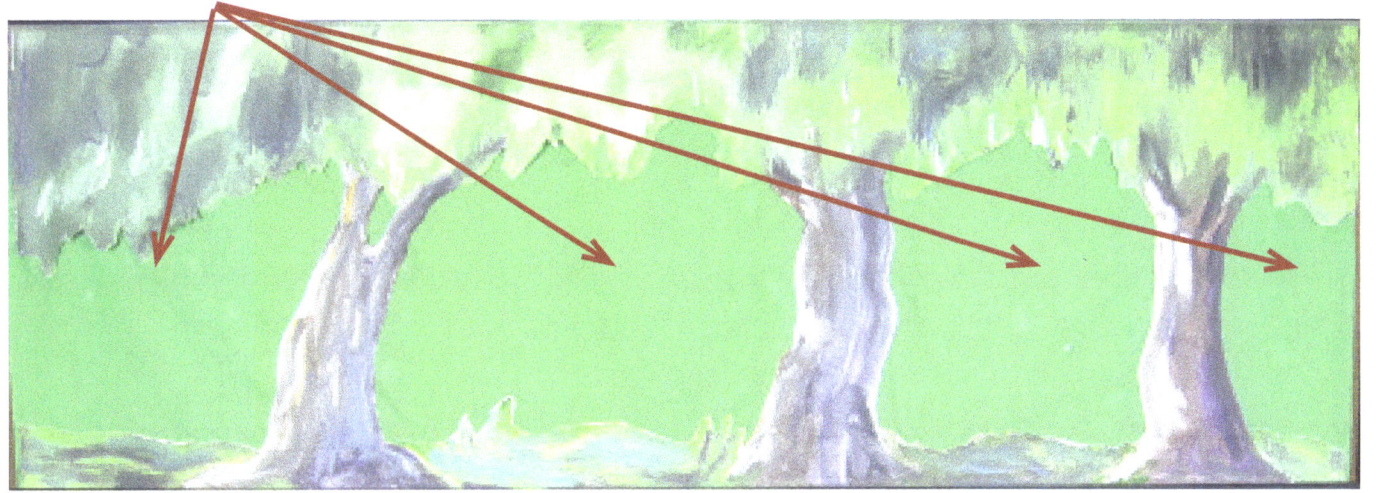

Woodsman's thicket

This is a prop that enables a puppet to exit centre stage.

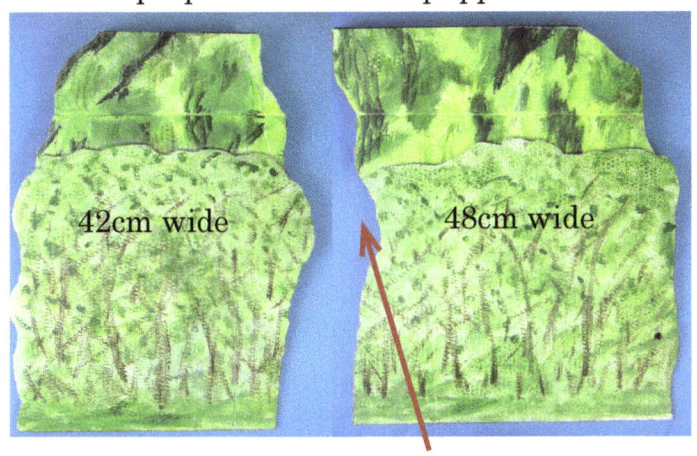

Both 72cm high

42cm wide   48cm wide   70cm wide

The thicket is divided in the middle. The left half hangs on the front rail and the right on the back scenery rail with an overlap in the middle.
The woodsman needs to be facing LRRH to exit through the gap and disappear down out of sight.
Then with the puppet and puppeteer out of the way LRRH can continue across the stage leave and circle round the back to come through again,

The prop needs to be full height in order to hang from the rail so the top part is painted as well as the thicket.

Wolf's tree

72cm high

70cm wide

Action around a centre prop.

Wolf can stand near the flowers talking to RRH, step around behind the tree and drop down.
RRH can go in front to the flowers. Then he comes up behind the tree, pops his head around it, comments, says good bye and goes off stage.

Doors are in many stories.

The Wolf, RRH and woodsman are all seen knocking and entering. Woodsman can take the wolf out. Grandma and RRH say goodbye at the door.
The 3 bears can go in and out the door.
Goldilocks knocks and comes in.

Simple door

Front | Back

Door opens forward so you see the puppet entering.

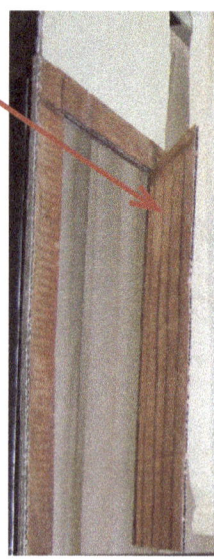

Velcro top and bottom to join onto side frame.

Porch frame

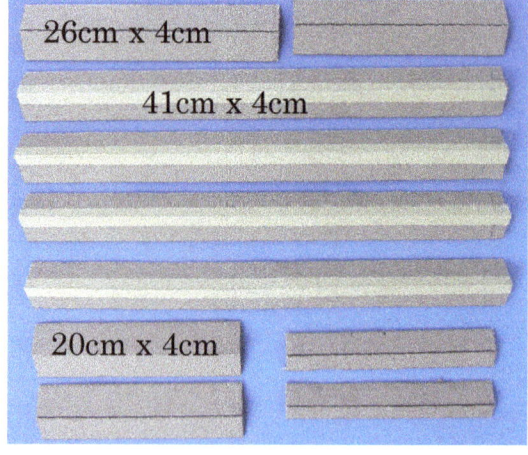

26cm x 4cm
41cm x 4cm
20cm x 4cm

1. Cut out card strips, bend and tape for the porch.

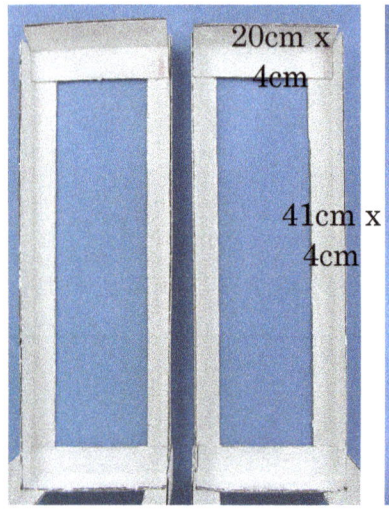

20cm x 4cm

41cm x 4cm

2. Glue side frames together.

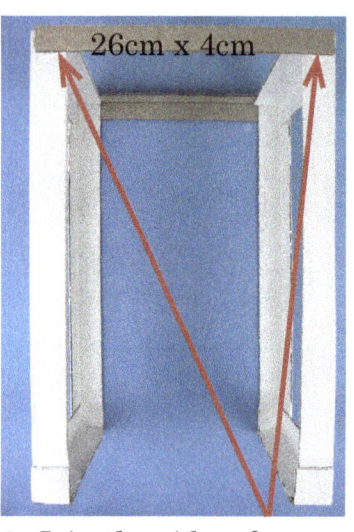

26cm x 4cm

3. Join the sides, front and back, at the top.

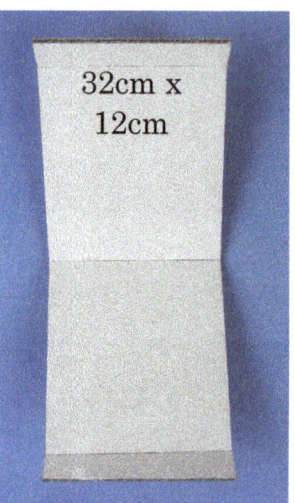

32cm x 12cm

4. Roof support

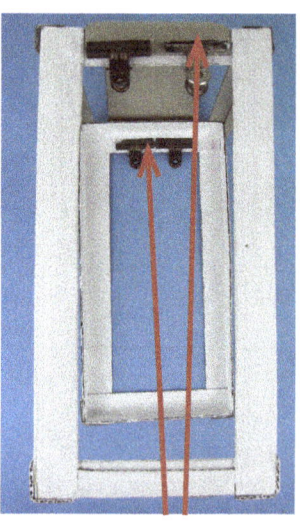

5. Glue it to sides. Clamp until dry.

Roof

The cores in the inside of corrigated cardboard.

6. Cut roof, running down the card coring. Fold front and back edge along a core.

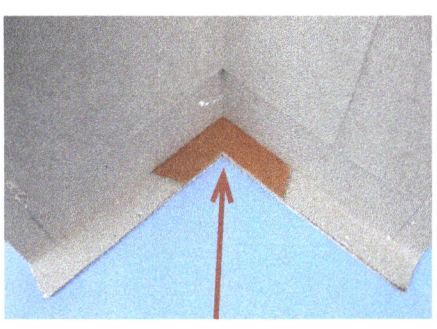

7. Bend roof peak, across coring, over a sharp edge.

8. Place on the roof support, mark centre front and back at peak. Cut off overlap.

9. Place roof peak on card, draw the angle, cut it out. Glue it inside the peak.

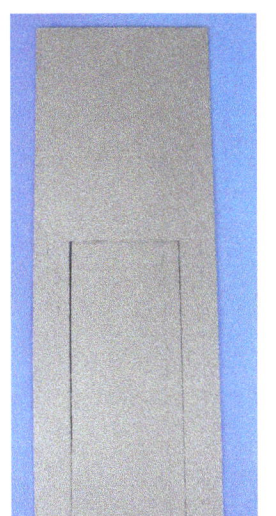

10. Glue roof onto roof support so it overhangs at the front . . . . .

. . .and is flush at the back.

Door

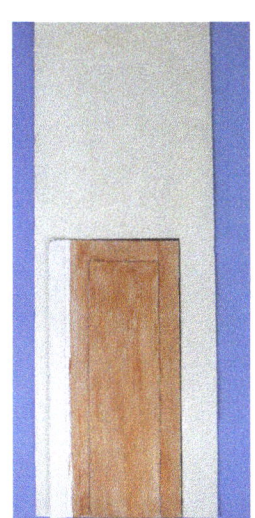
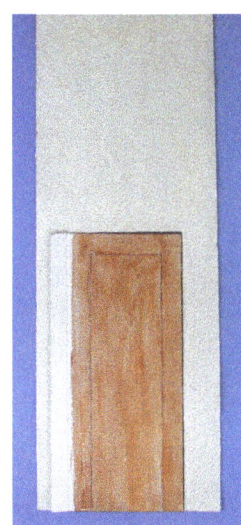

11. Cut out the wall, door 1 and door 2 with a hinge allowance. Glue doors together.
12. Glue on left inside, to open inwards, not into porch.
13. Undercoat both sides of the door and wall.
14. Paint both when porch roofing is decided.

Joining it together

The porch on the side of the house with a blue sky.

On a wall at the end of the house with a blue sky.

The room can have a ceiling.

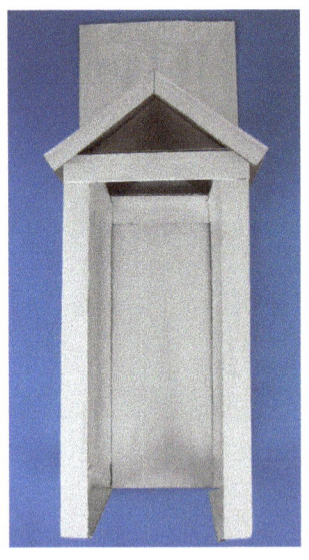

15. Only undercoat for bright colours, leave for dark.

16. Paint the porch.
17. Glue it to the wall backing.

Door opens away from porch.

This way where they come out of the house - RRH and GBM.

A 30cm x 20cm sheet of paper in a tight roll glued across top to rest on rails. Goes past edge.

Attachment points

Put velcro pieces on these bottom and top points to attach to the proscenium.

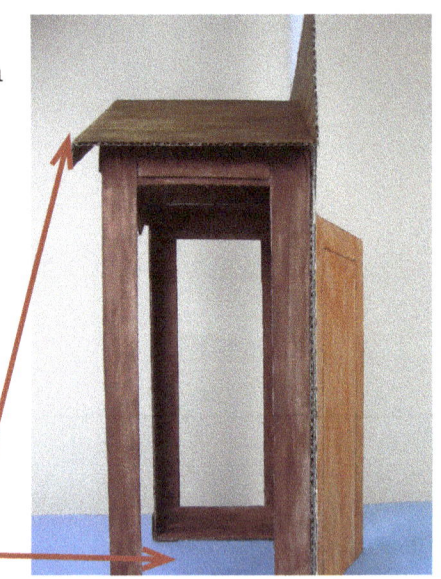

This way to come into house - 3 bears and LRRH.

Bed

The whole bed with pillows can be painted flat or made in 3D. The measurements give the sizes of these props. Cut and glue boxes and cardboard together for a 3D bed.

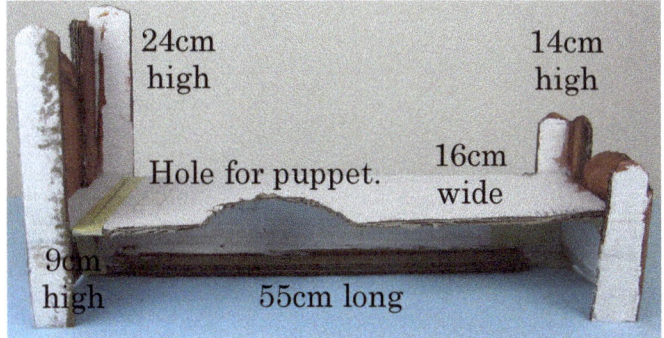

Paint the surfaces that will be seen.

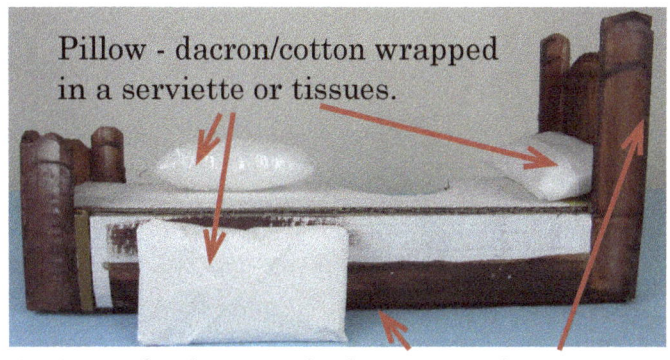

A piece of velcro on the bottom and one on the post attaches it to the proscenium.

Body shape in bed

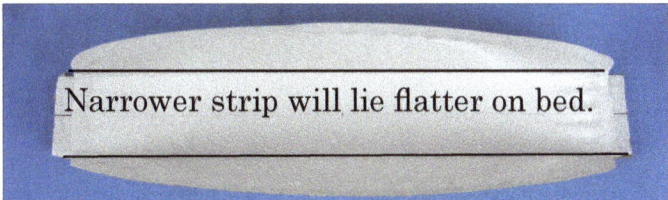

1. Glue cardboard plates onto card for body in bed. Thinner strip for a smaller Grandma.

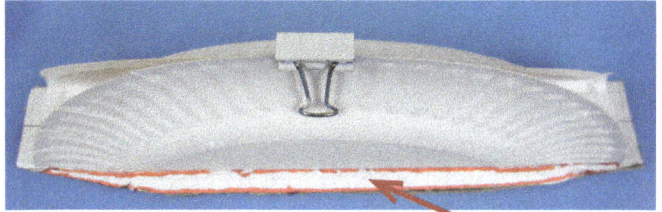

2. Glue together at top edge. Leave extra card on one side and cut off on the other.

3. Fold A4 sheet into 4, cut along fold lines.

4. Fold each strip in half.

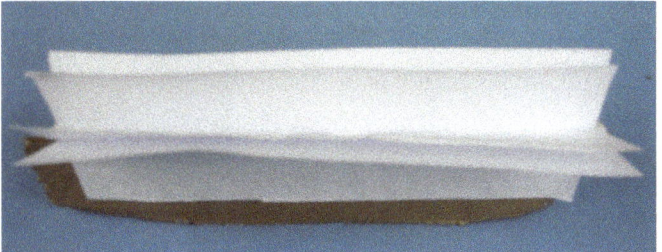

5. Glue 2 on the back side and 2 on front side of the bottom edge.

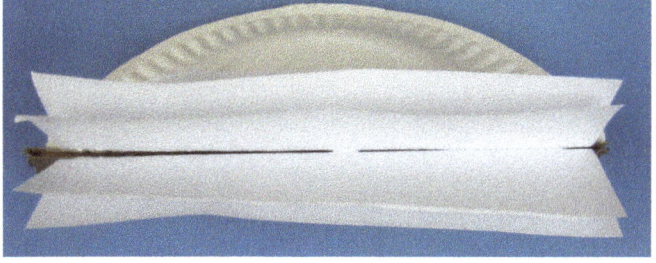

6. Glue onto the bed (2 towards front, 2 towards back) forming a double hinge,

Place it with the curve to the front.

Pull card edge back to stand it up on the bed.

4 Poster bed

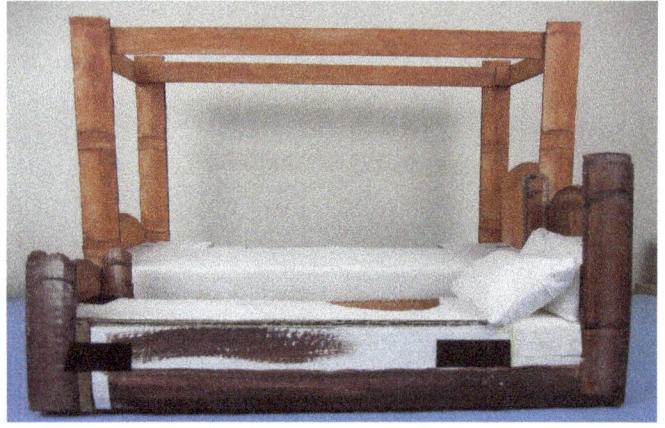
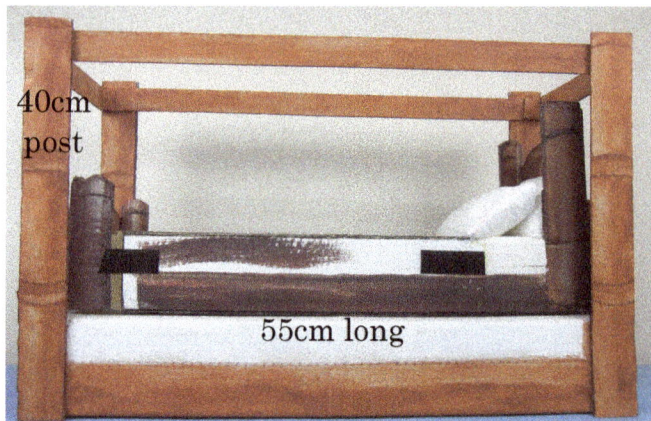

A four poster bed made 3cm longer, 3 cm wider, 1cm higher is very impressive.

Pillows and curtains.

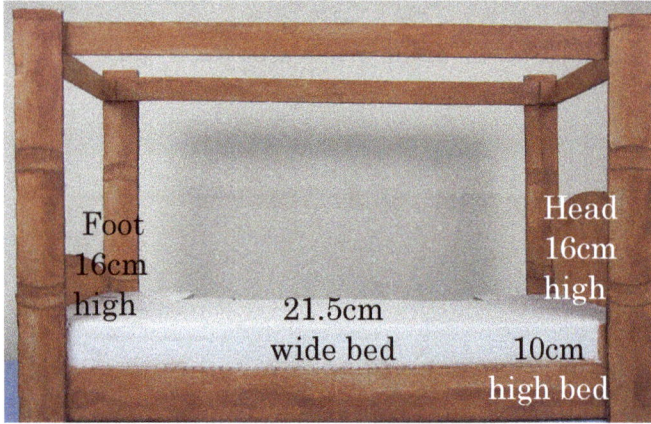

This is a simple box base with flat painted card for posts, top and bed ends.

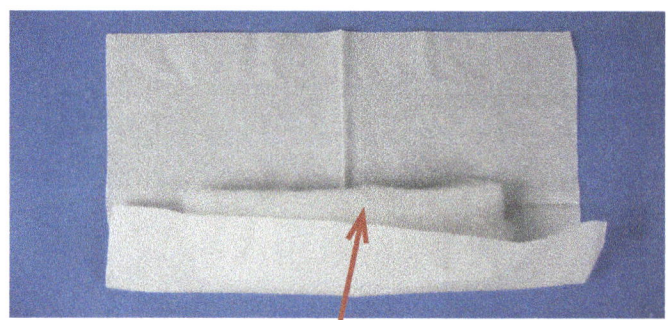

1. Place a piece of dacron on a serviette, fold in the 2 sides and stick it with glue.

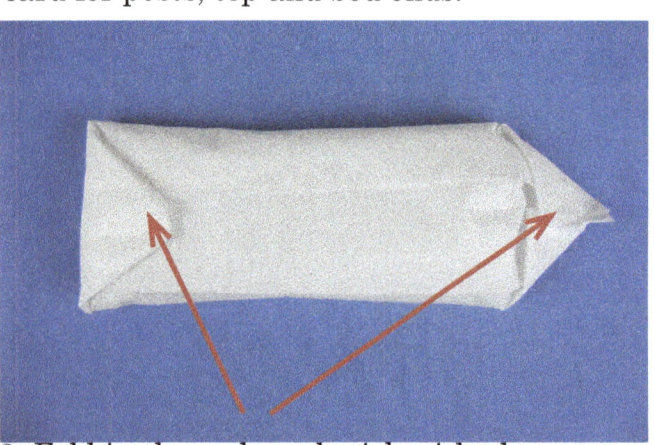

2. Fold in the ends and stick with glue.

3. Cut 2 pieces of material for curtains and 1 for a bedspread. Hem them.

4. Tack along near the top with double thread, gather it to fit where it is going.

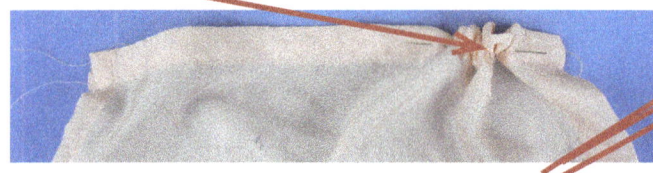

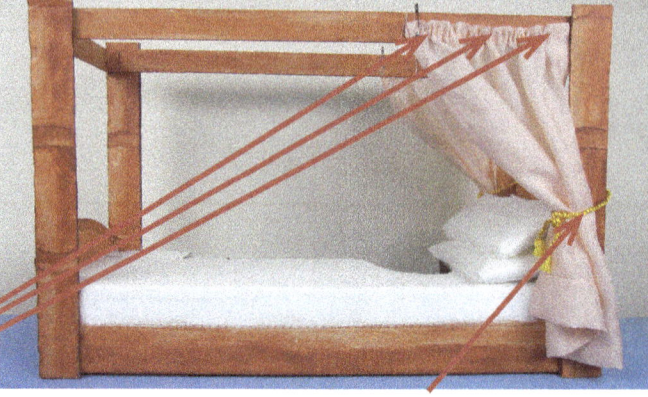

5. Oversew it to the top beam at 3 points.

6. Tie curtain back with cord/ribbon to post.

Bed can overhang on the front proscenium, put velcro pieces under the middle of the foot end and top head curtain rail. Gather top of curtain back further to see puppet faces.

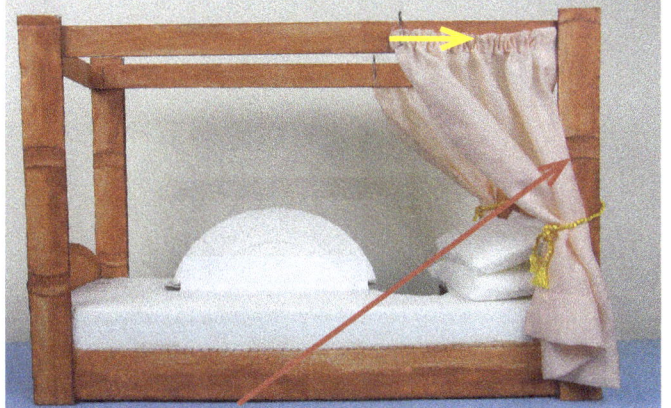
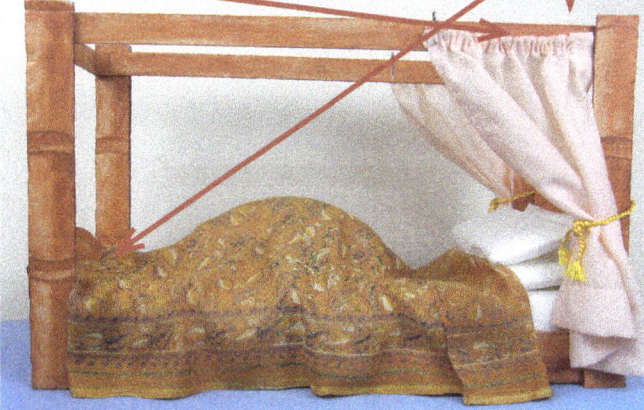

Put the tie higher up to see the faces.   Final result with bedspread.

Basket with flowers

1. Cut out template from paper or thin card.
2. Fold along dotted lines.
3. Fold in and glue in place.
4. Cut out handle and glue in place.
5. Paint the whole basket.
6. Paint a bunch of flowers on card.
7. Cut it out and keep it to place in basket.

Handle is 16cm x 1cm strip of cardboard.

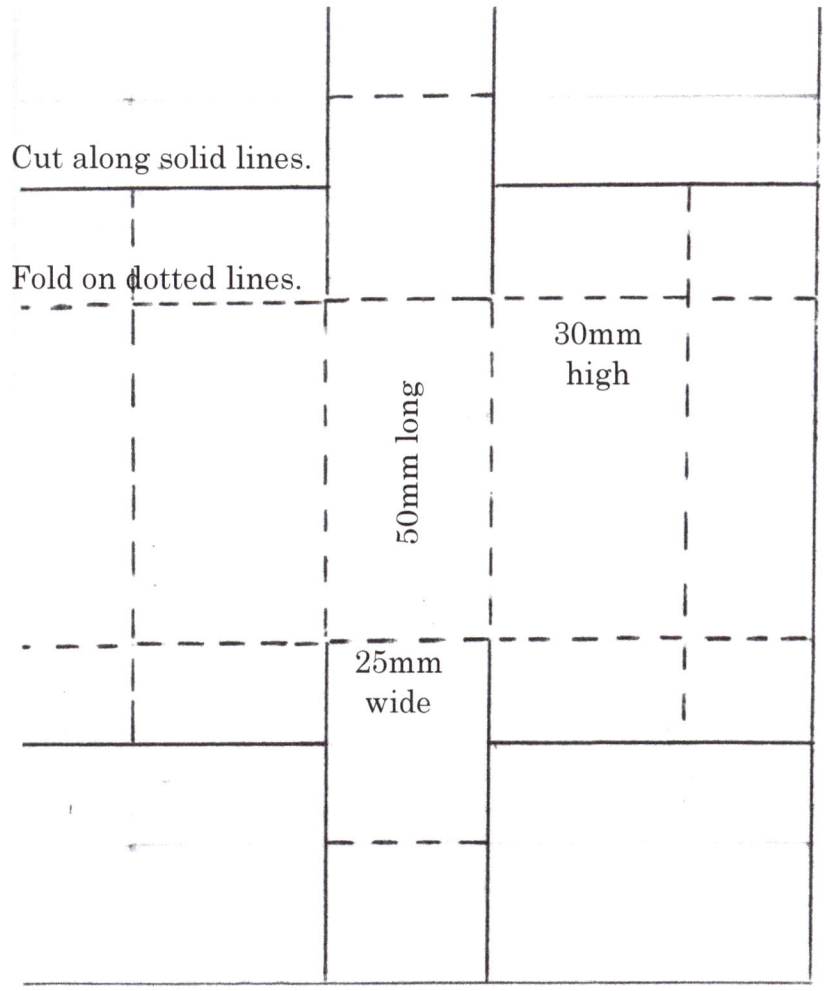

Cut along solid lines.

Fold on dotted lines.

30mm high

50mm long

25mm wide

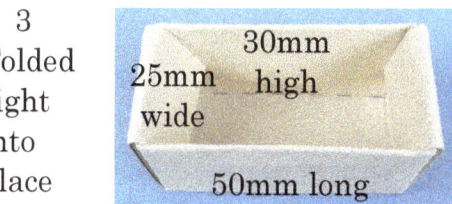

3 Folded right into place

30mm high
25mm wide
50mm long

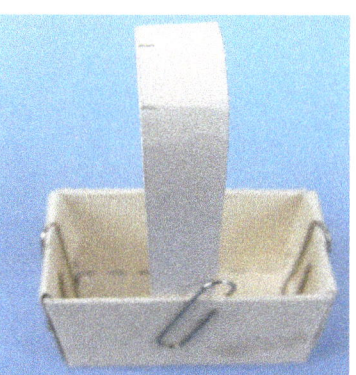

4 Handle and basket glued in place.

Basket and flowers painted Room for puppet hand behind.

Mothers comes to the door and calls. How does LRRH answer?
As she leaves mother says "Don't talk to strangers. Don't wander in the wood."
She skips along and repeats her mothers words as she goes.

How does she meet the woodsman? How does she chat with him?
Does he ask why she is in the woods alone? Does he warn, don't wander? etc.
How does she leave after he's gone into the thicket. Skip, walk, repeating warning, etc?

There's a tree? Does the wolf look ahead imagining her being a lovely sweet snack?
How does he meet her, talk to her, ask where she is going, point out flowers - slyly?
Peep around the tree.

The wolf knocks at the door, comes in frightening Grandma, and eats her.
After eating her he can voice his thoughts. He goes off stage looking for a disguise to put on.
Comes back in wearing a mob cap. Climbs slowly into bed as the body shape is turned up.

How does LRRH come in? Act and move around the bedroom?
She slowly gets near the wolf who jumps out of bed and eats her.
Delicious! Now I am sleepy. Tries to gets comfortable. Sleeps and snooorres.

Huntsman peeps in the door then creeps in and looks at the wolf.
The woodsman/huntsman cuts the wolf to let them out. Then he fills the wolf with rocks?
Chases him out, or kills him? How do you want to finish your story?

Making your puppet come alive

Practise with just the hand first. Pointer finger straight up.

The thumb out as one arm. Can put an extender on.

Second finger out as the other arm. Can put on an extender.

Fold the 4th and 5th fingers into the palm of the hand

The arm is straight out from the shoulder.

The forearm bent up at right angles at the elbow.

Keep the hand straight with the forearm at the wrist.

Nod the pointer. Wave the thumb or 2nd finger.

To clap hands or hold something put the thumb and 2nd finger together.

Lean back and laugh, tilt forward and bow.

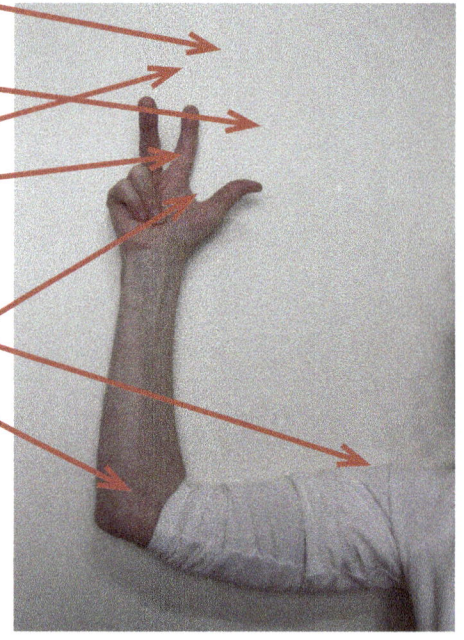

Walk the puppet across the stage making sure your arm stays upright, then run with it at a slight angle. To do this you have to walk and run yourself, with little steps.

Now put the head on your pointer.
Repeat all these actions.

Add the glove to the head and practise the movements.

Try other human actions eg. bending, sitting, picking something up and carrying it, dancing, etc.

Keeping your focus on the puppet, see how many actions you can do. Carry a basket or something else.

Practise in front of a mirror, watching your puppet in the mirror.

You are clever at doing and expressing lots of things with your hands all the time when you are talking. Do it with your puppet.

Making the story flow

Practise the script in a large open space, inside or outside, where the voice has to be projected to others a good distance away.

Speaking loudly makes you speak slower so the audience will hear the words better.

Exaggerate the expression in your voice, making it dramatic. It's drama!

Microphones behind the stage will pick up all the scene changes and movement noises.

No whispering or talking behind the stage. It will interrupt actors who are doing their best.

N.B. A VERY IMPORTANT RULE ~
NO ACTING ON STAGE UNTIL SCRIPTS ARE KNOWN!!!

It's impossible to hold a script and act a puppet, it will be lifeless.
Concentrate on the puppet and ad-lib the words if need be.

Videod rehearsals for the children to watch, and make adjustments are useful.
They can also watch and learn from each other's rehearsals.
Make backdrops and props which will enhance the actions.

Choreograph everything

Movement on stage ~
Especially when entering and exiting, moving around or crossing others.

Group actions to get unity and make a greater impact.
The team effort required for this is well worth the effort.
It gives the children a big boost in acting, confidence and fun.

Dance ~
Whether it is one, two, three or a group of puppets, these are important ~
The puppets are small so make the actions clear and exaggerated.
Set a pace that everyone can manage and so keep together.

Marching across together can be very effective IF done well.

Curtain openings and closing. Practise all of them.

Scenery changes ~
They are done by children not involved in the two scenes being changed.
Children remove and store used scenery in designated places.
Others bring in the new scenery in a planned order.
It is vital to practise these changes so they run like clockwork and keep the play's momentum going.

Puppets are sorted according to scenes or entrances, etc.

Everyone needs to know exactly where they have to be throughout the performance.

Practise curtain bows because they really add to the end of the show.

A prompt is needed at one side of the stage.

Music

If you want music in your play, choose it and use it when rehearsals start.

Children learning musical instruments in the school can have fun performing it.

It can be recorded for puppetry rehearsals and the performance.

Some extras worth considering

Design publicity and place it in the school or wherever you wish to advertise.

Take photos of the puppets and the scenes for your records.

Design and print a program advertising the puppeteers, scenes, etc.

A DVD of the production can be made to have for sale at the performance.
Have someone video the final performance.

The performance

Performances can be done for younger children in the school, for parents, relatives and anyone else in the community.

It is really beneficial doing several performances, 3 or 4 is excellent.

Sometimes a small charge can be made to recoop your costs or to go towards some needy group, adding even more value to what the children have achieved.

Review

The day after the performance have a get-together.

Ask the puppeteers to comment on what it has all meant to them.

Close with any relevant comments.

Plays

I hope you have tried many of the suggestions on p2 and throughout the book.
Puppetry provides wonderful opportunities to create and experiment with life situations.
Puppets are small, inexpensive and enable us to do some things we could not do as humans.

We laugh all the time when we are photographing the puppets. I hope you enjoy them too.
The puppeteer put the cat in the tree just like the Cheshire cat in Alice in Wonderland.

This manual has introduced the basics of simple glove puppetry ~

1. How to make glove puppet heads and bodies.
2. How to make and act smaller puppets.
3. How to dramatise the puppet characters.
4. How to increase the dramatic effects.

Extra acts are a valuable addition in between the wolf and each house scene.
At the end of the final scene there was the chance to dance and sing with our puppets.

We have learnt how to make and use a centre prop - the bridge.
This play showed us how to act the puppets in a confrontational scenario.

We now know how to act our puppets using the chairs at the table and with the beds.
We can use musical interludes, etc during scenery changes to add to the play's appeal.

A chase isn't just running. It can go at varying speeds and have interruptions. A small or large puppet can steal the show. Changing the props (any number) alters the location.

The two LRRH scenes gave us the opportunity to add in extra large props and acts that developed the characters, increased interest and built up the intrigue and suspense.

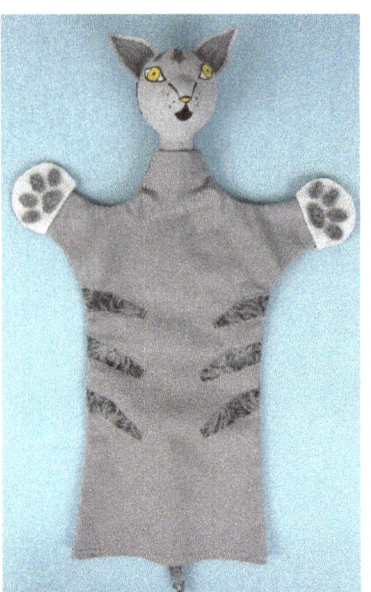

Everything has been kept basic.
With this foundation you can do far more detailed and elaborate puppetry.

Make more detailed, characterised or made up faces with stylish hair do's. Decorate the glove - like this cat.

3D scenery allows puppets to be and act in the backdrop, front prop, etc.
Put in additional scenes and acts within the play for more fun and story.
Using a little bit of lighting or music introduces a whole new dimension.

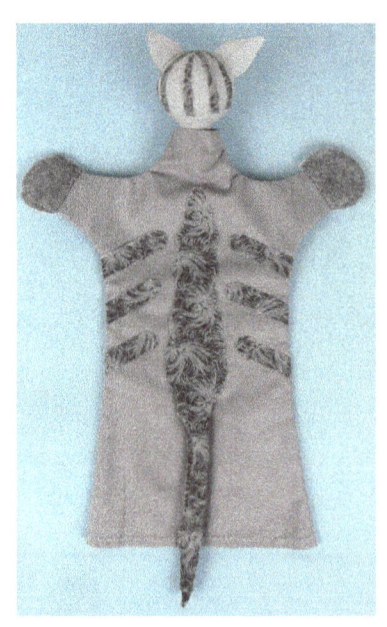

In Introducing Puppetry we made 3D cardboard plate puppets that we operated with 2 hands.

In Glove Puppetry we have made smaller puppets which go on one hand.

In Marionette Puppetry it's smaller whole body puppets, operated from above by both hands.

Just because he felt my slapstick
The policeman carts me off to jail.
Most people find it is quite comic,
A funny way to end a tale.
We've been on show since sixteen fifty
And people never get tired of us.
Everyone thinks we're pretty nifty
So our future is one great big plus.

The End

Appendix

Cost of puppet theatre materials for Introducing and Glove puppetry theatre.

Capral Qubelok

4 x 6.5m lengths	$16.00	=	$64.00
8 x rt<	$1.50	=	$12.00
4 x 'T' connectors	$1.50	=	$6.00
4 x 3 Way connectors	$1.50	=	$6.00
8 x end stoppers	80c	=	$6.40
	Total	=	$94.40

Bunnings

4 x 10cm right-angle brackets

4 x small right-angle brackets

6 x 85cm hinges

5mm x 6.5mm blind rivets

18 x 5mm x 38mm nuts and bolts

Small self-tapping screws

Spotlight

4m black block-out material (buy on special) or other material.

Velcro $18.00 for 20m roll = $40 or $60 (Tapes on line)

If curtains included

2 x 5cm x 5cm rt< brackets for the curtain rod

Curtain material, gather tape, hooks and rod or track.

Scenery rack

2 x 6.5m lengths Qubelok	$16.00	=	$32
8 x 3Ways @ $2.00 each		=	$16.00
	Total	=	$48.00

These are rounded prices I paid in 2020

If no money available, money can always be borrowed, a small charge made for seeing the performance and the loan repaid. Another very valuable experience for the group.

Shadow puppets will also use this theatre, so lots of uses for many years. (coming soon.)

First book in this series

Introducing Puppetry

Margaret Arney

Coming next Marionettes

for more information check out
www.puppetrytheatre.com

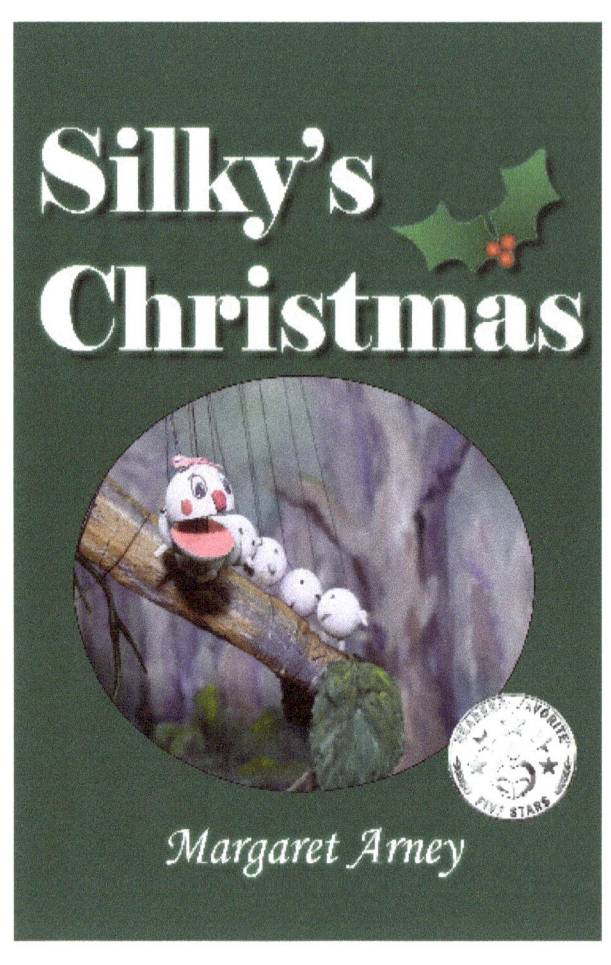

Available now

for more information check out
www.puppetrytheatre.com

www.ingramcontent.com/pod-product-compliance
Lightning Source LLC
Chambersburg PA
CBHW041713290426
44110CB00024B/2825